African Diaspora Research Project
Urban Affairs Programs
Michigan State University
East Lansing, MI  48824 -- USA

# IN SEARCH OF A BETTER LIFE

African Diaspora Research Project
Urban Affairs Programs
Michigan State University
East Lansing, MI 48824 -- USA

# IN SEARCH OF A BETTER LIFE

## Perspectives on Migration
## from the Caribbean

Edited by Ransford W. Palmer

*Foreword by Gordon K. Lewis*

New York
Westport, Connecticut
London

**Library of Congress Cataloging-in-Publication Data**

In search of a better life : perspectives on migration from the
  Caribbean / edited by Ransford W. Palmer.
      p. cm.
    Includes bibliographical references.
    ISBN 0-275-93409-8 (alk. paper)
    1. Caribbean Area—Emigration and immigration.   2. Great Britain—
Emigration and immigration.   3. Immigrants—Great Britain.
4. United States—Emigration and immigration.   5. Immigrants—United
States.   6. Canada—Emigration and immigration.   7. Immigrants—
Canada.   I. Palmer, Ransford W.
JV7321.I5 1990
304.8′09729—dc20        89-29658

Library of Congress Catalog Card Number: 89-29658
ISBN: 0-275-93409-8

First published in 1990

Praeger Publishers, One Madison Avenue, New York, NY 10010
An imprint of Greenwood Publishing Group, Inc.

Printed in the United States of America

The paper used in this book complies with the Permanent
Paper Standard issued by the National Information Standards
Organization (Z39.48—1984).

10  9  8  7  6  5  4  3  2  1

To my wife, Sally, whose support has made my research possible over the past twenty-five years.

# Contents

# Tables

# Foreword

The essence of Caribbean life has always been movement. It explains the energizing *brio* of Caribbean life in music and dance, sports, language, even religion and politics. It also explains, of course, the socioeconomic phenomenon of migration. Migration—as the vast, restless, circulatory movement of whole peoples—has its roots, historically, in the immediate post-Discovery period. For the first century of European colonization, migration meant the influx to the colonies of European peasants and the workers of the European seaports including the riffraff of London, Paris, and Madrid. After that came the African influx, organized by the Atlantic slave trade, which did not really cease in the islands until slavery abolition in Cuba in 1886. Following that, again, was the influx of Indian indentured labor, lasting for the period 1845–1917. Every person in the Caribbean has been a newcomer; and certainly by 1700, the region's identity had been established as a series of rich, picaroon, and polyglot societies, eclectic, porous, absorptive, peopled by a *dramatis personae* that included colonists, slaves, indentured *engagees*, Catholic and Protestant planters and merchants, heretics, Jews, felons, "poor whites," buccaneers, transported political prisoners, and the rest, all of them mingling in a fascinating exoticism under tropical skies.

The modern twentieth century has witnessed a similar migratory explosion, though of a different form and direction. The period may be conveniently divided into two time spans: the period between the Spanish-American War and World War II, and the post-1945 contemporary period. The first period witnessed the passage of West Indian workers to work on the Panama Canal construction, the efflux of Haitian cane-cutters to Cuba and Santo Domingo, the passage of West Indian sugar workers to Cuba, and even as far afield as Miami, as well as the settling of Cuban cigar workers in the towns of Southwest Florida. World War II brought a halt to some of these movements but, on the other hand, brought wartime employment and, for the English-speaking West Indians in the services, a taste for overseas places.

The second period, then, saw a resurgence of emigration, fuller in both volume and intensity and comprised of two major trajectories: intraregional and intercontinental. The intraregional movement has involved "small island" migrants from the Leewards and Windwards traveling north to the Virgin Islands tourist economy and south to the Trinidad-Netherlands Antilles oil economy. (It was in the latter during the war years that future political leaders such as Eric Gairy learned union organization and agitation.) The intercontinental movement has involved a greater flow of migrants to the metropolitan economies of France, England, Canada, and the United States.

Caribbean migration thus has certain distinctive features. It is at once intraregional and intercontinental. Yesterday it was facilitated by the steamboat, today by the airplane, spurred by the postwar advances in cheap and rapid air transportation. It is multiclass in character; the middle class and the affluent now emigrate almost as much as the poor. It involves at once economic refugees and political refugees, although there is a fine line between the two. Some of it is organized by government-to-government contract labor agreements, such as that involving Jamaican agricultural workers to the orchards of Florida and Pennsylvania; much more of it rests on the independent decision of the individual emigrant, in consultation with family and friends. Some of it is legal, some of it illegal, like the distinction between bonded and illegal aliens in the Virgin Islands economy. Some of it is long-term migration, some of it is short-term; the latter includes many Puerto Ricans who, as U.S. citizens, can come and go without any problem with immigration entry. As the saying goes, Puerto Ricans do not emigrate, they commute.

Above all, perhaps, and constituting an all-embracing feature of its migration, is the fact that the Caribbean can be seen as a frontier society—a seaborne frontier society—with all the irresistible urge to move out and move on characteristic of such a society.

Some of these features merit a little further attention. Much of the migration story is that of labor migration under capitalism, responding to the law of capitalism that dictates that the mobility of capital in the global economy gives rise to the mobility of labor. But all social strata join the process. Between 1962 and 1976, a total of 41,363 professional persons left home from the territories of Jamaica, Trinidad, and Tobago, including engineers, clerical workers, doctors and dentists, nurses, and pharmacists. Jamaican losses were particularly acute in the 1972–80 period, when many professionals, including business people, left the island because of their fear of Manleyite socialism. If we remember that in 1972 there were only 710 doctors serving a population of some 2.2 million, and that by 1976 the number had dwindled to 390, the serious nature of the brain drain can be appreciated. The damage is somewhat offset by remittances sent home, so that some small islands, such as Montserrat, are virtually remittance economies, but that does not compensate for the loss of precious skilled manpower and the financial investment that has gone into its preparation. The economic impact on the societies whose professionals leave can thus be severe. As Prime Minister Eric Williams was once moved to lament, there will soon be no West Indians left in the Caribbean.

Much of the literature on migration has concerned itself with the juxtaposition of the so-called "push" and "pull" factors in migration decision making: the "push" factors include poverty, massive structural unemployment and underemployment, severe shortages of the basic necessities of life (as in Guyana), and the political climate (as in Haiti). The "pull" factors include easy transportation, better employment opportunities, access to better health and educational services in the "receiving" economies, and, generally, the promise of a better lifestyle.

The main motive of emigration is the desire to better oneself. The psychology of migration is, indeed, as simple as that. No would-be migrant sits down and makes a rational calculus of "push" and "pull" factors; he or she simply knows the situation has become so desperate that something has to be done about it. He or she does not add up consciously the various compass points of the migration magnetic field. He or she simply knows, instinctively, that they are there.

The other side of the migration coin, of course, is the matter of how the migrant fares in the receiving country. In the Caribbean itself, the most optimistic reception is given to Grenadian immigrants in Trinidad, who are treated with a sort of genial disdain; after all, the most famous of them all is the calypsonian, The Mighty Sparrow, with whom Trinidadians can find no wrong. Other scenes are less pleasing. Haitians in the Bahamas are disliked because they do not speak English. "Down Islanders" in the Virgin Islands are seen as less-educated people by the "native Virgin Islanders," who are clannish. In both cases—since both societies are mainly black—it is a form of cultural rather than racial prejudice.

Racial prejudice is at work elsewhere, however. Smuggling rings in the Dominican Republic ferry illegal migrants in to Puerto Rico in flimsy craft across the treacherous Mona passage, where the migrants are captured and deported at the hands of the U.S. federal authorities. Illegal Haitian entrants, the tragic "boat people," received no better welcome in the 1970s, when only a handful of Puerto Rican human rights groups protested their prolonged incarceration in the old Fort Allen military compound. While Puerto Ricans, although overwhelmingly *mulate*, like to think of themselves as white and Spanish, they are treated with racial prejudice. Symptomatic of this is Governor Rafael Hernández Colón's remarks in Spain, denigrating the Indian and African elements in the Puerto Rican culture.

Then there is the problem of the political migrant. A case in point is that of the outspoken Guyanese journalist, Ricky Singh, who in recent years has been blacklisted, by means of the work permit system, by governments in Guyana, Trinidad, and Barbados. The case constitutes a violation of the principle of the freedom of movement of persons, which is at the heart of any regional entity like the Caribbean Community (CARICOM).

But the real battleground of migration is in the metropolitan countries of Canada, the United States, Great Britain, France, and Holland, where the Third World meets the First. A voluminous literature already exists on the topic, if only because it goes to the heart of the modern global race issue. For the migration explosion has set off a veritable demographic revolution worldwide. There are Haitians and West Indians in Canada; Surinamese in Holland; Haitians and French Antilleans in France; West Indians and Pakistanis in Britain; and a legion of Caribbean and Latin American groups in the United States, including West Indians, Puerto Ricans, Haitians, Colombians, Mexicans, and Venezuelans. The receiving countries, historically ethnocentric and potentially racist societies, have been confronted with the problem of becoming multiracial, multireligious, and multilingual societies. Only the United States has had a sufficiently long history of assimilating successive migratory populations to be able to cope with the problem.

Not surprisingly, then, the new immigrants have been faced with hostile antiforeigner attitudes, ethnic stereotyping, bias and prejudice in the employment, educational, health, and housing fields, and a sometimes vicious white backlash in national politics. At least in dual-language Canada, Haitians can find linguistic comfort in Montreal and West Indians the same in Toronto. Elsewhere, the picture is more difficult. Everywhere, immigrants are confronted with the contradictory attitudes of public opinion: on the one hand, they are welcome to the low-status jobs nobody else wants; on the other, they are pilloried for "taking away" jobs from the local working class.

Immigrants are particularly vulnerable if they are not naturalized citizens. To take a Caribbean example, there is the brutal exploitation of the Haitian cane workers in the almost slavery-like plantations of Santo Domingo; to take a North American example, there are the continuing scandalous housing encampments of West Indian agricultural workers in the fruit-growing areas of Florida and Pennsylvania, testified to by numerous federal and state investigative reports. Low pay, a grim housing shortage, and color and class prejudice combine to drive the immigrant populations into the inner cores of the decaying industrial cities, so that the European countries have seen the rise of American-type ghettos.

Not least of all is the sinister development of national "white only" political parties, associated with the names of Enoch Powell in Britain and Le Pen in France, whose main staple is the warning that white, Christian culture is being polluted by dark, alien forces.

It is instructive to look at the record of the two major receiving countries, Great Britain and the United States. It was the conventional wisdom in 1945 that England was the liberal society and the United States the racist society, and lecturing the Americans was the favorite pastime of the London media establishment. But the last 30 or so years have witnessed a curious reversal of roles. The United States has moved forward, with the civil rights movement and the Great Society legislation, to redress the historic injustices done to its nonwhite minorities, especially black Americans; but Britain, after 1962, passed a number of race relations acts step-by-step making entry for nonwhite immigrants more difficult, with the final end of destroying the old Commonwealth concept of a family of nations.

In Britain, figures like Powell have been able to make the "color problem" a central theme in the national politics, while in the United States, no politician who wants to succeed can afford to talk as did men like Governors Orville Faubus and George A. Wallace a brief generation ago. As America has become a more open society—there is the congressional Amnesty Law of 1986, which, although making a virtue of necessity, reveals American generosity at its best—England has become a more closed society. That is why in the Caribbean today, no one wants to go to England—and everybody wants to go to America.

In his 1906 book, *The American Scene*, Henry James described the teeming immigrant masses of the Lower East Side. Today, the masses are still there, although their origins have shifted from Europe to the Caribbean, Latin America, and Southeast Asia. How does the immigrant cope? In part, coping depends on what is sometimes euphemistically called the "host" society. Paradoxically, the closed character of English society, simply by being reluctant to assimilate immigrants, may thereby make it easier for them to retain their customs and values, while U.S. society, by its open invitation to "become" Americans, may all the more readily lead to their erosion. In any case, immigrants do not come culturally naked: they bring a lifestyle with them, and it helps them shape their coping mechanisms.

An extensive sociological literature has already described many of those mechanisms. There are the political clubs that avidly discuss politics back home. There are religious cults and sects such as Pentecostalism, *voudun*, and *santoria*, for Caribbean peoples are devoutly religious. There are institutes and organizations formed to lobby local councils and city agencies for a fair share of municipal services. There are student groups, such as the well-known West Indian Students Association in London, periodically addressed by visiting politicians from home. There are Caribbean *susu* savings clubs of African origin, where contributing members receive an occasional "hand" to help buy a television set, start a small business, or pay a house mortgage. Because Caribbean people are great letter writers, there is the letter to or from home; indeed, the imaginary humorous letter from some fussy aunt in New York or London or Toronto is the stock in trade of some Caribbean comedians. There are local immigrant newspapers as well as serious journals. There are restaurants and street market stalls where every staple food and dish of creole character can be bought. Not least of all, there are annual Carnival events, copying the tremendous *fete bacchanal* of Port-of-Spain.

As has been noted, there is a large scholarly literature on all this, but it is worth noting that there also exists another literature, usually fictive, written by immigrants themselves or by others interested in their cause. There is the Puerto Rican Bernardo Vega's *Memorias*, describing a lifetime of union organizing and agitation in the period between the two World Wars. There is Samuel Selvon's *The Lonely Londoners*, showing 'how West Indians love and work in a cold climate, cold socially as well as in terms of weather. There is Barry Levine's *Benjy Lopez*, a picaresque tale of "hustling" to "beat the system." There is George Lamming's *The Emigrants*, in which a boatload of emigrants talk endlessly about what they expect to find in England. There is E.R. Braithwaite's sentimental *To Sir, with Love*, describing the struggle of a black teacher in the East End London schools. There is also Vidia Naipaul's autobiographical account of his retreat from Trinidad into the solace of southern England. We still await, perhaps, the epic novel which, like John Steinbeck's *Grapes of Wrath*, will sum up the drama and the tragedy of the Caribbean diaspora.

Migration, in all its ramifications, raises serious questions about public policy making in both the sending and receiving societies. In the United States, for example, there is the profound question that concerns the very future of the society: will immigration continue to be absorbed by the old "melting pot" syndrome, or will nationalizing assimilationism give way to a polycultural society of separate but equal ethnic groups, as the Cubanization of Miami would seem to suggest? In any case, future public policy will certainly depend on the evolving majority-minority situation, for the very future of the American democracy lies at its heart.

For the Caribbean sending societies, there are problems of equal, perhaps even more, gravity. Migration is a function of a model of economic dependency and must therefore be perceived as a prime element in developmental planning. So far, individual Caribbean governments have adopted—as in the related matter of tourism—a laissez-faire attitude to migration (with the exception, of course, of Cuba, the only country with a state-controlled system).

Yet since the region is a single socio-economic-cultural area, such a unilateral and passive policy is clearly inadequate. Migration needs an effective regional plan, which will seek to maximize its advantages and minimize its disadvantages. Such a planning program would involve a number of high-priority goals. It means planning an ambitious rejuvenation of regional agriculture, if only because the neglect of agriculture and its consequent rural depopulization have been prime causes of emigration. It means that bodies like the Caribbean Community must liberalize their policies with respect to the free movement of persons so as to enlarge employment opportunities at home. It means a bold regional program of planned production for community consumption, which in turn means a serious reexamination of existing developmental schemes. Certainly, migration is here to stay, for it is part of human nature, human curiosity, the human nomadic instinct. It is as old as recorded history, going back at least to the Israelite exodus from ancient Egypt. But if the health, wealth, and happiness of the Caribbean peoples improve, fewer people may want to leave their ancestral homelands.

Gordon K. Lewis

# Preface

This volume examines the phenomenon of population migration from the Caribbean and the social, economic, and cultural adaptation of the immigrants to their new environments. The flow of Caribbean peoples to North America and Europe since the Second World War represents an expansion of the search for economic opportunities beyond the margins of the capitalist system, where American capital once beckoned them to Panama and Cuba, to the centers of that system, where the industrial economies face serious labor shortages.

The economic conditions that heralded the beginning of the mass migration of Caribbean labor in the nineteenth century are explored by Peter D. Fraser (Chapter 2). Twentieth-century postwar migration, however, is more than a movement of labor in search of jobs; it is also a movement of households. It therefore affects not only the economic well-being of members of the household but their social relationships as well, particularly the household role of immigrant women who actively participate in the labor force. As Patricia R. Pessar (Chapter 5), Monica H. Gordon (Chapter 6), and Aubrey W. Bonnett (Chapter 7) show, tensions tend to develop as the immigrant household adjusts to its new environment. I argue that the migration of households from the Caribbean is in fact a circular process, rather than a linear one (Chapter 1), set in motion when the economic disparities between sending and receiving countries induce one or more members of the household to migrate. The returning flow of remittances from these household members strengthens perceptions in the origin country of a better life abroad and helps to finance the reunification of the household as well as the migration of new households.

The adaptation of Caribbean immigrants to their new environment varies as one moves across the Atlantic. Mel. E. Thompson (Chapter 3) underscores the social and economic experience of Caribbean blacks in the United Kingdom, while Anthony H. Richmond and Aloma Mendoza (Chapter 4) find differences in educational performance on both sides of the Atlantic.

The book also examines the peculiar characteristics of illegal migration from the Caribbean to the United States. Based on data generated by the amnesty program of the Immigration Reform and Control Act of 1986 as well as data from the annual reports of the Immigration and Naturalization Service, Lisa S. Roney (Chapter 8) and I (Chapter 9) show that the majority of illegal aliens from the Caribbean entered the United States as temporary visitors and later violated the conditions of their visas.

The idea for this volume arose from discussions with Frances G. Henry of York University in Toronto. I am grateful to Professor Henry for the encouragement she provided in launching this project.

# I

## Origins and Destinations

# 1

# Caribbean Development and the Migration Imperative

RANSFORD W. PALMER

## INTRODUCTION

The Caribbean has been unable to achieve the kind of economic development that would widen the range of job opportunities and allow its economy to absorb the incremental growth of its labor force. As a result, emigration in search of job opportunities has been an enduring feature of the economic history of the region. Yet World Bank income data place the region among the more developed of the developing countries,[1] and indices such as literacy rate and infant mortality compare quite favorably with those of some developed countries.

The fact is that some of these indicators of development are themselves the cause of emigration. A high rate of literacy in a region with a high rate of unemployment means that the population can readily absorb and interpret information about job opportunities abroad. A low infant mortality rate may mean a high population growth rate, which may intensify the pressure to emigrate. Given the sharp inequality in the distribution of income that is typical of the region, a high per capita income by the standards of developing countries may mean a high standard of living for a small share of the population and a near subsistence level for the majority. The tension created by this disparity may be a cause of emigration.

The essential point here is that in examining the relationship between migration and development, one must probe beyond the accepted indices of development. The phenomenon of migration from the Caribbean is due not so much to the lack of development, but to the character of that development. It is the character of development that shapes individual expectations about lifetime household earnings. This chapter argues that migration is a circular process, and that this process is powered by the objective of maximizing the welfare of the household.

## CAPITAL AND MIGRATION FLOWS

The real measure of development is the extent to which it achieves a sustained improvement in the lot of the majority of the population. For these capital-scarce economies, the inflow of foreign capital is regarded as essential for achieving this objective, but often the development benefits resulting from foreign capital inflows have not been shared by the population at large. In other words, while foreign capital has stimulated growth, it has created a limited number of employment opportunities in countries where the unemployment rate is high.

Indeed, foreign capital has been known to stimulate growth and migration simultaneously. A classic case in point is the massive migration from Jamaica to Britain in the 1950s when large amounts of foreign capital flowed into the bauxite industry and light manufacturing. This was a capital-intensive kind of development that had little impact on the unemployment rate. What emerged from this process has been described in the center-periphery framework as an international counterflow of labor and capital—capital flowing from the center to the periphery to earn large profits and labor flowing from the periphery to earn higher wages.[2]

The reality, however, is more complicated. There is not just one but several counterflows. If we consider repatriated profits as "remittances" from capital, then there is a counterflow of remittances, one from immigrants in the developed country and one from capital in the developing country. There is also a counterflow of labor: skilled labor that accompanies capital moving one way and labor from the capital-receiving country moving the other way. Finally, there is a counterflow of capital, with the repayment of debt capital moving one way and foreign private capital moving another. The character of these flows varies over time as development progresses. A predominantly capital-labor counterflow may evolve into a counterflow of remittances as profits are repatriated and gainfully employed immigrants begin to send money home. Later, this may evolve into a capital-capital counterflow as the repayment of debt capital moves one way and new funding from abroad moves the other. Occasionally, these counterflows spawn migration eddies, as when Jamaican businessmen migrate with their capital to Miami and commute to Jamaica to run or to settle what is left of their businesses. At any point in time, elements of capital and labor can be found moving together. The expectation, however, is that capital should flow to the capital-scarce Caribbean and labor to labor-scarce North America. Given the power of the owners of capital to exploit, this expectation accommodates the notion of a conscious global strategy on the part of the metropolitan countries to keep the Caribbean under the control of international capitalism.[3]

Migration flows cannot be discussed only in relation to private capital flows because they are also affected by public investment at home as well. There is ample evidence that an increase in public investment in education has led to increased migration. In his analysis of 29 developing countries, Palmer found a significant positive relationship between public investment in education and the willingness of educated workers to emigrate from Third World countries to the United States.[4] Henry and Johnson have cited Guyana and Jamaica, where public investment in education has led to massive emigration. As they put it, "The mismatch between the educational system and the local economy has translated a great deal of investment into an involuntary gift to the North Atlantic countries."[5]

## MIGRATION AS A CIRCULAR PROCESS

On closer examination, the migration process is not a set of linear flows but a collection of circular movements. This is best observed by treating the household—as Patricia Pessar suggests in Chapter 5—as a unit of migration.[6] Looked at from this perspective, the purpose of migration is not just to maximize the lifetime income, both monetary and nonmonetary, of the individual but of the household as well.

The assumption of the maximization of lifetime household earnings is based on a normal expected life span of the income-earning members of the household. If social and political developments threaten to shorten that lifespan, as many Jamaican business owners felt when they were threatened with violence during the first Michael Manley regime, then the maximization objective is undermined. Thus, we contend that anything that impinges on the maximization of lifetime household earnings encourages migration.

When part of the household remains in the country of origin, the maximization of household income requires a counterflow of remittances to the part left behind. This part may include not only a spouse and children but other relatives as well. Thus, remittances are a necessary function of the income maximization objective.

Since the more members of the household who are employed, the higher the household income, and since employment opportunities are perceived to be greater and wage levels higher in the destination country, there is a tendency for able-bodied members of the household in the origin country to join the rest of the household in the destination country. As households are reunited in the destination country, the counterflow of remittances to the origin country will decline. The period of time from the initial breaking up of the household to its eventual reunification constitutes a complete migration cycle—a cycle dictated by the maximization of household income. Of course, there is no guarantee that when the household is reunited that it will stay united. (Aubrey W. Bonnett in Chapter 7 has described some of the marital and parental tensions that reunification often creates.) Nevertheless, the income maximization imperative tends to lead toward reunification, a goal that is encouraged by U.S. immigration law.

This theory of household migration makes it necessary to look at migration in three stages. The first stage is typified by the migration of the spouse to the destination country. The second stage is the settlement of the migrant in the destination country and the remitting of funds to the rest of the household in the origin country. And the third stage is the reunification of the household in the destination country. Thus, the migration flow is a collection of unique circles, each a fingerprint of a household movement.

Remittances, looked at through the prism of this theory, symbolize the incompleteness of the migration circle. As long as there are remittances, there are circles to be completed. While U.S. immigration policy encourages the completion of the circles, Caribbean countries would like to keep them open, not out of any wish to prevent the reunification of households, but to maintain the flow of remittances.

To the extent that older members of the extended family household do not migrate, remittances will continue to flow to the origin country. Thus, for many households, the circle will remain open until the older members in the origin country die. But even in this eventuality, the circle might still be incomplete as distant relatives lay claim to extended family status. It is for this reason that at any point in time, the migration flow is a collection of incomplete circles. When the circle is complete, the migration process ends.

## THE MOVEMENT

The gravitational pull of a large developed industrial country in close proximity to small developing economies dictates that there will be a flow of workers from the lower-income developing countries to the higher-income developed country. The evidence is overwhelming that the great majority of the people who voluntarily migrate from the Caribbean to the United States do so for economic reasons.

Because the migration decision is based on people's implicit calculations about the economic future of their households, it is instructive, therefore, to consider those factors that enter into this decision making. Some of these factors reside in the sending countries, others in the receiving countries. They may broadly be categorized as push and pull factors, respectively, with full recognition that both categories are in some way interrelated. The potential emigrants' assessment of these factors is conditioned by their life experience, as well as by the information received. The sources of information may include friends and relatives abroad, movies, television, magazines, books, newspapers, and, in some cases, potential employers. The information gathered may affect people's assessment of the push factors. They may feel that their household condition is worse than they thought before they received the information and they may therefore develop a greater urgency about deciding to migrate. Ultimately, each individual's assessment depends upon the particular set of push and pull factors he or she deems important, the quality of information received, and the ability to process that information in a way that minimizes risks to the household.

In general, the most important set of pull factors in the United States resides in the prospect of earning a comfortable livelihood in a social and political setting that is relatively free, safe, and stable. This prospect is not necessarily affected by cyclical variations in the unemployment rate in the United States. Empirical studies of the relationship between the rate of unemployment in the United States and the rate of emigration from the Caribbean have produced insignificant results.[7] The fact is that the perception of the United States as a land of opportunity transcends cyclical variations in its unemployment rate. For even in the worst post–World War II recession, the United States' unemployment rate was far below that of Caribbean countries.

While economic conditions in the sending country are considered the major push factor, the economic status of the emigrant is likely to be above average for the rest of the population. This is due partly to the requirements for obtaining a visa to enter the United States and partly because emigrants are some of the more resourceful people in the population. An applicant for a visa is usually required to demonstrate some means of support. For one who is not a dependent, this means that he or she must have accumulated some savings through some form of employment. It is more often the case that Caribbean immigrants to the United States who are not dependents are likely to have held jobs back in their home countries, or to have had opportunities of holding jobs, giving rise to the phenomenon that while high unemployment rates in the sending country may be a general determinant of migration to the United States, individual unemployment is not.

The paradox of migration from the Caribbean to the United States is that migration may occur even from those sectors of the economy generally considered to suffer from a shortage of labor, further aggravating the labor shortage problem. Thus, migration occurs in sectors of the Caribbean economy where unemployment is both high and low. Economic theory can help us to understand this phenomenon. We are not suggesting, however, that a complete explanation lies in the economic realm, only that economic theory offers us a powerful tool to examine the problem.

Why would workers migrate from a sector of the economy where there is a labor shortage, when such a shortage normally pushes wages upward? The answer is that the path to a higher equilibrium wage is strewn with structural obstacles. The extent to which a labor shortage may cause wages to rise depends on the competitive structure of the labor market and the strength of labor unions. If there is only one firm as employer and no organized labor, theory tells us that the wage rate that employer will pay is likely to be less than what it would pay if it had to compete with other employers for the same workers. When the sole employer is the government, as in the case of, say, nurses, wage rates resulting from a shortage of nurses may be capped by budgetary constraints. If the monopoly employer were a private profit-maximizing firm, it would pay the worker a wage rate less than the value of that worker's marginal product (that is, the additional output produced by an additional unit of labor), in contrast to a competitive employer who would pay a wage equal or closer to the value of the worker's marginal product. Where labor unions are strong, they have been able to bargain with major monopsonist employers for a share of the monopoly profits, thereby pushing wage rates up. However, the extent to which labor is organized diminishes as the firms get smaller.

The absolute size of the value of the worker's marginal product will depend on his or her productivity and the price at which the output is sold. Productivity, in turn, generally depends on the amount of capital the worker works with. In capital-intensive industries such as bauxite and oil, wage rates are higher than in other sectors of the economy. In these export industries, the value of the worker's marginal product is subject to foreign demand.[8] Therefore, the extent to which a labor shortage may increase wage rates may be constrained not only by the competitive structure of the labor market and the amount of capital that each worker has to work with, but also by the vulnerability of the product price to foreign demand. This means that the value of the marginal product would fluctuate because of fluctuating international prices, causing the gap between the wage rate and the value of the marginal product to vary even while a collective bargaining contract is in effect.

If, as we assume, each worker's objective is to maximize the lifetime earnings of his or her household, then he or she would want those members of the household who work to work with as much capital as possible in a competitive labor market where the wage rate is closer to the value of the worker's output and where product prices are relatively stable. If his current situation deviates substantially from this ideal, the household may be motivated to redefine its labor market to include employers in the United States, thereby making its perceived market more competitive and each worker potentially more productive. This perception must then be translated into reality, which requires the household to go abroad, where it would expect to increase its earnings. In many households, the first to migrate is the woman (see Bonnett, Chapter 7, and Monica H. Gordon, Chapter 6).

## Employment and Migration

We noted earlier that while general unemployment is a determinant of migration, individual unemployment is not. This needs further explanation. High unemployment rates in a particular occupational group suppress the income growth in that group, in that way placing a constraint on maximizing its household income. Thus, the glacial force of unemployment pushes the employed abroad. The Jamaican data suggest that this glacial force has been particularly effective in low productivity occupational groups such as "clerical, sales, and kindred workers" and "craftsmen, foremen, and kindred workers," whose unemployment has hovered around 23 percent.[9] Migrants from these two occupational groups average 12 to 15 percent of the annual migration of workers from Jamaica.

If the migration of employed workers is the result of slow wage rate growth brought about by high unemployment rates, then the antidote to migration lies in policies that reduce the general unemployment rate.

The public policy initiative required to accomplish this has not been forthcoming because Caribbean governments have been reluctant to recognize migration as a problem. Whenever migration is seen as a problem for the sending country, it is invariably migration from the top, that is, the migration of highly skilled workers. Caribbean governments have routinely encouraged migration from the bottom to relieve the high unemployment rates among their unskilled labor forces and to ensure a continuous flow of remittances in the years ahead. But even when migration from the top is regarded as a problem, it is not viewed with any great urgency because the public policy initiatives required to induce highly skilled workers to stay home or to return home are more difficult to implement than hiring substitute workers from abroad. The Michael Manley government in the 1970s took temporary workers from Cuba while announcing to its own population that there were five flights to Miami. In a sense, this willingness to use foreigners is analogous to the buy or lease problem businesses face. It is often easier to lease the equipment than to buy it. A policy to induce skilled workers to stay home is like buying equipment, only in this case it is human capital equipment, while hiring foreigners on a temporary basis is like leasing equipment. There are, however, obvious benefits from ownership, not the least of which is the development of an indigenous capacity to produce and, along with it, the ability to replicate and expand that capacity.

## SETTLEMENT

It is generally believed that most Caribbean immigrants entertain thoughts of returning home later in life, perhaps to build a house, establish a business, or just to retire. This view allows one to think of Caribbean immigrants not as an integral part of their new society but as sojourners whose primary purpose is to accumulate enough assets to provide them with a comfortable living when they return home. Implicitly, this raises questions about the ability of these immigrants to be settlers and therefore to contribute to the development of their new country.

The truth is that while some of the remittances sent home are ostensibly in preparation for the day when they will return, few immigrants ever return to live out their old age in a country where their children and immediate relatives do not live.[10] Thus, the dream of returning to live on social security or accumulated savings usually evaporates into the reality of dying in their adopted country. And the remittances they have sent back over the years have only served to keep the migration flow alive.

The fact is that the great majority of Caribbean immigrants eventually become settlers, albeit urban ones. Their greatest concentration is in New York City, where 41 percent of the Jamaicans and 80 percent of the Dominicans live (see Table 1.1). They tend to settle where the cost of housing is affordable and where there is an existing immigrant stock. Forty-five percent of the Jamaicans in New York City live in Brooklyn (Kings County) and 80 percent of the Dominicans in New York City live in the county of New York (which includes Manhattan Island) (see Table 1.2).

In Brooklyn, the concentration of West Indians changes the cultural tone of the area as small businesses and social organizations spring up to service the new immigrants. The concentration of immigrants in a particular part of the city, welded together by the culture and music of home, can operate as an important gateway into the larger American society for many newcomers or it can be a zone of isolation that provides little contact with the outside world and little encouragement to do so. The fact that these enclaves never seem to disappear does not mean that the immigrants have not assimilated into the larger society. Indeed, this migratory process goes on all the time as investment in education and hard work begin to pay off in the form of better jobs and higher incomes. The arrival of new immigrants will replace those who

**Table 1.1**
**Caribbean Population in the United States, New York State, and New York City, 1980**

| Country | United States* | New York State | New York City | N.Y. State as % of U.S. | N.Y. City as % of State | N.Y. City as % of U.S. |
|---|---|---|---|---|---|---|
| West Indies | 1,192,910 | 463,759 | 414,032 | 38.9 | 89.3 | 34.7 |
| Cuba | 500,564 | 56,895 | 46,880 | 11.4 | 82.4 | 9.4 |
| Dominican Republic | 155,930 | 131,313 | 124,088 | 84.2 | 94.5 | 79.6 |
| Jamaica | 223,652 | 107,130 | 90,756 | 47.9 | 84.7 | 40.6 |

*Persons who reported single ancestry.

*Source:* U.S. Department of Commerce, Bureau of the Census, *General Social and Economic Characteristics, New York, 1980 Census of the Population* (Washington, D.C.: U.S. Government Printing Office, 1983); U.S. Department of Commerce, Bureau of the Census, *Ancestry of the Population by State: 1980* (Washington, D.C.: U.S. Government Printing Office, 1983).

**Table 1.2**
**Distribution of New York City's Caribbean Population by County, 1980**

| County | Bronx | Kings | New York | Queens |
|---|---|---|---|---|
| West Indies | 760,936 | 161,142 | 98,352 | 91,774 |
| Cuba | 5,123 | 7,391 | 15,983 | 17,941 |
| Dominican Republic | 16,689 | 19,847 | 64,045 | 23,316 |
| Jamaica | 24,809 | 40,717 | 5,630 | 19,325 |

Source: U.S. Department of Commerce, Bureau of the Census, *General Social and Econom-ic Characteristics, New York, 1980 Census of the Population* (Washington, D.C.: U.S. Government Printing Office, 1983); U.S. Department of Commerce, Bureau of the Census, *Ancestry of the Population by State: 1980* (Washington, D.C.: U.S. Government Printing Office, 1983).

have left, keeping the enclave alive until the supply of new immigrants falls to a trickle.

Immigrants inherit no assets; they must create them if they are to be successful. Indeed, the success of any immigrant group in America depends not only on hard work but ultimately on the amount of real and financial assets they are able to acquire and hand down to their children later. West Indian immigrants, by virtue of their history, are property-owning people. In urban America, where virtually all of them live, the small business is an important symbol of property ownership. Like oth-er ethnic groups before them, many West Indian immigrants have used the small business as a vehicle for social and economic advancement in their new society. The assets inherited by subsequent generations have helped to establish them in the mainstream of American life.

It has been argued that the amount of assets an immigrant group accumulates is inversely related to the political and economic cost of returning home.[11] This has been used to explain why Cubans have a greater incentive than other Caribbean immigrants to accumulate as-sets. One is led to conclude that since the accumulation of assets indi-cates success on the part of the immigrant, the cost of returning home must be considered the reason for that success. This view, of course, is simplistic because many middle-class Cubans brought capital with them, making it easier for them to accumulate capital in their new country. Capital accumulation is slower when immigrant groups rely entirely on wage income, even when they practice a high rate of saving.

For the new immigrants entering the United States today, the urban environment is a tougher place to make a living than it was for their predecessors. But the prescription for upward mobility remains the same: hard work and investment in education. Over the years, West

Indian immigrants have demonstrated a remarkable ability to adjust to their new work environment, a phenomenon attributed to factors ranging from their language to their determination to fulfill the purpose of their immigration, that is, to improve their standard of living.[12] As English speakers, they arrive with communicating skills. As descendants of property-owning freed slaves and indentured servants, they come with a long experience of property ownership and a taste for accumulating wealth. All of these attributes are reinforced by their origins as nationals from independent sovereign states.

The success of the immigrant abroad is shared by the country of origin. This sharing has an intense emotional dimension, especially in achievement in spectator sports and in the field of entertainment. But it is no less genuine in other areas of achievement. This feeling also carries over for second-generation immigrants who achieve high positions in public as well as private life.

The prosperity of Caribbean immigrants as a group has implications for the balance of international payments of their origin countries. Not only does it increase the flow of remittances, but it also expands the market for certain Caribbean goods and services such as food and airline service. Food, like music, is a cultural link with the country of origin, and the national airline is a flying umbilical cord. British West Indian Airways and Air Jamaica are heavily used by West Indian immigrants on their return visits.

The perception of the United States as a land of opportunity is reinforced by the remittances sent back to relatives. Remittances, therefore, perform a dual role: they provide household income support on the one hand and, on the other, they strengthen perceptions about economic opportunities in the United States. This in turn encourages household reunification in the United States. In addition to remittances, return visits to relatives and friends also strengthen the migration impulse. The visit is perceived by the visited as a demonstration that the visitor has acquired enough discretionary income or enough credit to finance the trip. For people who are struggling to acquire basic necessities, the visit further underscores the perception that things are better over there. To the visitors, the trip may be less of a demonstration that they are doing well than a psychological need to reacquaint themselves with the romantic images of their ancestral home, which they have carried around with them during the years of adjustment in the United States.

## ASSESSMENT

Since the monopolistic structure of national labor markets in the Caribbean tend to constrain the maximization of lifetime household earnings, development strategy should try to make those markets more competitive by diversifying the production structure of national economies. However, such an effort by every individual Caribbean country would result in wasteful duplication, especially because the limits of diversification in the smaller islands would be reached quickly. It is for this reason that a common market arrangement with no obstacles to labor mobility offers the best option. It provides the benefits of diversification without the waste of duplication. If national labor markets are to become more competitive, labor mobility across national boundaries is essential. The great fear of such mobility is based on the premise that the poorer islands will export their unemployment to the richer ones, depressing wage rates and taking jobs away from nationals. This will be the outcome only if the total number of jobs remains fixed and if job creation continues to depend disproportionately on the production of one or two export commodities. When the oil-dependent Nigerian economy fell into a slump because of declining oil prices in the early 1980s, the Nigerian government forcibly repatriated thousands of Ghanaians to Ghana. Although there was no formal common market arrangement between the two countries, the incident indicates how threatening labor mobility is perceived by a country whose economy is vulnerable to fluctuations in the earnings of its major export. The lesson from this experience is that labor mobility among countries is better accommodated in a context of diversification and growth.

Diversification is generally interpreted to mean a widening of the range of productive activities so that the economy is not overly dependent on the production of one or two commodities or services. It must not only provide a shock absorber for international market fluctuations, but it must also create new linkages that allow firms to add more value to the final production. If this occurs, then lifetime earnings will be enhanced because workers will be in a better position to exploit the concessionary access to North American and European markets. The net result would be a wider range of job opportunities, which would enhance the prospect for greater lifetime incomes.

While diversification of Caribbean economies will ensure a more stable development path, the region's development will continue to be influenced by the United States' economy as a supplier of capital and as a market for the region's export. The value of the worker's marginal product will still be determined largely externally, but because the nature of the exports will be different, this value will be more predictable. This predictability combined with the reduction of unemployment rates will enhance lifetime earnings and reduce the incentive to migrate.

When this condition is achieved, the problem of an excess supply of labor will disappear. An excess supply of labor is an effect of inadequate development: it does not have a life of its own. A policy that encourages migration is a policy that deals with the effect rather than the cause.

Development removes the excess supply of labor without removing the population. If migration is perceived as providing a country with breathing space to develop, then as development takes place, there should be less need for such breathing room. But if the protection that migration provides against rapidly rising population rates is perceived as permanent, then the incentive for governments to make difficult decisions to accelerate development may be weakened.

## CONCLUSION

In the context of our theory of migration as a circular process, development in the Caribbean would have its greatest impact on the first stage of this process, either by preventing a migration decision or by inducing the migrant to return home before the second stage begins to develop. However, once the process begins, it is difficult to stop. Migrants' knowledge of a larger market for the services of their households is irreversible. Their return to the countries of origin will depend on their assessments of the opportunity cost of doing so. It is entirely possible that only part of the household will return, reopening a closed migration circle. But as long as the household remains a household, there will be a tendency toward reunification. If the household disintegrates, then new households will be created with possibly new migration circles.

## NOTES

1. World Bank, *World Development Report* (New York: Oxford University Press, 1988).

2. Elizabeth M. Petras, "The Global Labor Market in the Modern World Economy," in Mary Kritz, Charles B. Keely, and Silvano M. Tomasi, eds., *Global Trends in Migration: Theory and Research on International Population Movements* (New York: Center for Migration Studies, 1981), pp. 44–63.

3. Hilbourne Watson, "Theoretical and Methodological Problems in Commonwealth Caribbean Migration Research: Conditions and Causality," *Social and Economic Studies* 31:1 (March 1982): 165–206.

4. Ransford W. Palmer, "Education and Emigration from Developing Countries," in Lascelles Anderson and Douglas M. Windham, eds., *Education and Development* (Lexington, Massachusetts: Lexington Books, 1982), pp. 113–28.

5. Ralph Henry and Kim Johnson, "Migration, Manpower, and Underdevelopment of the Commonwealth Caribbean," in Robert A. Pastor, ed., *Migration and Development in the Caribbean: The Unexplored Connection* (Boulder, Colorado: Westview, 1985), pp. 273–88.

6. A few economic studies have examined the family as a unit of internal migration. The most relevant of these is by Jacob Mincer, "Family Migration Decisions," *Journal of Political Economy* 86:5 (October 1978): 749–74. While its findings may have limited applicability to international migration between the

Caribbean and the United States, it does underscore the importance of the maximization of family earnings.

7. Ransford W. Palmer, *Caribbean Dependence on the United States Economy* (New York: Praeger, 1979).

8. Clark M. Reynolds, "Caribbean Basin Interdependence: The Future Movement of People and Goods," in Robert A. Pastor, ed., *Migration and Development in the Caribbean: The Unexplored Connection* (Boulder, Colorado: Westview, 1985), pp. 395–408.

9. Statistical Institute of Jamaica, *The Labour Force* (Kingston: The Government Printer, 1976–85); Planning Institute of Jamaica, *Economic and Social Survey* (Kingston: The Government Printer, 1976–85).

10. Hymie Rubenstein, "Return Migration to the English Speaking Caribbean: Review and Commentary," in William F. Stinner, Klaus de Albuquerque, and Roy S. Bryce-Laporte, eds., *Return Migration and Remittances: Developing a Caribbean Perspective* (Washington, D.C.: Research Institute on Immigration and Ethnic Studies, 1982), pp. 3–34.

11. George J. Borjas, "The Earnings of Male Hispanic Immigrants in the United States," *The Industrial Relations Review* 35 (1982): 351.

12. Thomas Sowell, *Race and Economics* (New York: David McKay, 1975).


## SELECTED BIBLIOGRAPHY

Borjas, George J. "The Earnings of Male Hispanic Immigrants in the United States." *The Industrial Relations Review* 35 (1982).

Henry, Ralph, and Kim Johnson. "Migration, Manpower, and Underdevelopment of the Commonwealth Caribbean." In Robert A. Pastor, ed. *Migration and Development in the Caribbean: The Unexplored Connection.* Boulder, Colorado: Westview, 1985, pp. 273–88.

Mincer, Jacob. "Family Migration Decisions." *Journal of Political Economy* 86:5 (October 1978): 749–74.

Palmer, Ransford W. *Caribbean Dependence on the United States Economy.* New York: Praeger, 1979.

_____. "Education and Emigration from Developing Countries." In Lascelles Anderson and Douglas M. Windham, eds. *Education and Development.* Lexington, Massachusetts: Lexington Books, 1982, pp. 113–28.

Petras, Elizabeth M. "The Global Labor Market in the Modern World Economy." In Mary Kritz, Charles B. Keely, and Silvano M. Tomasi, eds. *Global Trends in Migration: Theory and Research on International Population Movements.* New York: Center for Migration Studies, 1981, pp. 44–63.

Planning Institute of Jamaica. *Economic and Social Survey.* Kingston: The Government Printer, 1976–85.

Rubenstein, Hymie. "Return Migration to the English Speaking Caribbean: Review and Commentary." In William F. Stinner, Klaus de Albuquerque, and Roy S. Bryce-Laporte, eds. *Return Migration and Remittances: Developing a Caribbean Perspective.* Washington, D.C.: Research Institute on Immigration and Ethnic Studies, 1982, pp. 3–34.

Reynolds, Clark M. "Caribbean Basin Interdependence: The Future Movement of People and Goods." In Robert A. Pastor, ed. *Migration and Development in the Caribbean: The Unexplored Connection.* Boulder, Colorado: Westview, 1985, pp. 395–408.

Sowell, Thomas. *Race and Economics.* New York: David McKay, 1975.

Statistical Institute of Jamaica. *The Labour Force.* Kingston: The Government Printer, 1976–85.

Watson, Hilbourne. "Theoretical and Methodological Problems in Commonwealth Caribbean Migration Research: Conditions and Causality." *Social and Economic Studies* 31:1 (March 1982): 165–206.

World Bank. *World Development Report.* New York: Oxford University Press, 1988.

# 2

# Nineteenth-Century West Indian Migration to Britain

PETER D. FRASER

This chapter examines the size and demographic composition, the principal domestic and foreign causes, and the significance of population movements from the British Caribbean to other countries in the nineteenth century. It also examines the effect of these population movements on the British Caribbean itself.[1]

## PRINCIPAL DOMESTIC AND FOREIGN CAUSES OF MIGRATION

At the root of nineteenth-century West Indian migration—as with so much else in Caribbean history—was sugar. After Emancipation and Apprenticeship (1834–38), these territories had to adjust to the new regime of free labor in unfavorable international economic circumstances. Sugar prices, fairly strong in the period 1835–46, fell sharply, then maintained a plateau for almost the next 40 years, when they once more sank until revived by World War I. Thus, although British Caribbean sugar production had almost doubled between 1839–43 and 1899–1903, it was worth only about two-thirds of its 1839–43 value by the end of the century. The chief reason for the drop in price was the enormous expansion of world sugar production, especially of beet sugar, which was heavily subsidized by European governments. Cane sugar production also expanded in the nineteenth century, with production equaling or exceeding the six million tons of beet sugar produced annually in the years 1899–1903. The Brussels agreement of 1902 removed the subsidies but failed to raise prices, since the annual average production of both cane and beet sugar in 1909–13 exceeded eight million tons.[2]

The British Caribbean failed to keep pace with this production expansion. In the years after the end of Apprenticeship, 1839–43, these territories produced 16 percent of the world's cane sugar and 15 percent of all sugar. By 1899–1903, their share was 5 percent of cane sugar and 2 percent of all sugar (see Table 2.1). Immediately before World War I, in 1909–13, these figures were down to 2 percent and 1 percent, respectively. By the end of the nineteenth century, therefore, the British Caribbean territories had become marginal producers of sugar, and their production levels had little influence on price levels, a situation far different from that of the eighteenth and early-nineteenth centuries. Even within the British Empire, their position was marginal: by 1909–13, Mauritius produced more sugar than all the British Caribbean territories combined. Within the Caribbean itself, Cuban production in those same years was almost nine times that of the British Caribbean, and the Dominican Republic, a marginal producer until the 1880s, was producing almost half as much sugar by that time.

This decline of the British Caribbean sugar industry had its roots in competition from cheaper producers of cane sugar such as Cuba and the artificially cheap beet sugar exports from European producers. (Though West Indian proprietors complained of Cuban access to supposedly cheaper slave labor, natural fertility of the soil was a bigger advantage.) The dismantling of British imperial protection in the 1850s and 1870s occurred when beet sugar exports were expanding rapidly. The British Caribbean throughout the nineteenth century failed to attract capital in sufficient quantity to modernize the sugar industry to face competition; the exception to this was in British Guiana, where significant modernization did occur.

Both proprietors and imperial officials, however, saw labor as the

**Table 2.1**
**British West Indian Sugar Production, 1839–1903 (Five-Year Averages)**

| Years | Tons | % of Total World Sugar Production from Cane | % of Total World Sugar Production |
|-------|------|------|------|
| 1839-1843 | 129,000 | 16 | 15 |
| 1859-1863 | 200,000 | 14 | 11 |
| 1869-1873 | 237,000 | 14 | 9 |
| 1879-1883 | 271,000 | 14 | 7 |
| 1889-1893 | 283,000 | 10 | 4 |
| 1899-1903 | 242,000 | 5 | 2 |

Source: Noel Deerr, The History of Sugar, 2 Vols. (London: Chapmen & Hall, 1949).

main—and sometimes the only—problem. They complained incessantly of the unavailability and unreliability of the ex-slaves and their descendants, and they experimented with labor from Europe, Africa, and China before settling on the Indian subcontinent as the chief source of labor in the sugar industries of Trinidad and British Guiana. These continual complaints are probably not unconnected with the failure to attract capital, since the picture painted of territories in decay with unwilling workers was hardly an inducement for investors.

The chief problems of labor supply after Emancipation seem to be creating a new type of labor relations and the question of wages. The transition from a slave labor to a free labor system involved profound changes from both sides and the former slaveowners proved to be the slower learners. Indeed, the quest for a new, immigrant labor force had more to do with questions of labor control than with labor shortages, since the conditions of indentureship maintained the dominance of employer over employee that proprietors had enjoyed under slavery. Adjustment became trickier when sugar prices fell from 1846 onward. Wages followed downward, and the labor supply for the sugar plantations began to contract, exacerbating further problems of adjustment. The interaction of these features explains the failure of the British Caribbean to expand its sugar industry at the same pace as its competitors[3] (see Table 2.2).

The result was that the British Caribbean became quite different from what it had been prior to Emancipation. Then, with the exception of the smallest islands, exports mainly of sugar dominated economic activity; in Jamaica and British Guiana, other plantation crops such as cotton and coffee were preeminent. By the end of the nineteenth century, three main types of economies could be distinguished: the plantation-dominated economy, the mixed economy, and the small-to-medium economy. In the first category belonged Barbados and St. Kitts, the oldest British Caribbean possessions, as well as the newest, Trinidad and British Guiana; in the second was Jamaica, even during slavery the most complex of the economies as well as the largest; and in the third, Grenada. The last two categories were created by the decline of the sugar industry in Jamaica during the nineteenth century and the collapse of sugar in the last three decades of that century in Grenada, St. Vincent, Dominica, and Montserrat. Such was the importance of sugar that there was large-scale emigration in all these territories, with the exception of Trinidad and British Guiana.[4]

Had there been alternatives to sugar with the capacity to absorb the labor released by the decline of individual sugar operations, emigration would have been much reduced. In the nineteenth century, the only reliable alternative activities were other export crops, mining, and small farming. Bananas became important in Jamaica right at the end of the

**Table 2.2**
**Sugar Production (Tons) of Individual Territories, 1839–1903 (Five-Year Averages)**

| Territory | 1839-1843 | 1859-1863 | 1869-1873 | 1879-1883 | 1889-1893 | 1899-1903 |
|---|---|---|---|---|---|---|
| Barbados | 15,000 | 33,800 | 35,400 | 47,200 | 57,200 | 44,000 |
| Jamaica | 33,200 | 25,600 | 25,600 | 24,200 | 21,000 | 17,600 |
| St. Lucia | 2,400 | 4,400 | 5,400 | 6,600 | 5,000 | 4,600 |
| St. Kitts & Nevis | 5,800 | 9,600 | 12,400 | 12,800 | 17,000 | 13,200 |
| Antigua | 8,800 | 10,000 | 9,600 | 10,000 | 14,400 | 9,800 |

*Source:* Noel Deerr, *The History of Sugar*, 2 vols. (London: Chapmen & Hall, 1949).

nineteenth century; gold mining had its boom at the end of the century in British Guiana, then a recipient of immigrants; and small farm production of food crops for domestic consumption (and occasionally for export) increased, although it was dependent on the availability of land. In islands such as Barbados and St. Kitts, where plantations monopolized land, small farming could not expand; even in Jamaica, where it did expand, small-scale agriculture failed to absorb surplus labor. No solutions seemed to exist for the twin problems of declining sugar production and increasing population.

During slavery, populations in these territories grew through the importation of new slaves as sugar developed. Population figures also increased naturally after Emancipation in most of the colonies, with major exceptions in Barbados (where natural increase preceded Emancipation) and Trinidad and British Guiana (where post-Emancipation immigration spurred population growth). These increases multiplied the effects of a static or declining demand for labor, especially since the alternative activities provided fairly weak demand. The full effect of this process was evident at the end of the century (see Table 2.3).

If the nineteenth century proved a difficult time for the British Caribbean, elsewhere in the Americas it was a time of expansion. In the second half of the century, the economies of Mexico, Central America, the Hispanic Caribbean, and Venezuela expanded as their export sectors were modernized. Workers from the British Caribbean were recruited for three main sectors: export agriculture, infrastructural development, and mining.

A certain irony emerges here: while proprietors of British Caribbean sugar plantations complained of labor shortages, West Indians emigrated to work on the sugar plantations of St. Croix (from the 1860s onward to the twentieth century); they contracted themselves to Puerto Rican planters (in the 1860s and 1870s); and they began to move to the nascent sugar industry in the Dominican Republic (from the 1880s onward). So too the workers of Barbados and the Leeward Islands moved to the developing sugar industries in Trinidad and British Guiana. And by the last two decades of the nineteenth century, the new banana industry in Costa Rica was proving attractive to West Indians.[5]

The expansion of international trade and new economic activities led to the development of infrastructure, thereby increasing demand for labor. The Panama Railway, built in the 1850s, created the first easy link between the Atlantic and Pacific Oceans, making travel between the East and West coasts of the United States quicker and less hazardous; it also marked the beginning of U.S. hegemony in Central America. Twenty years later, West Indians were helping to build a railway in Costa Rica and, in the next decade, one in Mexico. In the 1880s and 1890s, they were involved in the construction of the Panama Canal. Although initial

**Table 2.3**
**Population of the British Caribbean for Selected Years, 1844–1911**

| Territory | 1844 | 1861 | 1871 | 1881 | 1891 | 1901 | 1911 |
|-----------|------|------|------|------|------|------|------|
| Barbados | 122,198 | 152,727 | 162,042 | 171,860 | 182,306 | * | 171,983 |
| Jamaica | 377,433 | 441,264 | 506,154 | 580,804 | 639,491 | * | 831,383 |
| St. Lucia | 21,001 | 26,674 | 31,610 | 38,511 | 42,220 | 49,883 | 48,637 |
| St. Kitts & Nevis | 32,748 | ** | 39,872 | 41,001 | 43,873 | 42,556 | 43,303 |
| Antigua | 36,178 | ** | 34,344 | 34,321 | 36,119 | 34,178 | 32,269 |

Source: Census Reports.

efforts by the French failed, the successful U.S. attempt in the new century involved even larger numbers of British Caribbean laborers.[6]

Mining proved attractive to West Indian migrants, as small numbers could be found in Venezuela by the 1870s. In 1882, a few thousand workers from "the British and French West Indies" were found by the Venezuelan Inspector General of Mines. French Guianese gold fields lured thousands of St. Lucians during the worldwide gold mining boom in the 1890s.[7]

As the migration to Haiti shows, some West Indians moved to jobs in the service sector. By the late nineteenth century, nearly all the coachmen in Port-au-Prince were Jamaicans.[8] The failure of the plantation sector to expand depressed the demand for skilled and unskilled urban, as well as rural, labor. Urban tradesmen migrated from Kingston and Spanish Town in large numbers during the first Jamaican movement to Panama, while Barbadian migrants to the rest of the British Caribbean were often teachers or policemen, and women migrants were often petty traders or domestic servants. The white emigrants who left Barbados for "Europe, the United States and other parts of the world" at this time on the whole also went to urban occupations.[9]

Any explanation of West Indian migration resting only on economic difficulties within the British Caribbean and the expansion without would be incomplete. Much must remain unexplained, for the emigration phenomenon, while commented on, was not studied in any great detail by colonial governments and was sometimes totally neglected by the census officials, as happened in the 1901 St. Lucia Census.

Destination countries, too, show a dearth of records of individual migrants preventing the sort of detailed examination that can provide nuanced explanations for migration decisions. Among the rare autobiographical accounts is that of Mary Seacole:

> Early in the same year [1850] my brother had left Kingston for the Isthmus of Panama . . . where he had established a considerable store and hotel. Ever since he had done so, I had found some difficulty in checking my reviving disposition to roam, and at last persuading myself that I might be of use to him (he was far from strong), I resigned my house into the hands of a cousin, and made arrangements to journey to Chagres.[10]

Yet, we can draw some conclusions about the economic and other motivations of migratory laborers. Higher wages outside the British Caribbean were clearly an inducement to emigrate. Wages on the Panama Railway in the 1850s were three times those in Jamaica. When wages in Barbados and the Leeward Islands were less than a shilling a day around 1870, Venezuelan mines paid just over seven shillings for a 12-hour day, rising to over 13 shillings for 8 hours by 1882. Clearly, such differences were a powerful inducement to leave, even for those who were employed, despite the often-arduous conditions in foreign mines, on plantations, and on infrastructural projects. Equally clear is the fact that higher wages are not by themselves a full explanation of migration. If they were, in conditions of almost unrestricted labor mobility such as prevailed at the time, wage rates would be equalized and the inducement to migrate would have disappeared. Other considerations were at work.[11]

Recent writers have laid great stress on migration being one sign of West Indians' search for independence from the domination exercised by plantation owners; others have stressed the creation of a migration tradition or a psychological predisposition among West Indians to migrate. Both of these features played a part in the nineteenth century migrations. Migrants were mainly younger adults who could vote effectively with their feet against the restrictions of politics and society. Similarly, the more people who migrated, the more information was made available to those who had stayed behind concerning the possibilities of financial success overseas or the chances of living fuller lives than the British Caribbean afforded. Yet basically the struggle against the elite revolved around the issues of the control of limited resources, whether land or labor, and the limited economic, social, and political opportunities available to black West Indians at home.[12]

## SIZE AND DEMOGRAPHIC COMPOSITION

The size of nineteenth-century migrations is difficult to estimate due to the patchy contemporary records. But we will make the attempt, first setting out estimates from various noncensus sources and then from census sources.

In the early 1850s, Panama attracted 4,000–5,000 Jamaicans; by July, 1854, some 2,000–3,000 males had already left the island. Haiti in the 1860s and 1870s was the destination of approximately 2,000–3,000 West Indians. St. Croix in the Danish Virgin Islands was said to have about 5,000 West Indians working on its sugar plantations at the time of the 1878 disturbances. The mines of Venezuela and French Guiana, in the 1880s and 1890s, respectively, were estimated to have about 2,000 West Indians each. In the 1880s, Costa Rica probably drew about 800 migrants a year, with the total dropping to 500 annually in the 1890s. In Mexico, the haciendas of the 1880s had perhaps 200 West Indians while the railways employed several hundred in the late 1890s. Around 500 West Indians each year, from the 1880s, went to the Dominican Republic. Panama, as in the following century, was the great magnet: nearly 84,000 Jamaicans and about 15,000 other West Indians migrated there between 1881 and 1889, when the French canal project was at its height.

(This figure assumes that nearly all Jamaican migrants went to Panama in those years.)

The census reports do not shed much additional light. The Dominica and Grenada censuses of 1881 reported unspecified numbers of migrants to the Venezuelan mines. The 1891 censuses of the Bahamas and St. Lucia were more precise, indicating that 85 migrants journeyed from the Bahamas to Central America and Haiti and 1,710 men left St. Lucia for Panama. The Antigua census of 1871 estimated a loss of approximately 1,600 to St. Croix, Trinidad, and elsewhere. By 1911, the Barbadian census estimated that 48,600 people—32,000 men and 16,000 women—migrated between 1891 and 1911, with probably 50 percent of the loss occurring in each decade. Based on 1881 and 1891 census figures, Gisela Eisner estimates a net migration of nearly 24,000 Jamaicans; for the period between the 1891 and 1911 censuses, almost 43,500 migrated, nearly all after 1904.[13]

All the evidence suggests that a large majority of the migrants were males between the ages of 21 and 45 (see Table 2.4). The loss of both men and women in their most productive years and the imbalance between the sexes played a decisive role in reducing population growth. Continuing internal economic pressures combined with success or failure abroad meant that in the late-nineteenth and early-twentieth centuries such demographic conditions became the norm throughout the British Caribbean. Slower population growth, or even population loss, helped to ensure that the endemic economic crisis never became epidemic. Migration reached epidemic proportions in the twentieth century, with further significant demographic effects.

## THE EFFECTS OF MIGRATION ON
## THE BRITISH CARIBBEAN

The first and most notable effect of nineteenth-century migrations was on population growth. The population of the British Virgin Islands actually fell between 1844 and 1891; in that same period, the population of Antigua increased by only a few hundred. Most territories did experience population growth, but it is notable that British Guiana and Trinidad, which outstripped the others, did so through immigration. (We are omitting British Honduras, with its exceptional history.) St. Lucia, Grenada, and Jamaica experienced lesser degrees of immigration. Little attention was paid to the effects of migration until the end of the nineteenth century; since financial constraints prohibited the 1901 census in all the territories, the full impact of migration at the time remains unknown. By 1911, however, the impact of migration to Panama made further neglect of the phenomenon impossible (see Table 2.5).

**Table 2.4**
**Sex Ratios (Males per 1,000 Females) by Age for Barbados, Jamaica, and St. Lucia for Selected Years, 1861–1911**

| Age | 1844 | 1861 | 1871 | 1881 | 1891 | 1911 |
|---|---|---|---|---|---|---|
| | | | Barbados | | | |
| 21-30 | 750* | 800 | 690 | 660 | 700 | 380 |
| 31-40 | - - | 760 | 730 | 660 | 640 | 500 |
| 41-50 | - - | 790 | 680 | 710 | 650 | 600 |
| | | | Jamaica | | | |
| 15-29 | 990** | † | † | 929 | 849 | 851 |
| 30-54 | - - | † | † | 950 | 901 | 890 |
| | | | St. Lucia | | | |
| 20-29 | 800*** | † | 960 | 940 | 810 | 620 |
| 30-39 | - - | † | 1,010 | 970 | 900 | 710 |
| 40-49 | - - | † | 1,030 | 1,030 | 910 | 840 |

*18+
**20–40
***16+
†Not available.

Source: Census Reports for Barbados and Jamaica; George W. Roberts, The Population of Jamaica (Cambridge: Conservation Foundation/Cambridge University Press, 1957), p. 72.

When authorities became aware of the extent of emigration, they noticed its effects on the sex balance of the population. The 1891 Barbados census took note of the exodus of males in this fashion: "the withdrawal . . . of persons of that age and sex most valuable in the community." This orthodox piece of Victorian sexism refers to the increasing presence of females in the Barbadian agricultural labor force. The figures in Table 2.6 show that in 1844, a rough equality existed: from 1861 onward, females outnumbered males to an increasing extent, even though males always outnumbered females up to the age of 15.

Table 2.7 shows the contrast between Trinidad and Tobago. In the former, there were slightly more than twice as many men as women engaged in agriculture, while in the latter, men were outnumbered by women.

**Table 2.5**
**West Indian Populations, 1844 and 1891**

| Territory | 1844 | 1891 | Percentage Change |
|---|---|---|---|
| British Honduras | 10,000 | 31,471 | 214.7 |
| Trinidad & Tobago | 73,023 | 218,381 | 199.1 |
| British Guiana | 98,133 | 270,865 | 176.0 |
| St. Lucia | 21,001 | 42,220 | 101.0 |
| Grenada | 28,923 | 53,209 | 84.0 |
| Jamaica | 377,433 | 639,491 | 69.4 |
| Montserrat | 7,365 | 11,762 | 59.7 |
| St. Vincent | 27,248 | 41,054 | 50.7 |
| Barbados | 122,198 | 182,867 | 49.6 |
| St. Kitts & Nevis | 32,748 | 47,662 | 45.5 |
| Dominica | 22,469 | 26,841 | 19.5 |
| Antigua | 36,178 | 36,819 | 1.8 |
| Virgin Islands | 6,689 | 4,639 | - 30.6 |

Source: Census Reports.

The figures for Jamaica in Table 2.8 confirm that general picture but also illustrate another effect of emigration on agriculture: the great increase in the number of planters, that is, small holders, between 1891 and 1911. Evident, too, is the sharp growth in the predominance of men. The populations of towns appear to have been mainly female.

**Table 2.6**
**Gender Division of the Agricultural Labor Force of Barbados by Age for Selected Years, 1844–1911**

| Year | Under Age 15 | | Over Age 15 | |
|---|---|---|---|---|
| | Male | Female | Male | Female |
| 1844 | -- | -- | 14,576* | 15,429* |
| 1861 | 4,010 | 3,539 | 15,228 | 19,478 |
| 1871 | 3,072 | 2,735 | 18,947 | 23,323 |
| 1881 | 3,078 | 2,662 | 18,426 | 23,804 |
| 1891 | 2,303 | 1,768 | 18,502 | 24,434 |
| 1911 | 1,939 | 1,491 | 14,216 | 22,017 |

*18 and over.

Source: Census Reports.

**Table 2.7**
**Gender Division of the Agricultural Labor Force of Trinidad and Tobago, 1891 and 1901**

| Year | Trinidad | | Tobago | |
|------|----------|--------|--------|--------|
|      | Male     | Female | Male   | Female |
| 1891 | 44,474   | 21,119 | 2,307  | 2,755  |
| 1901 | 49,550   | 23,227 | 2,149  | 2,538  |

Source: Census Reports.

The effect of the nineteenth-century migrations on social life, especially family life, must have been considerable. This, of course, is even harder to comment on than the volume of migration. Records are not readily available, although there are scattered references concerning the distress of families left behind. Temporary separations sometimes became permanent due to desertion, death, or the inability of the migrants to escape harsh conditions, including binding labor contracts. All this suggests that stresses on West Indian family life were considerable by the end of the nineteenth century.

The political effects must also remain speculative. If the migrants felt they would receive little economic justice at home, they often felt they had been denied justice pure and simple abroad. The fate of those West Indians killed during the St. Croix disturbances of 1878 illustrates the precariousness of life abroad. Many petitions from migrants in Haiti and elsewhere in the nineteenth century showed West Indians appealing to British norms of justice and British protection from foreign insult

**Table 2.8**
**Gender Division of Agricultural Laborers and Planters in Jamaica, 1891 and 1911**

| Year | Laborers | | Planters | |
|------|----------|---------|----------|--------|
|      | Male     | Female  | Male     | Female |
| 1891 | 114,910  | 123,353 | 19,365   | 10,247 |
| 1911 | 68,333   | 81,078  | 80,690   | 31,852 |

Source: Census Reports.

and injury. Whether or not the migrants returned home with a heightened sense of the proclaimed standards of British justice, not always in evidence in the British Caribbean, does not appear so far in the records. Further study of political organizations in the late-nineteenth century might reveal the influence, if any, of returning migrants. It is quite possible that these people, able to purchase land or improve their property and well placed to benefit from the new export crops of the late century, had a conservative effect on political life. The continuing loss of workers must have retarded the development of workers' organizations, since continuity in membership would have been difficult to achieve. In contrast to their effect in the twentieth century, there is little evidence of the effect of emigré communities on the political life of the British Caribbean. One case worth noting, however, is that of Joseph Love, the Bahamian who influenced Marcus Garvey; he ultimately settled in Jamaica after living in the United States and Haiti.[14]

The economic effects of the migrations were far-reaching. The plantocracy complained about the lack of labor while large numbers of laborers migrated. Migration undoubtedly made life more difficult for owners but helped to maintain wage levels, which remained low up until World War I. Although throughout most of this period migration removed surplus labor, at the end of the century workers migrated who might have been able to find employment at home. Both skilled and unskilled labor migrated. The failure of domestic wages and salaries to rise does suggest that the area was producing a surplus of both types of labor, skilled due to the development of education and unskilled as a result of the contraction of the sugar industry and the growth of the population.

The departure of migrants meant that a safety valve operated in two distinct ways. The removal of surplus labor ensured that challenges to the prevailing economic system were minimized and postponed the necessity of reconstructing it to provide its inhabitants a livelihood within the British Caribbean. The response of the elite to migration was ambiguous: while they complained about labor shortages, they recognized that migration was a necessity. A second safety valve was provided by the repatriation of migrants' earnings. If living standards were maintained at low levels by the removal of the reserve army of surplus laborers, they were also sustained by the remittances of these same migrants. Cessation of work on the Panama Canal in 1884 was reported to have led to a drop of over £20,000 in money circulating in Jamaica the following year (although not all that can be attributed to migrants' remittances). Between 1868 and 1875, Barbadians remitted £10,000 from British Guiana.[15]

Migration also established trading links between Jamaica and Panama and between the Bahamas and Haiti. The link with Panama has remained an important one for the sale of ground provisions. Migrations, especially to construction projects such as railways and the Panama Canal undoubtedly also helped by upgrading the skills of West Indians.[16] Finally, migration became an integral part of British Caribbean economies, with the Barbadian pattern becoming the common one. What had started as a tactic for the workers in their struggle with the owners for economic security and independence became in the twentieth century a grand strategy.

## THE SIGNIFICANCE OF NINETEENTH-CENTURY MIGRATIONS

The nineteenth-century migrations from the British Caribbean contained in miniature the same elements as those in the twentieth century. Their origins lay in economic problems within the British Caribbean and expanding opportunities outside, although they were much more closely tied to the fortunes of the sugar industry than later migrations. Political considerations figure much more prominently in some of the post-1960s migrations than they ever did in the previous century. It must not be forgotten, however, that white West Indians migrated in the nineteenth century for sociopolitical reasons as much as for economic ones, and doubtless black West Indians did not choose Haiti merely for its economic possibilities. Yet there is no real equivalent in the nineteenth century of the politically inspired outward flow of people from Guyana and Jamaica during the 1960s and 1970s.

Nineteenth-century migrations also differed in destination. Geographically, destinations were confined to the Caribbean and Central and South America. Twentieth-century migrants would continue to go to these regions, but the great majority would move to Canada, the United States, and Britain. This also marks a difference in the types of receiving society: in the nineteenth century, they were countries in which an expanding capitalism transformed agriculture; in the twentieth, they are established centers of industrial capitalism. The beginnings of this change can be observed in the tiny flow of people to North America and Britain before 1900. The nineteenth-century migrations established enduring links with other countries in the hemisphere. Panama recurs in the history of West Indian migration from the 1850s to the 1940s, but West Indian communities, although small, are well established in other Central American countries. The comparatively unknown migration to Haiti prefigures the better-known, although equally small, migrations to Africa in this century. The Dominican Republic remained a destination for West Indians from the 1880s to the 1930s; today, Venezuela is an important destination for small numbers of people. The nineteenth-century migrations established regions beyond British control and with languages other than English as possible destinations for migrants in parallel with destinations inside the British Caribbean.

If the nineteenth century started the tradition of migration for West Indians, it also helped entrench migration as an integral feature of the British Commonwealth economic system. The pressure to act energetically to transform the economies as compensation for the decline of sugar was relieved in a number of ways. Surplus labor was removed, sometimes permanently; population growth slowed and was sometimes halted; and poverty was relieved and social mobility achieved through the remittances of migrants. But migrants, by going to expanding economies, contributed to the economic difficulties of the British Caribbean by assisting the development of competitors—sugar in the Dominican Republic and bananas in Costa Rica, for example. This is another way of saying that capital was invested outside the British Caribbean, sometimes by British investors, while the homelands of the migrants were not treated similarly.

The nineteenth century also established the major pattern of West Indian migrations: migrants that were seen, and saw themselves, as temporarily resident in their destinations. Their work on the Panama Canal projects, Mexican and Costa Rican railways, and sugar and banana plantations was mainly seasonal, though in the course of time, especially on the larger plantations, permanent communities were formed. In the twentieth century, seasonal migrations continue, despite a tendency toward settlement, specifically in the industrialized centers of the Northern Hemisphere. Settled communities were much larger in the twentieth century than in the previous one. Another pattern established in the nineteenth century was the movement of people from one destination to another or from one project to the next. For example, migrants would move from Haiti to the Dominican Republic or from railway building to banana plantations in Costa Rica. In the twentieth century, this trend can be found in movement from Panama to the United States or from Britain to North America. Then, too, in the nineteenth century came the beginnings of the West Indian brain drain among colored and black West Indians following the loss of qualified white West Indians in the eighteenth century.

As they were in the nineteenth century, Jamaica and Barbados have been the major exporters of people in the twentieth century. Other prominent exporters of people in the nineteenth century, such as the British Virgins and Antigua, remain so in this century. Last century's centers of immigration, chiefly Trinidad and Guyana, became twentieth century emigration centers, especially Guyana in the 1960s. We should not forget, however, that even in these two centuries, those two countries lost over a quarter of their Indian indentured immigrants, resulting in substantial outward flows even in the 1800s.[17]

Emigration from the British Caribbean in the nineteenth century was a universal phenomenon; it also involved the French Antilles. The twentieth century is witnessing the continuing movement of peoples from Haiti, Puerto Rico, Cuba, the Dominican Republic, and the Dutch Antilles. Nineteenth-century West Indian migrations appear, therefore, to be the first signs of an enduring crisis in the political economy of the Caribbean.

## NOTES

1. The reader's attention is directed to the following valuable resources: Elizabeth Thomas-Hope, "The Establishment of a Migration Tradition: British West Indian Movements to the Hispanic Caribbean in the Century after Emancipation," in Colin G. Clarke, ed., *Caribbean Social Relations*, University of Liverpool Monograph Series No. 8 (Liverpool: University of Liverpool Centre for Latin-American Studies, n.d.) and Dawn I. Marshall, "The History of Caribbean Migrations: The Case of the West Indies," *Caribbean Review* 11:1 (Winter 1982): 6–9 and 52–53, provide good surveys of nineteenth and twentieth century movements; Orlando Patterson, "Migration in Caribbean Societies: Socioeconomic and Symbolic Resource," in William H. McNeil and Ruth S. Adams, eds., *Human Migration: Patterns and Policies* (Bloomington, Indiana, and London: American Academy of Arts and Sciences/Indiana University Press, 1978) provides an interpretation; studies on particular movements include Olive Senior, "The Panama Railway," *Jamaica Journal* 44 (n.d.): 67–77; "The Colon People: Part One," *Jamaica Journal* 11:3 and 4 (March 1978): 62–71; and "The Colon People: Part Two," *Jamaica Journal* 42 (September 1978): 88–103, all excellent; Lancelot S. Lewis, *The West Indian in Panama: Black Labor in Panama, 1850–1914* (Washington, D.C.: University Press of America, 1980); Velma Newton, *The Silver Men: West Indian Labour Migration to Panama, 1850–1914* (Mona, Jamaica: Institute of Social and Economic Research, 1984); Quince Duncan and Carlos Melendez, *El Negro en Costa Rica*, 3rd edition (San Jose: Editorial Costa Rica, 1976); Jeffrey Casey Gaspar, *Limon, 1880–1940, Un estudio de la industria bananera en Costa Rica* (San Jose: Editorial Costa Rica, 1979), which contains much information about West Indians; two fine studies by Bonham C. Richardson, *Caribbean Migrants: Environment and Human Survival on St. Kitts and Nevis* (Knoxville, Tennessee: University of Tennessee Press, 1983) and *Panama Money in Barbados, 1900–1920* (Knoxville, Tennessee: University of Tennessee Press, 1985), the latter useful on nineteenth-century migration, as well as his "Human Mobility in the Windwards in the Late 19th Century," a paper presented at the Workshop on the Caribbean Diaspora, London University Institute of Commonwealth Studies, June 1987; Victor C. Dahl, "Alien Labor on the Gulf Coast of Mexico, 1880–1900," *The Americas* 17:1 (July 1960): 21–35; Peter D. Fraser, "British West Indians in Haiti in the Late Nineteenth and Early Twentieth Centuries," *Immigrants and Minorities* 7:1 (March 1988): 79–94.

2. Noel Deerr, *The History of Sugar*, 2 vols. (London: Chapmen & Hall, 1949).

3. R. W. Beachy, *The British West Indian Sugar Industry in the Late Nineteenth Century* (Oxford: Basil Blackwell, 1957).

4. Douglas Hall, *Free Jamaica 1838–1865: An Economic History* (New Haven, Connecticut: Yale University Press, 1959); Gisela Eisner, *Jamaica, 1830–1930: A Study in Economic Growth* (Manchester: Manchester University Press, 1961); Douglas Hall, *Five of the Leewards 1834–1870* (St. Lawrence: Caribbean University Press, 1971); and, for specific countries, see William A. Green, *British Slave Emancipation: The Sugar Colonies and the Great Experiment, 1830–1865* (London: Oxford University Press, 1976) and his "Push Factors: Nineteenth Century Backgrounds to the Caribbean Diaspora," paper presented at the Workshop on the Caribbean Diaspora, London University Institute of Commonwealth Studies, June 1987, for the wider picture.

5. Along with works cited in Note 1, see Andres Ramos Mattei, "La imigracion contratada de las islas Britanicas en el Caribe a la industria azucarera Puertorriquena: 1860–1880," paper presented at the tenth Conference of the Association of Caribbean Historians, College of the Virgin Islands, St. Thomas, U.S. Virgin Islands, 1978; Patrick E. Bryan, "The Question of Labor in the Sugar Industry of the Dominican Republic in the Late Nineteenth and Early Twentieth Centuries," in Manuel Moreno Fraginals, Moya Pons, and Stanley L. Engerman, eds., *Between Slavery and Free Labour: The Spanish Speaking Caribbean in the Nineteenth Century* (Baltimore, Maryland, and London: The Johns Hopkins University Press, 1985); for the Danish Virgin Islands, see *F.O. 22/423* (Kew, Surrey, England: Public Records Office, Foreign Office, n.d.), for instance.

6. See works cited in Note 1, especially Senior and Gaspar.

7. *F.O. 80/286*, p. 141; and, for French Guiana, Richardson, "Human Mobility."

8. Benoit Joachim, *Les Racines du Sous-developpement en Haiti* (Port-au-Prince: Impremerie H. Deschamps, 1980), p. 101.

9. Hall, *Free Jamaica*, pp. 221–22; Richardson, *Panama Money*, pp. 100–104; *Barbados Census Report 1881*, p. 4.

10. Mary Seacole, *Wonderful Adventures of Mrs. Seacole in Many Lands*, Ziggi Alexander and Audrey Dewjee, eds., 2nd ed. (Bristol, England: Falling Wall Press, 1984; orig. ed., 1857), pp. 62–63.

11. Green, "Push Factors"; *F.O. 80/286*; Senior, "Colon People: Part Two."

12. Thomas-Hope, "The Establishment of a Migration Tradition."

13. Census Reports; Eisner, *Jamaica, 1830–1930*; and George W. Roberts, *The Population of Jamaica* (Cambridge: Conservation Foundation/Cambridge University Press, 1957), pp. 133–39.

14. Fraser, "British West Indians."

15. Senior, "Colon People: Part Two," p. 102; Richardson, *Panama Money*, p. 104.

16. Senior, "Colon People: Part Two," pp. 101–103.

17. K. O. Laurence, "Immigration into the West Indies in the 19th Century," in *Caribbean History 3* (St. Lawrence: Caribbean University Press, 1971), p. 57.

## SELECTED BIBLIOGRAPHY

Beachy, R. W. *The British West Indian Sugar Industry in the Late Nineteenth Century*. Oxford: Basil Blackwell, 1957.

Bryan, Patrick E. "The Question of Labor in the Sugar Industry of the Dominican Republic in the Late Nineteenth and Early Twentieth Centuries." In Manuel Moreno Fraginals, Moya Pons, and Stanley L. Engerman, eds. *Between Slavery and Free Labour: The Spanish Speaking Caribbean in the Nineteenth Century*. Baltimore, Maryland, and London: The Johns Hopkins University Press, 1985.

Dahl, Victor C. "Alien Labor on the Gulf Coast of Mexico, 1880–1900," *The Americas* 17:1 (July 1960): 21–35.

Deerr, Noel. *The History of Sugar*. 2 vols. London: Chapmen & Hall, 1949.

Duncan, Quince, and Carlos Melendez. *El Negro en Costa Rica*. 3rd ed. San Jose: Editorial Costa Rica, 1976.

Eisner, Gisela. *Jamaica, 1830–1930: A Study in Economic Growth*. Manchester: Manchester University Press, 1961.

Fraser, Peter D. "British West Indians in Haiti in the Late Nineteenth and Early Twentieth Centuries," *Immigrants and Minorities* 7:1 (March 1988): 79–94.

Gaspar, Jeffrey Casey. *Limon, 1880–1940, Un estudio de la industria bananera en Costa Rica*. San Jose: Editorial Costa Rica, 1979.

Green, William A. *British Slave Emancipation: The Sugar Colonies and the Great Experiment, 1830–1865*. London: Oxford University Press, 1976.

_____. "Push Factors: Nineteenth Century Backgrounds to the Caribbean Diaspora." Unpublished paper presented at the Workshop on the Caribbean Diaspora, London University Institute of Commonwealth Studies, June 1987.

Hall, Douglas. *Five of the Leewards 1834–1870*. St. Lawrence: Caribbean University Press, 1971.

_____. *Free Jamaica 1838–1865: An Economic History*. New Haven, Connecticut: Yale University Press, 1959.

Joachim, Benoit. *Les Racines du Sous-developpement en Haiti*. Port-au-Prince: Impremerie H. Deschamps, 1980.

Laurence, K. O. "Immigration into the West Indies in the 19th Century." In *Caribbean History 3*. St. Lawrence: Caribbean University Press, 1971.

Lewis, Lancelot S. *The West Indian in Panama: Black Labor in Panama, 1850–1914*. Washington, D.C.: University Press of America, 1980.

Marshall, Dawn I. "The History of Caribbean Migrations: The Case of the West Indies." *Caribbean Review* 11:1 (Winter 1982): 6–9 and 52–53.

Mattei, Andres Ramos. "La imigracion contratada de las islas Britanicas en el Caribe a la industria azucarera Puertorriquena: 1860–1880." Unpublished paper presented at the tenth Conference of the Association of Caribbean Historians, College of the Virgin Islands, St. Thomas, U.S. Virgin Islands, 1978.

Newton, Velma. *The Silver Men: West Indian Labour Migration to Panama, 1850–1914*. Mona, Jamaica: Institute of Social and Economic Research, 1984.

Patterson, Orlando. "Migration in Caribbean Societies: Socioeconomic and Symbolic Resource." In William H. McNeil and Ruth S. Adams, eds. *Hu-*

man *Migration: Patterns and Policies*. Bloomington, Indiana, and London: American Academy of Arts and Sciences/Indiana University Press, 1978.

Richardson, Bonham C. *Caribbean Migrants: Environment and Human Survival on St. Kitts and Nevis*. Knoxville, Tennessee: University of Tennessee Press, 1983.

———. "Human Mobility in the Windwards in the Late 19th Century." Unpublished paper presented at the Workshop on the Caribbean Diaspora, London University Institute of Commonwealth Studies, June 1987.

———. *Panama Money in Barbados, 1900–1920*. Knoxville, Tennessee: University of Tennessee Press, 1985.

Roberts, George W. *The Population of Jamaica*. Cambridge: Conservation Foundation/Cambridge University Press, 1957.

Seacole, Mary. *Wonderful Adventures of Mrs. Seacole in Many Lands*. Ziggi Alexander and Audrey Dewjee, eds. 2nd ed. Bristol, England: Falling Wall Press, 1984; orig. ed., 1857.

Senior, Olive. "The Colon People: Part One." *Jamaica Journal* 11:3 and 4 (March 1978): 62–71.

———. "The Colon People: Part Two," *Jamaica Journal* 42 (September 1978): 88–103.

———. "The Panama Railway." *Jamaica Journal* 44 (n.d.): 67–77.

Thomas-Hope, Elizabeth. "The Establishment of a Migration Tradition: British West Indian Movements to the Hispanic Caribbean in the Century after Emancipation." In Colin G. Clarke, ed. *Caribbean Social Relations*. University of Liverpool Monograph Series No. 8 (Liverpool: University of Liverpool Centre for Latin-American Studies, n.d.).

# 3

# Forty-and-One Years On: An Overview of Afro-Caribbean Migration to the United Kingdom

MEL. E. THOMPSON

June 22, 1988, marked the fortieth anniversary of large-scale labor migration from the Caribbean to the United Kingdom. On that same date in 1948, the S.S. Empire Windrush landed at Tilbury Docks with 492 Jamaicans on board. Needless to say, their coming was deemed tremendously newsworthy, as witnessed by these reports, "Jamaicans arrive to seek work. . . . Among them are singers, . . . pianists, boxers and a complete dance band . . . "[1] and "[there] were law students, dockers, potential chemists and scientists, who had left their homeland because of the difficulties of getting employment there."[2]

The mirror effect of this lack of employment opportunities in Britain's Caribbean colonies was the extreme labor shortage in the Metropole at that time. With this in mind, the London *Evening Standard* greeted these extra hands with the headline, "WELCOME HOME," and went on to say, "Officialdom, at both government and local levels, moved swiftly to make the Jamaicans feel welcome and find them accommodation and work. Jobs were found immediately for 202 skilled men; the others did not have to wait long."[3]

The above, however, is grossly misrepresentative of the underlying feelings and ultimate general response of the British government and people to the economic implosion of black labor. The ensuing large-scale immigration to Britain served to expose various latent contradictions in the society at both the ideological and practical levels. This immigration also exposed the many inconsistencies in the nation's attitudes to the issue of race. The presence of large numbers of black labor migrants forced a reevaluation of British political ideologies. According to Rex and Tomlinson:

> During this period [of black immigration] there was a slow and painful
> abandonment of ideals in the face of rising racial tension. Notions which
> would have been dismissed as morally disgraceful by nearly all parties in
> the early 1950's became the unspoken ground assumptions of the most
> respectable politicians and leading writers by the end of the 1960's.[4]

Blacks on their doorstep were certainly a different thing than blacks
four thousand miles away, and the humanitarianism that Britain so
boastfully claimed to have been behind the final abolition of slavery was
sadly lacking when the descendants of the slaves finally came home to
mother. Again quoting Rex and Tomlinson, "The actual contingencies
which the [black] settlement created, produced responses which were,
perhaps, latent in the structure of British society, but which were at
odds with the ideologies of conservative imperialism, liberalism indi-
vidualism, and international socialism"—ideologies that were instrumental in informing the philosophical debates during the shaping of the
British nations.[5]

This chapter examines, first, the socio-politico-economic factors surrounding the implosion and incorporation of Afro-Caribbean migrants
into the British economy. In an attempt to locate the views of migrants
within the spectrum of migration debates, some ethno-biographical material will be used, this taken from a study done by the author in the
West Midlands in 1984. This will help to bridge the gap between theoretical discussions and the perceptions/experiences/stories of the migrants. Second, by looking at various theoretical debates and raising
sometimes "controversial" views, we will attempt to come to grips with
the basic problems of migration when it relates to groups of people who
are perceived to be extremely different from the natives.

## DEFERRING TO PRAGMATISM:
## IMPLOSION OF COLONIAL LABOR DURING THE WAR

Caribbean immigration was not as laissez-faire as contemporary writers
had assumed. During the war, the British government decided that,
despite labor needs, black people should be kept from British shores.
According to Sherwood, "The Colonial Office sent secret telegrams to
all the Colonial Governors on 24th December 1939, telling them that it is
not desired that non-European British subjects should come here for
enlistment."[6]

This directive, however, could not be nonnegotiable, due largely to
Britain's labor-starved condition as the war progressed. More significantly, strict adherence to this directive could have led to mass labor
unrest and political upheaval in the colonies on a scale previously un-

known because, by 1939, much discontent existed, fueled by large-scale unemployment occasioned by the worldwide Depression.

Moreover, discontent within the colonies might well have shifted from their "home governments" to the mother country had Britain continued to refuse to recruit colonial labor, thus fanning the flames of the desire for independence. Lord Moyne may well have had that in mind when he wrote to the secretary of state for employment in September 1941:

> For political reasons, I attach great importance to the proposal [to bring over West Indians]. The people of the West Indies are eager to take an effective part in the War effort but so far it has not been possible to give them much opportunity, and there is a danger of the spread of frustration and "unwantedness."[7]

Could it be then that Britain, deferring to pragmatism, took action that would act as a panacea to her "wards"? Whatever the reason, shortly after that letter, labor began to be recruited from the West Indies into munitions industries mainly in the North, where there were more of "their kind." It was assumed that injecting these people into the labor force would not cause major dislocations, which seemed inevitable had the migrants gone where no indigenous blacks lived. On a more cynical note, however, Sherwood suggested that, "given the documented difficulties Blacks in the area historically faced, the 'experiment' of importing even a small number of West Indian workers would prove a failure and hence no more would need to be brought to the UK."[8] Despite the deterring effects such placements were meant to have, the very familiarizing experiences they gained, together with legislative changes in Britain's immigration policy, meant that the die was irretrievably cast for further migration to Britain at the end of the war.

## EXPLAINING AN ANOMALY: THE 1948 BRITISH NATIONALITY ACT

With Britain's obvious aversion to importing black labor, how then were West Indians able to enter the country in increasingly large numbers in the post-1948 through early-1962 period? The answer to this lies in the anomalies inherent in the British Nationality Act of 1948, which—by default—granted to all Commonwealth citizens the same legal rights accorded to all British citizens.

Prashar, in his work on British nationality law, indicates that "under the existing Imperial Act of 1914, everybody born within the allegiance of the Crown in any part of the Empire was a natural born British subject. This so called 'common code' had been intended to confer equality of citizenship throughout the Empire."[9] To a certain extent, both the Imperial Act of 1914 and the 1948 Nationality Act were enacted specifically to enable Britain to keep a hold on parts of her dominion where attempts were being made to establish their "coming of age" as nations, thus breaking the British imperial hold. In conferring British citizenship on existing and former colonial subjects, these acts were intended to circumvent citizenship policies of independent countries, thereby rendering them impotent in cases where former colonial citizens wished to claim British citizenship. According to Prashar, the Commonwealth citizenship conferred in 1948 meant that "citizens of independent countries like Canada or India, or British dependencies like Hong Kong, or Britain herself, are all alike 'British Subjects' or 'Commonwealth Citizens' (whether their governments wish it or not!)."[10] Commonwealth citizens, therefore, who wished to activate their right to the privileges of British citizenship could do so without any kind of referral to their own governments. As Prashar further stressed:

> the very interchangeability of the expressions "British subjects" and "Commonwealth citizens" and the use of the word "British" to describe a citizen of an independent Commonwealth country have tended to confuse Parliament, the press and the general public about the real meaning of British citizenship.[11]

It was these citizenship constructs that enabled people from the Anglo-Caribbean regions who still held colonial status to enter Britain.

Bearing in mind the lengthy and continued reluctance to admit black colonial subjects into Britain, one could be forgiven for questioning the rationality for the expansiveness of the act. This questioning can, however, be dispensed with by considering, first, that the most immediate contemporary concern was to enable Britain to maintain some hold on "acceptable" former colonial citizens—mainly Canadians—who, given the privilege of having dual citizenship, might be relied on to uphold British interests in the future.

Second, if the British had overtly excluded their black colonial citizens, it would have been too reminiscent of Nazi racism, against which they had just inflicted a crushing defeat. In addition, such a policy could have speeded up liberation struggles in areas where Britain still wished to maintain a stranglehold, though in the resource-drained Caribbean, independence would have been willingly conceded if imperial protocol had not demanded a more orderly retreat.

Third, legislation is not irreversible; it can be repealed or amended. This was the considered recourse with which Britain dealt with the anomaly created by the immigration of blacks to the country as a direct result of the 1948 British Nationality Act.

## WAR RECRUITS – THE PRECURSORS OF WEST INDIAN MIGRATION TO THE UNITED KINGDOM

By emphasizing the postwar period, many writers failed to give significance to the West Indians who went to work in Britain as members of the war recruitment groups. Their going broke the psychological barrier that prevented most potential labor migrants from the Caribbean from considering England as a possible place to seek work. These recruits were instrumental in paving the way for others to follow when normalization occurred. In addition, a rarely mentioned fact is that these recruits were the first West Indian migrants to enter Britain in large numbers to seek work. Many who enlisted did so because of a basic desire to fulfill economic needs, therefore becoming the precursors of the labor migrants.

Douglas Manley stressed in 1955 that the "discovery of Britain as an outlet for migration is the most important feature of the War period."[12] His father, Norman W. Manley, emphasized, as prime minister and minister of development in 1960, the contribution of war recruits in terms of their effect on the employment level in Jamaica:

> With the outbreak of World War II in 1939 came a substantial amount of relief from the heavy pressure of unemployment. About 10,000 men volunteered for the Services and of these about 7,000 went overseas, mainly into the Royal Air Force.[13]

War volunteers contributed to the sending economies by reducing the unemployment level and by increasing the supply of foreign exchange and contributing to the well-being of those left behind by their remittances of money and goods.

## FAMILIARITY BREEDS DEMYSTIFICATION

While in the United Kingdom, many recruits worked in coal mines and in areas close to industrial centers such as Birmingham. These recruits were able to familiarize themselves more fully with everyday life in England because they were in regular contact with civilians. When they returned home, they could relate to friends and relations their experiences in Britain and, importantly, could inform people about the availability of jobs. (So great was the labor need, in fact, that many refugees were encouraged to stay and help in the reconstruction program.)

Due to the slowness of the demobilization of West Indians after the war—in 1948, three years after the war's end, a troop ship with 200 demobilized Jamaicans on board was just preparing to leave England—these men were conversant with the often-heated debates taking place in Parliament regarding the country's dire need for labor. They were aware that several members of Parliament had pleaded for a change in the law regarding alien immigration, which would allow an easier flow of people into Britain. Though relatively small in numbers, war recruits were instrumental in helping to break down the mystique surrounding Britain by acting as "agents of diffusion." They were the pioneers of West Indian migration to the United Kingdom and, as British subjects, did not perceive that they had problems in obtaining employment, although many writers and indeed the recruits themselves claimed that the racism that was unleashed against them during the 1950s and the years that followed was partly cloaked during the war.

The following is an extract from the 1984 West Midlands Interview Data (WMID) recounting the encounters with racial prejudice by recruits during the war:

> As West Indians when we came here first . . . I will never forget that . . . about three or four old ladies asked us if we were prisoners of war! But I put it down to a lot of ignorance.
>
> We had a hard time down there. . . . They never use to coloured and even when you get your pass on weekends and you go out . . . you are a stranger into a place and if you ask for directions before you'd get shown . . . they would run away from you! Oh yes, ah not telling you no lies! Well, you feel lost! As you go along you find that it never improve. We couldn't understand why they acted that way because we thought these people knew about the West Indies . . . as we been taught about England . . . all the coal fields and things . . . all day long we've been hearing about coal fields in school and the different counties in England, and when I came here and found that the majority of the people at the time don't even know where the West Indies is.
>
> I'm telling you, it was very tough and we got to break barriers down, just by going out night after night until people get use to us.[14]

So aggrieved did these recruits feel about their treatment in England that, according to WMID respondent Mr. Marks, there was "a big trouble" when the Norwegian ship in which they returned reached Jamaica:

> Being as the lads was that roughly treated up here [in the United Kingdom], they said they going to have it the other way when they land in Jamaica. . . . I'm telling you what I know! . . . So when they get to find out they [were] going to start a riot on the boat, the captain turn the boat back and . . . couldn't come into Kingston because a lot of them would not have got demobbed. . . . They did want to jump the boat and go right to their home.[15]

It is almost inconceivable that these returning soldiers would not have informed people about their adverse experiences in England. Whether those listening would have been able to interpret the meaning, however, was a different matter, especially when, unlike black Americans, the majority of Afro-Caribbean people had never themselves experienced overt white racism, either as rural workers or in a modern urban/industrial context. This is true because the majority of them, unlike their slave forefathers, did not come into direct contact with white people. Mr. Downs, another of the WMID respondents, was in Jamaica at the time the recruits returned and later traveled to England to seek employment. I asked him whether he was aware of racism before he came to the United Kingdom and he said no and then told the following story:

> He was walking downtown one day when he saw a large crowd of people, and they were making so much noise as they laughed that he went to see what was going on. In the middle of the crowd was a soldier who had obviously recently returned from England. The soldier told them how English people drank many cups of hot tea. At that, the people laughed loudly because for someone living in a tropical country such as Jamaica, the thought of people drinking several cups of hot tea was certainly something they found hilarious. The soldier then went on to talk about how they asked him if he had a tail and whether people in his country lived in trees. At this, people almost fell about with laughter![16]

When asked whether he did not feel a sense of unease about this and didn't the listeners interpret this to be racist, Mr. Downs said they did not understand. Like the many cups of tea, this was put down to the quaintness of the English and to their ignorance. The majority of West Indians did not associate racism with Britain, and they were not prepared for it in the way they would have been had they gone to the United States and seen racism in practice. The Jamaicans, in short, did not know how to deal with racism when they encountered it—especially in a British context.

## RELUCTANT BONDING—UNITED KINGDOM CAPITAL AND BLACK LABOR

Three months after being demobilized in Jamaica, WMID respondent Mr. Marks was back in England. He had received £50 from the Jamaican government but, like many others, no land, although, according to him, some men got as much as 20 acres and a house. He contacted a lawyer but then decided to return to the United Kingdom. When asked why he had decided to come back to England, bearing in mind the dissatisfaction he had previously experienced, he replied:

> Because you mostly in the camp . . . among soldiers, you don't know what civvi street life is like . . . 'cause it is entirely different . . . and you don't know what you going to put up with in civvi street. . . . You would never know what most of the people [are] like.[17]

The passengers on the Windrush were to have a taste of what "civvi street" would be like while they were still on the Atlantic Ocean. Sam King, one of the returnees, reported:

> As we got closer to England there was great apprehension on the boat because we knew the authorities did not want us to land. . . . We heard on BBC News that if there was any disturbance on the immigrant ship, HMS Sheffield would be sent out to turn us back. I saw a man crying over the side because he thought we would be turned round. We heard there was consternation in Parliament and that newspapers like the *Daily Graphic* and the *Express* were saying we should be turned back. On the boat there was sadness about this. . . . We knew we were not wanted.[18]

Despite Britain's obvious reluctance to encourage immigration of these labor migrants, however, with their legal access assured, it was inevitable that the postwar economic expansion in Europe would act as a magnet to people from less prosperous regions of the world. As Peach points out, "It is not that poverty is new in the South, it is that industrial prosperity, on its present scale, is new in Northern Europe."[19] Further, developments in the twentieth century that gave rise to the internationalism of fast, relatively cheap information and transport technology meant that the process of bonding labor to capital was effected more swiftly since the last world war. The returning demobilized recruits in 1948 were closely followed by what might be termed "peer group" recruits. As time progressed, the migration of dependents and single women swelled the ever-increasing ranks from the West Indies.

Laissez-faire governmental response continued to be more apparent than real. Unknown to would-be migrants, the British government instructed their colonial governments to apply delaying tactics in an attempt to deter the free flow of migrants from the black-peopled colonies. Furthermore, even before the introduction of work permit conditions, Britain sent out instructions that passports should be issued only if proof of employment were available.[20]

These migrations to Britain, as well as being indicators of economic deprivation in the migrants' homelands, must be juxtaposed with Britain's chronic need for manpower and the legal and moral rights of Caribbean peoples as British colonials and later as Commonwealth citizens to exploit this for their own gains. In a way, the migration of large numbers of colonials to the metropolis must be seen as the final stage in the colonization process. The colonized capitulate completely to the political, economic, and psychological domination of the colonizer. This is one of the most serious aspects of colonialism. It is possible that at this stage, to quote Mabogunje:

> In place of traditional self-confidence, the people [are] reduced to a state of imitative dependence, a highly degraded state associated not only with

an inability to provide themselves adequately with the material means of sustenance but also with the loss of cultural and psychological integrity.[21]

By the time mass migration begins to take place from the periphery to the center, the immigrants often feel gratitude for being allowed to "use" the metropole for their advantage, thus often experiencing a strong sense of obligation toward the core—at least initially. Despite immigration, however, the migrants are still pawns and, through various anti-immigrant restrictions, overt and otherwise, they are controlled by the ultimate power of the core to bring in labor and expel it at will.

## SETTLEMENT

From the 1940s to the mid-1960s, at least, a period of contradiction existed. At the beginning of the 1940s, black workers found themselves in demand in factories where their labor contributed to the war effort, but, even so, employers and coworkers often resisted their presence.[22] The color bar, according to Little, also meant "the refusal of lodgings, refusal of service in cafes, refusal of admittance to dance halls, etc., [and] shrugs, nods, whispers, comments, etc., in public, in the street, in trams and in buses."[23]

As labor migrants, West Indians were given the worst jobs at the lowest pay and had to live in low-grade inner city housing—many of them in neighborhoods that had been slums long before the workers entered the country. For example, the city of Birmingham, which attracted a large number of Afro-Caribbeans because of its desperate labor needs, was regarded as being in urgent need of a housing program long before the inflow of postwar labor migrants.

A study undertaken by the Bournville Village Trust in 1941 stressed that 64 percent of Birmingham's 268,608 dwelling houses were of pre-1914 construction. In 1938, the medical officer of health had reported that "17,500 houses were unfit for human habitation and ought to be demolished within the next five years." The study went on to stress that

> many unofficial observers would regard this figure as too low. On a broader definition of the term "unfit for human habitation," there can be no difficulty in justifying some such number as 50,000 to 70,000 dwellings as being ripe for demolition as soon as the necessary houses can be built to replace them.[24]

In 1955, local authorities in the United Kingdom had estimated that 853,000 units were representative of the total of unfit houses in their wards. By 1967, however, a housing survey of England and Wales reported that in Birmingham alone, "30,000 families are on the waiting list, and 6,500 families apply each year. Over 50,000 people are overcrowded, over 40,000 homes are unfit for human habitation, and nearly 60,000 households have no access to a hot water tap."[25] From this we may judge that slums were forming at an alarming rate, certainly faster than suitable housing could be erected.

On a national level, the situation was similar—and in places even worse than Birmingham. As late as 1966, a Labour party white paper stated, "In Great Britain some three million families still live in slums, near slums, or in grossly overcrowded conditions."[26] The paper further stressed that to rectify the severe housing shortage, 3,700,000 houses were needed immediately and that an additional 180,000 houses would be needed each year. The severity of the national problem was emphasized as well in the 1967 housing survey of England and Wales, which indicated that no less than 5.5 million people lived in houses "unfit for human habitation." Further, an additional 13–14 million people lived in substandard housing—some requiring demolition. In short, "40% of dwellings in England and Wales were either totally unfit or substandard, or lacking amenities."[27]

Into this situation came the postwar migrant laborers. The shortfall between supply and demand, and the fact that there was no attempt to organize housing for the immigrants, resulted in "New Commonwealth" migrant workers experiencing some of the worst effects of inadequate housing. As this situation became apparent and the need for government action evident, it was used to fuel racist allegations, due to the tendency to equate macro housing shortages with perceived micro welfare requirements. Thus Grieve's assertion on the homeless in London during the early 1960s has universal relevance:

> When the homeless become a topic for public discussion, accusation and counter-accusation, there is debate and speculation as to whether the homeless are "feckless ne'er do wells" or "ordinary decent Londoners". There are echoes here of the Victorian insistence upon the distinction between "deserving" and "undeserving" poor. The research team found that the homeless were more likely to be decent than ne'er do well, but, in any case, there is little point—or humanity—in attempting to separate the victimised from the feckless and unvirtuous if the object is to help one but not the others.[28]

Social destitution, as is universally the case, had little to do with individual fecklessness. That the housing "problem" was exacerbated with the arrival of postwar labor migrants is a reflection of the short-sightedness of the local and national governments in maintaining an adequate house building/renewal program. This had been the case from the previous century. What is more alarming, however, is that conditions for black people have not improved in any significant way—more than

40 years later. They have been consistently discriminated against with regard to access to council housing stock.

As they faced discrimination from private landlords, many Afro-Caribbean migrants, through their imported practice of "pardners" (informal money-saving schemes), were able to raise down payments on low-grade housing, much of it due for demolition. Unfortunately, unlike previous immigrants starting out this way, many black labor migrants have not been able to achieve upward mobility to escape the ghetto. Indeed, Karn has commented that several "inner-city home owners live in housing conditions considerably worse than those in the worst council housing stock."[29]

## LABOR MARKET EXPERIENCE

On entering any labor market, most immigrants, especially those from a rural background, lack an awareness of and, indeed, a commitment to the specific types of work available in an industrial society. For many, as we have noted, this migration to foreign labor markets must be seen as pragmatic bids to raise money for economic enhancement back home. To some extent, therefore, it is true that—in the earliest stages of migration—it is "a job" and, more importantly, "the remunerations" from it, that are of greatest value. This does not mean that migrant laborers make conscious decisions to accept the worst type of jobs available in the receiving country. What it does mean is that they are usually ignorant of the specific labor market dynamics; many believe they would at least be able to obtain the kind of work they did back home, if not better.

When, however, these migrants are faced with the realities of the type of work available to them as black, powerless workers in the United Kingdom, it is possible that in the short run, while returning home is still regarded as a viable ambition, the adverse effects of alienation and anomie could be counterbalanced by the very temporary nature of their existence. For example, unlike indigenous British workers, the migrant can suspend notions of work-related prestige and job satisfaction until returning home. Of more lasting relevance is the fact that even while still in the core country, the immigrant can gain prestige if the focus is removed to the periphery where the actual or anticipated material achievement of the work effort is realized. Thus it is not uncommon to hear individual Afro-Caribbean migrants refer to their "many acres of land *back home*," "ten-apartment house *back home*," or to the fact that they "come off better table" than someone who is perceived to be of "lower origin," yet in the United Kingdom appears to have done comparatively better than the commentator. Until "mere existence" begins to take on a settlement nature, the very transitory nature of the migrant's existence often necessitates a curtailment or deferment of social requirements and obligations. It is this ability to defer gratification that contributes to their elasticity, rendering them more suited than indigenous groups to meet immediate needs in the labor market. At the same time, though, they can be more easily segmented and more easily exploited.

Integral to most accusations about immigrant groups during their presettlement period is the belief that they will inevitably form a cheap source of labor and compete against existing host groups for jobs. This argument finds greatest expression in localities where, due to declining or transitional industries, fears—based on real or imagined factors—are ever present.

A common feature in British industrial evolution is the failure of indigenous groups to identify the process of industrial change. People such as Mishan believe that the injection of New Commonwealth labor migrants delayed the introduction of new technology to the detriment of the country.[30] Intriguingly, however, Duffield, in his work on Indians in the foundry industry, emphasized this false generalization about New Commonwealth immigrants. He stressed that whereas indigenous groups were reluctant to leave their old skilled and semiskilled jobs in declining industries,

> [as] a general rule, immigrant workers were absorbed as a part of the process of change and modernisation. Their social role was not, as conventional theories suggest, to help maintain backward production methods. Modernisation created many new manufacturing and service jobs—jobs which, although some were not particularly pleasant, had not existed before.[31]

This procedure led to de-skilling of indigenous, as well as imported, workers. This phenomenon of mechanization accompanying sectional de-skilling is a recurring feature in capitalist productivity methods. Black workers, like their indigenous counterparts, were de-skilled; on entry they were restricted to the lowest paid sectors of the employment market and, as noted by Brown, this is still very much the case today. He emphasizes that, among other inequalities, black workers are congregated in the most vulnerable service areas of employment, are the most prone to adverse fluctuations in the trade cycle and the resultant unemployment; are more likely to work night shifts; and earn proportionately much lower wages than their white peers.[32]

## ORGANIZED LABOR AND BLACK MIGRANTS

Technological change facilitated a connivance of union and management to subjugate migrant laborers. Duffield emphasized that from the late 1940's the foundry unions were able to impose a new skill hierarchy upon the mechanised forms of production then developing. This hierarchy mapped out in advance the social places that Asian workers would be forced to occupy. From this perspective, the arbitrary standards and spurious technical thresholds created by labour bureaucracies and used to oppress workers in general, become an essential and organic mechanism of racial oppression.[33]

Antiblack sentiments have been greatest during periods of economic decline or in transitional stages in industrial development. These are often viewed as justified antimigrant labor sentiments, "legitimized" as being the attempts of workers to safeguard themselves against capitalist exploitation through the phenomenon of imported labor. Consequently, throughout British immigration history, trade unions have often been in the vanguard of anti-immigration abuses.

Analyses of trade union responses to black imported labor have been approached from different theoretical perspectives. On the one hand there is what might be identified as a class structural approach. This is based on the premise that it is the requirements of a capitalist economic system that encourage the formation and exploitation of various strata within the society, with black people forming at least a substrata, if not the lowest level. What is inherent in this system is the apparent need for each stratum to relate parasitically to those below for its own well-being. Thus writers such as Castles and Kosacks[34] and Miles[35] emphasize that the class perspective is germane to understanding the position of black people in the European trade union movement. Through the real or perceived built-in competition in capitalist modes of production, capitalism creates factions among the many sections of the proletariat, and through a divide and rule strategy renders them more easy prey for exploitation.

On the other hand, there is what might be termed a race relations approach, which suggests that British society is innately ethnocentric and racist and that trade unions, like all other institutions within the political economy, are inevitably permeated with these characteristics. This view maintains that it is only by catherizing itself through education and, more importantly, through legislative measures to deter discrimination, can black people ever obtain equity with the wider society.

Needless to say, neither of the above approaches is totally exclusive. What is of relevance here is the fact that trade unions have consistently failed to defend black workers and have often been in the forefront of antiblack practices. Thus a study by the Greater London Trade Union Resource Unit points out that

the experience of Black trade unionists within the labour movements is often a reflection of the experience of Black workers within employment as a whole. Black people are more likely than white people to be unemployed, or if in work to be clustered at the lower ends of the scale of pay and power. As trade union members, even though a higher proportion of Black people join unions than white people, they are less likely to be represented at senior levels of union structure, and their particular struggles are often ignored.[36]

According to Wrench, the trade union movement has failed its black members through "a general lack of awareness of the issues of race and equal opportunity and the particular circumstances of ethnic minority members, which may not manifest itself as racism but in effect lessens the participation of Black members in the union."[37]

Until 1955, both the General Council and the Trade Union Congress (TUC) appeared to ignore the whole area of immigration, discrimination, and racism. That year was a watershed because a TUC resolution for the first time condemned racial discrimination. This move, however, seemed to spring from a desire to incorporate in order to control. Members were concerned that immigrants would form a pool of cheap labor and thus undermine trade union bargaining power.

Despite this positive action in 1955, trade unions, through their mouthpiece of the TUC, were at best strangely silent and at worst openly obstructive during the immigrant maligning and legislatively restricting period running from the 1960s through the early 1980s. Initially, the general response of the TUC to racism within the unions was that this "would be best overcome by immigrants increasing their efforts to integrate."[38] In the same vein, the TUC opposed both the 1965 Anti-Discriminatory Race Relations bills and the 1968 Race Relations Act, stressing that "voluntary organizations such as itself and the CBI [Confederation of British Industry] should supervise such integration rather than the state."[39] In the same year, however, they did support the Commonwealth Immigration Bill, under the Labour government, though they did not speak out against the 1971 Tory Immigration Act. (The latter was devised to restrict the entry of blacks into the United Kingdom.)

In 1973, the TUC approved a resolution to call on a future Labour government to repeal the 1971 Immigration Act. It was never repealed, but, by approving this resolution, the TUC, in actuality, recognized the effects of racism on blacks and also recognized that the unions and, more importantly, the government (rather than the disadvantaged groups themselves) had an obligation to assist in eradicating racism. Two years later, the TUC established an Equal Rights Sub-committee and a Race Relations Advisory Committee. Previously, race relations concerns were dealt with by the international department, implying that the problems and solutions were external to Britain, rather than emanating from internal policies and practices.

From the late 1970s to the early 1980s, the TUC took on a more positive antiracist stance as a result of the National Front's political actions, evidenced by local union activities and electoral victories. Through the publication of their Black Workers Charter in 1981, the TUC Workbook on Racism in 1983, and the TUC/CRE (Congress for Racial Equality) Code of Practice for Trade Unions in 1984, the organization appears to have accepted its responsibility to stand against anti-immigrant and racist discrimination.

Despite this, there is no doubt that there is a long way to go before black trade unionists can feel confident in the knowledge that they will obtain equality of opportunity through the traditional labor organizations. The intransigence on the part of indigenous trade unions has resulted in factionalism as black workers have resorted to caucusing among themselves to safeguard their own interests.[40]

Any concessions and changes in union policy today in support of black workers were achieved either through the unions' bid to incorporate blacks in a further attempt to subjugate them or, more importantly, through the struggles of black workers themselves. These unions have consistently failed to examine existing rules and procedures that are discriminatory to black workers—rules such as the "last in, first out policy," as well as union policy to support the tenure of the black member whose job is at risk in a dispute involving two members. Thus in cases of race or gender abuses where the laws have been contravened, the unions often end up supporting racist or sexist perpetrators on the grounds that their jobs are at risk. Further, by failing to utilize the imported expertise of migrant labor trade unionists, British trade unions have inadvertently restricted progress of trade unionism and radicalism generally.

## A BID FOR ECONOMIC INDEPENDENCE: AFRO-CARIBBEAN ENTREPRENEURIAL INVOLVEMENT

Generally, the involvement of Afro-Caribbean people in business in the United Kingdom has not attracted much research attention until fairly recently. This increased interest must be seen in the context of the government's attempt to turn the country into a nation of small businesses to combat contracting industrialization. There is a tendency to compare the seeming "great success" of the Asians with the "underachievement" of Afro-Caribbean people in the area of business. Education, business expertise, and "natural ability" are often held as the main factors responsible for the perceived supremacy of the Asian in business. The educational achievement levels of the two groups show that whereas 15.2 percent of the Indian men possessed post "A" level General Certificate of Education (GCE) professional and graduate qualifications, among the general population and the Afro-Caribbean population, the figures were 8.7 percent and 2.6 percent, respectively. Of the Afro-Caribbean women, 10.2 percent had achieved this level. This was 0.7 percent higher than that of Indian women and seven percent above that of Afro-Caribbean males. Several studies have identified factors in the British educational system as partly responsible for this situation.[41]

If formal qualification is a measure of one's ability to succeed in business, the data cited here show that Afro-Caribbean men are most destined to fail in business. Ward and Reeves, in explaining the apparent leadership of Asians above Afro-Caribbean people in the business world, referred to the 1971 Census figures, which highlighted Asian supremacy in qualification and positional attainment. Nineteen percent of the Indian males were employed in the "administrative, managerial, professional, and technical" category, compared to 4 percent for the Afro-Caribbean males; in "clerical, sales," the figures were 12 percent and 4.1 percent, respectively.[42]

Table 3.1 outlines the most recent statistical analysis of the employment categories of the various immigrant groups in Britain in 1986. While the figures reveal that Afro-Caribbean people are still lagging behind "Asians" and white groups in the top employment echelons, there was, nevertheless, an appreciably noticeable upward mobility when compared with the 1971 figures. It must be stressed, however, that while there is obviously room for hope, a large number of black migrants are achieving this mobility within ethnic enclave enterprises, and this cannot therefore be used to measure the degree of equitable incorporation of black workers in the society as a whole.

Other factors believed to contribute to the relatively poor business performance of Afro-Caribbeans compared to Asians include the fact that the former number approximately one-third of the latter population in Britain. Thus, in terms of controlling sections of the market through specific ethnic demands, the Asians are at an obvious number advantage. While this thesis may accurately describe the contemporary situation, which can be explained partly through geographical settlement—both in terms of work and residence—language, and ethnic encapsulation, to gain long-term credibility, it needs to assume that retailers have a monopoly over buyers in their own ethnic groups, that monopoly control cannot be effectively penetrated by "nongroup" people, and that for the long-term survival of the business, cultural demands will remain inelastic.

Entrepreneurship is not new to people from the Caribbean. Tables 3.2

**Table 3.1**
**Percentage Distribution of Employment by Race and Sex of Workers 16 and Over, 1984–86**

| Category | West Indian & Guyanese | | Indian | | Pakistani & Bangladeshi | | White | |
|---|---|---|---|---|---|---|---|---|
| | Male | Female | Male | Female | Male | Female | Male | Female |
| Professional | 3 | 0 | 13 | 4 | 5 | -- | 7 | 1 |
| Employers & Managers | 4 | 2 | 17 | 5 | 13 | -- | 19 | 8 |
| Other non-manual | 15 | 55 | 17 | 42 | 9 | -- | 18 | 53 |
| Skilled manual | 47 | 5 | 33 | 13 | 39 | -- | 37 | 8 |
| Semi-skilled manual | 21 | 50 | 16 | 32 | 28 | -- | 13 | 21 |
| Unkilled manual | 9 | 7 | 3 | 3 | 5 | -- | 4 | 8 |

Source: Labour Force Survey, 1986: Series LFS No. 6 (London: Her Majesty's Stationery Office, 1986).

**Table 3.2**
**Entrepreneurial Activities in Jamaica of West Midlands**
**Interview Data Respondents, 1984**

| Type of Activity | Males<br>(N=24) | Females<br>(N=21) |
|---|---|---|
| Baking | 2 | 1 |
| Butchering | 1 | - |
| Cabinet making | 3 | - |
| Carpentry | 2 | - |
| Cook (Chinese food) | 1 | - |
| Dressmaking/sewing/<br>  embroidery/tailoring | 2 | 8 |
| Farming/agriculturalist/<br>  cultivator | 16 | 2 |
| Higglering/paper bag<br>  making | - | 4 |
| House painting | 2 | - |
| Kindergartden teacher | - | 2 |
| Pipefitting | 1 | - |
| Roof shingle making | 1 | - |
| Stone masonry | 2 | - |

Source: West Midlands Interview Data (1984).

and 3.3 show that by far the majority of migrants from the 1984 West Midlands Interview Data had taken part in various entrepreneurial pursuits at some stage, both in the Caribbean and in the United Kingdom. The complexity of motivating forces underlying the unmistakably high involvement of the WMID respondents in small proprietorships is worth exploring, due to its potential for micro- as well as macroimplications. There is a notion that the ambition for independence, which a small business seems to confer, is somehow basic to human nature; thus entrepreneurial pursuits are deemed to be natural human responses. An extension of this idea could be that because migrants are often among the most enterprising section of any society, they enter the receiving country already imbued with entrepreneurial zeal. Consequently, one could logically expect them to become involved in any activity, including small businesses, that they believe capable of aiding their bid for capital accumulation and—for many—quicker return home. It could be further argued that the entrepreneurial pursuits listed in the tables are in line with a tradition of peasant and artisan proprietorship common throughout the world. In these cases, they are often purely pragmatic bids for economic survival in the midst of depleted resources and economic and social underdevelopment.

**Table 3.3**
**Outcome of Entrepreneurial Activities in the United Kingdom of West Midlands Interview Data Respondents, 1984**

| Type of Activity | Males (N=24) | Females (N=21) | Outcome* |
|---|---|---|---|
| Grocery shop (full-time) | 2 | 2 | F |
| Barber (full-time) | 1 | - | S |
| Bakery (1 full-time; 1 part-time) | 2 | - | F |
| Off License (financial partner) | 2 | - | F |
| Holiday Magic (part-time) | 2 | - | F |
| Market stall holder (full-time) | - | 2 | S |
| Home sewing (intermittently full-time and part-time) | - | 2 | U |
| Part owner of house | 1 | - | S |
| No entrepreneurial activity | 4 | 15 | - |

*S=Successful
F=Failed
U=Unable to determine

Source: West Midlands Interview Data (1984).

The involvement of WMID respondents in one-person activities is due to a number of complex interrelated factors comprising the need for economic subsistence in the absence of alternative employment outlets. There is undoubtedly also a strong desire to be one's own boss or to be involved in innovative activity.

Forty-two percent of the male respondents became engaged in entrepreneurial activities in the United Kingdom, compared to an overall total of 75 percent while in Jamaica. The Jamaican involvement, however, showed an even division between those who were involved in full-time proprietorship and those involved on a part-time basis. The lower U.K. involvement nevertheless indicates that full-time entrepreneurial activities (17 percent) exceeded part-time (12.5 percent). Of the U.K. entrepreneurs, 12.5 percent were not actually involved in using their labor to work the capital but instead had invested money while they themselves were engaged in other labor pursuits. This straight "capitalist" tendency cannot be explained in terms of traditional working-class proprietorship; such clearly speculative attempts to make money without personal labor input are more akin to the petit bourgeois method of capital accumulation. This validates the view that attempts to localize and predict attributes and behavioral norms of particular groups may be conceptually flawed when applied to specific groups, especially for mi-grant workers, who are often classified as appendages, and unwelcome ones, of the indigenous working class. While in terms of remuneration and vulnerability to exploitation, it is difficult to differentiate them from the working class, their heritage as rural land-owning peasant farmers and artisans, owners of factors of production, controlling the rhythm of work, as innovators in the ways in which they earn their living and in several cases employing others, mean that their aspirations and actions are often not strictly working class, despite professed loyalties. It is, therefore, not surprising, but must be seen within their tradition, to find migrant laborers purchasing properties, even as members of coopera-tives, in their attempts to exploit money-making possibilities.

Entrepreneurial activities were undertaken by 29 percent of the fe-male WMID respondents. Of this total, 19 percent were engaged on a full-time basis, while 10 percent worked full- and part-time intermittent-ly. These figures contrast greatly with female respondents' entrepre-neurial activities prior to emigration from Jamaica. There, 43 percent were engaged in entrepreneurial activities. Of this group, 24 percent reported they were fully self-employed, while 19 percent claimed partial self-employment. The females were involved in stereotypical activities such as setting up a grocery shop, holding a market stall, and sewing at home.

Scrutiny of each individual business run by the interview respondents in the United Kingdom reveals that only three—the barber and the two bakers—could be termed specifically "ethnic" enterprises. The bakers produced hard-dough bread, buns, patties, and so forth, specifically for the Afro-Caribbean market, although increasingly the products were purchased by other ethnic groups as those people became more adven-turous in their choice of food. In the same way, the barber specialized in cutting Afro-Caribbean hair, predominantly males; he did however boast that he had white clients also, including, he emphasized, a doctor from the hospital close to his shop.

When questioned about the outcome of their activities in the United Kingdom, 80 percent of the males said their businesses had failed, while only 2 percent could boast success. Of the females, 33 percent claimed failure, while another third said it was difficult to determine the level of success. Women who sewed for private individuals, for example, re-ceived irregular payments, making it necessary for them to seek alterna-tive forms of work on an intermittent basis. Each market stall holder in the sample felt that her business was successful. One of them sold clothes, and she attributed unqualified success to her endeavor. The other sold Afro-Caribbean food and, although she was successful, she pointed out that at times she found it strenuous to make a living in competition with white market stall holders who also sold "ethnic" food.

She felt they often resorted to undercutting methods, thus contributing to her lack of progress.

Lord Scarman believes that black business development can be a panacea for many of the wrongs suffered by blacks in Britain, whether they experience a sense of underachievement, alienation, or racism. In the Scarman Report, he observes:

> The encouragement of Black people to secure a real stake in their own community, through business and the professions, is in my view of great importance if future social stability is to be secured. . . . I do urge the necessity for speedy action if we are to avoid the perpetuation in this country of an economically dispossessed Black population. A weakness in British society is that there are too few people of West Indian origin in the business, entrepreneurial and professional class.[43]

Scarman's views are increasingly repeated, especially in the strong capitalist climate of Prime Minister Thatcher's Britain. The government has been encouraging the population at large to "set up on their own" to combat unemployment. For Afro-Caribbean people, the pressure to prove their worth has never been more intense, and the medium of business is the chosen testing ground. Some Pan-African adherents and sympathizers also argue that it is only through separate development of a strong economic base that black people can begin to redress the negative power relationship between themselves and the larger, predominantly racist white society. Black people have become caught up in the desire to display "black success." However, this cooptation of Thatcherite ideology that business success is a measure of individual group worth implicitly results in the acceptance of the converse, that inability to display overt business success is a sign of individual or group failure.

Apologetic black people and their "liberal/socialist minded" white supporters, on the other hand, are quick to point out in defense that blacks from the Caribbean have not had a tradition of the type of individual capitalism practiced in most advanced economies and that forms of cooperative capitalism might be more successful. Here, they argue, black people would be able to develop their own capitalist institutions without having to be controlled by, or compete with, white or Asians.

Today's call for individual responsibility and self-determination is made by the government in response to this era of postindustrial decline. Like its birth, the decline of industry will cause intense social distress through economic dislocations. Some of these are evidenced in the phenomenon of "a divided nation," whereby in Britain there are regional pockets of obvious material wealth juxtaposed by others in advanced stages of industrial urban decay.

The nineteenth-century predecessors of Thatcher's government were mindful of the potential for social unrest caused by the existence of a situation of rich juxtaposed by poor inter- or intraregional variations. Thus, while philosophizing to validate the right not to become their brother's keepers, they also devised laws to protect and uphold the sanctity of property. In any eventuality, state compulsion was to be effected in an attempt to get people to shoulder their own responsibilities. Consequently, the 1834 New Poor Law was enacted. By this piece of legislation, the government assumed the barest responsibility for social welfare—this to be administered only when would-be recipients had been totally degraded by the ravages of poverty. The extent of relief and the conditions under which assistance was given further dehumanized the individual to make the deterrence more effective.

Why this preoccupation with the past century? The agenda has been set by the present Conservative government, and it is crucial to understand the ramifications of this for black people, particularly for Afro-Caribbeans, who form a virtual subclass in British society. Capitalism of the nineteenth century—for which Mrs. Thatcher so longs—was ushered in by the "Christian" capitalist pioneering entrepreneurs of the seventeenth and eighteenth centuries, aided by a mass of resources Europeans were able to accumulate through militaristic expropriation. Their economic pursuits were goaded on by an intensity that only strong emotions such as fear could instill—fear that underachievement or failure was a sure sign of God's dissatisfaction, whereas success was a sign of divine approval. Such approval could be gained only by good works within the individuals' specific "calling." This latter part is of particular relevance, for it was this that should pacify those who, despite hard and laborious work, were unable to reap similar benefits that the "business person" reaps. If these persons could not achieve, then God was displeased with them or they were striving outside their "calling." It was opportune for the capitalists and the government of the day to have the people accept these doctrines. While, according to Marx, they acted as an opiate against the harshest realities of poor people's existence, they were also a protection mechanism for those who were making conspicuously large profits against a backdrop of intense economic and social hardships for the majority of the people.

## IMMIGRATION AND "NATION" POLITICS

The politicization of racism is a phenomenon that certainly existed prior to the fourth decade of the twentieth century, when large-scale labor migrations of "New" Commonwealth citizens to Britain took place. Racism, however, is often cloaked, partly because of the way in which students of various academic disciplines have tended to name the symptoms rather than the disease itself. Prejudice and xenophobia are usually discussed as though they were "natural" human reactions and are usually referred to in isolation from their effects on recipient groups. This abstraction of the debate from the resultant effects tends to dull the impact of the knowledge that immigrants are often subjected to vile abuses and inhumane treatments.

In the same vein, notions of nationalism are often used to explain or excuse the behavior of sections of the host group toward an incoming group. Again, nationalism is seen as some kind of tangible inalienable commodity with advantages accruing to owners of the particular nationality. Nationalism, however, is a many-dimensional construct having implications for "in" as well as "out" groups.

Within British geographical boundaries, the move from a feudal, pyramidally structured society where the monarch and the ruling elite formed a small peak of privileged ethno-centric (culture-centric) group to a more egalitarian society was achieved through lengthy struggles as people wrestled to be among the deference-receiving groups at the top or simply to obtain a reasonable level of subsistence. This struggle has continued throughout most of Britain's historical development, with varying degrees of tension. These internal struggles are no less than micro and regional ethnocentric sparrings based on the groups' experiential notions of culture. Sumner has been credited with being the first to define ethnocentrism as a

> view of things in which one's own group is the center of everything, and all others are scaled and rated with reference to it. . . . Each group nourishes its own pride and vanity, boasts itself superior, exalts its own divinities and looks with contempt on outsiders.[44]

The stratified nature of British society and the levels of exploitation inherent in capitalism provide the perfect opportunity for nationalism to be intermittently redefined, both with reference to the various groups within the country's geographical boundaries and to external groups as well.

Prevailing ideologies of nineteenth-century Britain enabled poverty and attempts by the poor to relieve themselves of capitalist exploitation to be defined as forms of cultural degeneration and therefore potentially disruptive to the status quo. This gave credibility to the penal punishment of transportation as a temporary banishment that allowed "nationals" to retain their "rights to British soil" from afar, reclaimable when they had regenerated themselves culturally by exhibiting tangible economic results through enterprising activities or labor. Ethnocentrism maintained, therefore, that for poor British nationals, incontrovertible residential rights were not automatic, despite "ownership" of citizenship accorded by ancient rights—jus soli (by virtue of being born on British soil).

Internal micro and regional ethnocentrism sets a precedent for reactions to "out groups," in cases of macro-ethnocentrism and racism. Macro-ethnocentrism compares and grades "out groups" according to values placed on such things as clothing, language, and methods of production.[45] Thus, both the Irish and Jews suffered from macro-ethnocentrism on their entry into nineteenth-century Britain. Each came into British society as a subclass, and there was undoubtedly a notion of cultural superiority underlying their reception. The *Report on the State of the Irish Poor* in Great Britain in 1836 stressed:

> The Irish emigration into Britain is an example of a *less civilized* population *spreading* themselves, as a kind of sub-stratum, *beneath a more civilized community*; and, without excelling in any branch of industry, obtaining possession of all the lowest departments of manual labor.[46]

Of the Jews, White commented in the 1890s:

> The *typical foreign immigrant* we wish to exclude *is an incapable*; he belongs to no trade union; he is the person who makes the lives of the Jewish Board of Guardians a burden; he *speaks no English, learns no skilled trade, and is destitute of qualities that enrich civilized communities*.[47]

In other words, these groups had nothing to offer and should be excluded, or at least separated from, the host groups to prevent the "spread" of degeneration. There is also no doubt that the language of racial supremacy featured very strongly in the responses to Jewish and Irish immigrants of the nineteenth and early-twentieth centuries; these groups were seen as being at a lower evolutionary stage than the indigenous population. Similar, and stronger, sentiments were later expressed in postwar years, when Britain's great need for imported labor attracted black excolonial labor.

When differing physical features, especially skin color and other biologically determined features, are involved in group interaction, the effects of macro-ethnocentrism become more virulent and are usually referred to as racism, the latter regarded as a continuum of the former. Preiswerk and Perrot quote Albert Memmi's definition of racism as "the valorization, generalized and definitive, of real or imaginary differences, which profits the accuser to the detriment of his victim in order to justify his privileges or his aggression."[48]

There is no doubt that ethnocentrism is an integral part of racism and, as we have seen in relation to the earlier nonblack immigrants to Britain, the newcomers were often abused through racist language. Nevertheless, the anti-Irish and anti-Jewish reactions were examples of ethnocentrism, not racism. Racism, inflicted by Europeans on other (i.e., black) groups, is usually based on skin color and facial features.

Reactions against the Irish and Jews were in some measure similar to those experienced by black immigrants in the postwar years. However, the more ethnocentrically different immigrants are perceived to be, the greater will be the reaction against them. The Irish and Jews are not so physically identifiable as the black immigrants; consequently, in time they can be absorbed into the society, thereby escaping some of the most overt forms of racism. For black immigrants, however, even if they desired complete assimilation, it would not be possible—except for generations of mixed breeding, an option seriously considered during the early European occupation of Australia. (This was only one "solution" to the aboriginal "problem," another being hunting them as wild animals.) In the "civilized" world of the 1960s Britain, the law would deal with this problem.

Thus, since the 1950s, a series of political debates and the enactment of laws have resulted in "Britain, more than most countries in the world [being] a country marked by racialist practice and racist theory."[49] Racism was able to do what no other force in the country could—unite all white classes in the society. This, therefore, served to expose the fallacy and simplistic explanation of certain left-wing interpretations that the race question is merely an extension of the class "problem" and not germane to an understanding of the position of black people in white capitalist society. Call it lack of sophistication, cynicism, or realism, the majority of black people in Britain do not believe that the racist treatment meted out to them has much to do with simply their economic role or class position in this society. In a strange way, such explanations are at best naive and at worst racist in that they have assumed the right to designate class positions or fail to acknowledge that among black immigrants there are also members who in their own countries are considered to be from the middle and upper classes. These people have achievements and aspirations similar to indigenous classes in the United Kingdom yet suffer racial abuses irrespective of their class status.

The following aptly captures British hegemonic reactions in the presence of a perceived "undesirable" out-group. By the mid-1970s, according to Rex and Tomlinson:

> whatever the humane traditions of conservatism, the concern for human rights of liberalism, or the internationalism of the unions and labour, there was effective agreement amongst the majority of each of those parties that coloured immigration must be limited and that any special effort to help coloured immigrants to overcome discrimination was electorally unprofitable. At best, immigrants were to be tolerated, but, on the whole, the consensus was that this was a dangerous element outside normal politics and outside the normal class system. The immigrants were frequently treated as scapegoats for the economic ills which beset the community, and, if they occasionally engaged in outbursts of violence or

joined in the often ill-considered attempts of the extreme left to defend them against the National Front, they were blamed as much as anyone for the breakdown of law and order.[50]

Traditionally, the severity of inevitable social changes that take place with each new wave of immigrants is often cushioned by the fact that within a relatively short period of time, the newcomers are assimilated (though often only partially) into the wider society. This is usually achieved by "admonishment," sometimes brutal wresting, from the wider society, pragmatism by the newcomers, or by a slow, conscious abandonment as cross-socialization takes place. Gutman notes that in the 1890s, Jews in the United States were told, "Hold fast, this is most necessary in America. Forget your past, your customs, and your ideals . . . do not take a moment's rest. Run, do, work, and keep your own good in mind."[51] He further indicates that "distorted perceptions and fears of new American workers" led to the newcomers being urged to "assimilate" quickly or face a "quiet but sure extermination." Those who retained their alien ways "will share the fate of the native Indian."[52]

As mentioned previously, black immigrants cannot assimilate to the extent that they are not easily identifiable, even if they so desired. Therefore, the most attainable and contemporarily acceptable outcome is mutual coexistence. And yet the general apathy, overt rejection, and tendency of the native British groups to view black people as "barbaric and pathological," together with the use of legislation to ensure that blacks remain "un-British," work against this. There appears, moreover, to be a strange process taking place, whereby black people are denied "real British" identification yet prevented from self-identification. Thus, on February 2, 1989, Conservative MP Terry Dicks wrote in the *Tatler*, "I don't believe in the phrase Afro-Caribbean. They are West Indians and that's where they came from. If they want to go back to Africa then we can give them some ladders and they can climb up the trees if they want to."[53]

The paranoia created from the 1950s onward led to stringent immigration laws intending to keep out blacks and to retain the Anglo-Saxon stock. These laws have placed the onus on dependents to prove they have legitimate rights to join their loved ones. This has led to abuses of the basest kind and a contravention of immigrants' basic rights. From a position of relatively open-door policy and an invitation to former colonial citizens to enter the country, Britain has moved full circle and is now virtually closed to nonpatrials (i.e., non–Anglo-Saxon stock). Black immigration had exposed Britain to microscopic scrutiny, and she was found sadly lacking. Almost involuntarily, the hypocritical cloak of racial tolerance that she had worn so long, fell off. It was no doubt received with ironic satisfaction by countries such as South Africa and

the United States, which had so often been upbraided by Britain because of their overt racism against the black members of their societies.
"King George Niggers" who had escaped the worst of U.S. racism simply
because they claimed protection under the British crown, came "home"
and found that the protection was no longer there, once they were on
British soil. In fact, they eventually found that the legislature was used
to curtail their entry into their "homeland."

In commenting on Britain's antiblack legislation, Fryer writes:

> It's the first step that counts. The 1962 Act was a piece of discriminatory
> legislation whose "obvious intention" was to reduce the total annual flow
> of Black people into Britain. Its "unstated and unrecognized assumption"
> was that Black people were the source of the problem. From this assump-
> tion everything else flowed and would flow—including, as Stuart Hall has
> pointed out with justified acerbity, all those liberal television programmes
> on the "problems" of "race relations," every word and image in which are
> "impregnated with unconscious racism" since they are "precisely predi-
> cated on racist premisses."[54]

Having just emerged from six years of war—purported to be against
racist Nazi protagonists—Britain, the acclaimed anti-Nazi victor, found
it possible to engage in racist, antiblack rhetoric and policy implementa-
tion akin to those for which the Nazi foes had allegedly been van-
quished. To obtain a clearer understanding of this apparent contradiction, one may turn to Toynbee:

> In bringing in a well-deserved verdict of "guilty" against German prison-
> ers at the bar of Divine Justice, the rest of the Western World was pro-
> claiming its own guilt in the same breath; for, when a non-German majori-
> ty of a Western community had done its best to clear itself of complicity in
> German crimes by making the most of the German people's peculiar aber-
> rations from the main path of the Western Civilization's moral and politi-
> cal progress in the Modern Age, these non-German Westerners could not
> deny, in the last resort, that those horrifying aberrant Germans were still
> bone of their bones and flesh of their flesh.
>
> A Western nation which, for good or evil, had played so central a part in
> Western history . . . could hardly have committed these flagrant crimes if
> the same criminality had not been festering foully below the surface of life
> in the Western World's non-German provinces.[55]

The potential, then, for the vilest abuses and inhumane behavior is
contained in the very fabric of Western societies. Toynbee's observation
is of more contemporary relevance when one considers the international trend to politicize and institutionalize racism rather than exorcise it.
This phenomenon led the European Parliament to publish its *Declaration Against Racism and Xenophobia* in 1987.[56]

## CONCLUSION

Afro-Caribbean people entered the United Kingdom amid severe contradictions. The country was in dire need of manual labor, and yet the government and unions contrived to keep them out. Together with capitalist employers, the government and the unions ensured that once entry was gained, Afro-Caribbean people would be relegated to the lowest social class position—for some, a subclass within the society. Through collusion of various state agencies, these workers have been stigmatized and penalized extensively. The government, like its nineteenth-century forebears, continues to be plagued by xenophobia and a belief in the miasmatic role of immigrants, whom it perceives as being very different from the native population.

The dilemma that the injection of black labor migrants created is evidenced in the government's intransigence in response to racial discrimination and abuses. On the one hand, there is a strong desire to remove the problem, hence the recurring nonsensical talks of repatriation. On the other hand, needing to exhibit some semblance of a civilized society, minor concessions are made, such as the 1976 Race Relations Act, which, although outlawing racial discrimination, is weakened by the absence of meaningful state monitoring systems, a shortage of resources, and a resolve on the part of the government not to introduce effective positive action measures such as employment quotas to redress some of the wrongs of the past. It may be that a change can come about only when Britain looks inward in an attempt to acknowledge that the cause, and hence the cure, for its actions of gross inhumanity, such as racism, lies within the very fabric of British society.

## NOTES

1. "Jamaicans Arrive to Seek Work," *Times* (London), June 23, 1948, cited in Lambeth Council, *Forty Winters On* (London: Lambeth Council, 1988), p. 7.

2. "Driberg tells the Jamaicans Britain is no paradise," *South London Press*, June 25, 1948, cited in *Forty Winters On*, p. 5.

3. P. Fryer, *Staying Power, Black People in Britain Since 1504* (Atlantic Highlands, England: Humanities Press, 1984), p. 372.

4. J. Rex and S. Tomlinson, *Colonial Immigrants in a British City* (London: Routledge & Kegan Paul, 1979), pp. 36–37.

5. Ibid., p. 37.

6. M. Sherwood, *Many Struggles—West Indian Workers and Service Personnel in Britain (1939–45)* (London: Karia Press, 1985), p. 5.

7. Lord Moyne, cited in Sherwood, *Many Struggles*, p. 60.

8. Sherwood, *Many Struggles*, p. 58.

9. Usha Prashar, cited in A. Dummett, *British Nationality Law: Runnymede Trust's Guide to the Green Paper* (London: Runnymede Trust, 1977), p. 7.

10. Ibid.

11. Ibid., pp. 7–8.

12. Douglas Manley and Clarence Senior, *A Report on Jamaican Migration to Great Britain* (Kingston: The Government Printer, 1955), p. 7.

13. Norman W. Manley, *Ministry Paper No. 33, Appendix No. LXXVII, Restriction of Immigration to the United Kingdom* (Kingston: The Government Printer, 1961).

14. Mr. Marks. This is a pseudonym for a respondent in a series of interviews taken by the author for an ethnographic study of Jamaicans in the West Midlands, Britain. Data from the interviews are referred to as the West Midlands Interview Data (WMID) (1984).

15. Ibid.

16. Mr. Down. Also a WMID pseudonym.

17. Mr. Marks.

18. Sam King, cited in Lambeth Council, *Forty Winters On*, p. 8.

19. Ceri Peach, *West Indian Migration to Britain: A Social Geography* (London: Oxford University Press, 1968), p. xiii.

20. See Public Record Office (PRO), Colonial Office Records (COR) 1066, Item 2, *Working Party on the Employment in the United Kingdom of Surplus Colonial Labour, Papers*, "Possibility of Employing Colonial Labour. . . . " (London: His Majesty's Stationery Office, 1948); PRO, Cabinet Papers: CAB 129/40, CP (50) 113, *Coloured People from British Colonial Territories* (London: His Majesty's Stationery Office, 1950), p. 3; and PRO, CAB 128/17, CM (50), *Coloured People from British Colonial Territories* (London: His Majesty's Stationery Office, 1950), p. 77.

21. Akin L. Mabogunje, *The Development Process, A Spatial Perspective* (London: Hutchinson, 1980), p. 49.

22. For further discussion, see Fryer, *Staying Power*.

23. Kenneth Little, "Colour Prejudice in Britain," *Wasu*: X/1 (May 1943), p. 28; cited in Fryer, *Staying Power*, p. 577.

24. Bournville Village Trust Research, *When We Build Again: A Study Based on Research into Conditions of Living and Working in Birmingham* (London: George Allen & Unwin, 1941), pp. 51–54.

25. Des Wilson, *I Know It Was the Places Fault* (London: Oliphants, 1970), p. 18.

26. Labour Party, *The Housing Programme for England and Wales*, White Paper (London: Her Majesty's Stationery Office, 1966).

27. Wilson, *The Places Fault*, p. 18.

28. John Grieve, cited in Wilson, *The Places Fault*, p. 24.

29. V. Karn, J. Kemeny, and P. Williams, *Home Ownership in the Inner City: Salvation or Despair? Studies in Urban & Regional Policy, 3* (Aldershot, England: Gower Publishing, 1985), pp. 55–57.

30. E. J. Mishan, *Economic Issues in Immigration: An Exploration of the Liberal Approach to Public Policy in Immigration* (London: The Institute of Economic Affairs, 1970).

31. M. Duffield, *Black Radicalism and the Politics of De-Industrialisation: The Hidden History of Indian Foundry Workers* (Aldershot, England: Gower Publishing, 1988), pp. 2–3.

32. Colin Brown, *Black and White Britain: The Third PSI Survey* (London: Heinemann, 1984), pp. 293–303.

33. Duffield, *Black Radicalism*, p. 3.

34. S. Castles and G. Kosacks, *Immigrant Workers and Class Structure in Western Europe* (London: Oxford University Press, 1973).

35. R. Miles, *Racism and Migrant Labour* (London: Routledge & Kegan Paul, 1982).

36. South East Region Trades Union Congress Race Working Party, *Black Workers and Trade Unions* (London: Caledonian Press, 1986), p. 1A.

37. John Wrench, *Unequal Comrades: Trade Unions, Equal Opportunity and Racism*, Policy Papers in Ethnic Relations No. 5 (Coventry, England: Centre for Research in Ethnic Relations, Warwick University, 1986), p. 4.

38. South East Region Trades Union, *Black Workers and Trade Unions*, p. 6A.

39. Ibid.

40. For information on black union caucusing, see Labour Party Black Section, *Black Agenda* (London: privately published, 1989), pp. 32–36.

41. See Brown, *Black and White Britain*; Lord Swann, *Swann Report: Education for All: Great Britain, Committee of Inquiry into the Education of Children from Ethnic Minority Groups* (London: Her Majesty's Stationery Office, 1985); and J. Eggleston, *The Educational and Vocational Experiences of 15–18 Year Old Young People of Minority Ethnic Groups* (Keele, England: Department of Education and Science, University of Keele, 1984).

42. R. Ward and F. Reeves, "West Indian Business in Britain," in R. Ward and R. Jenkins, eds., *Ethnic Communities in Business* (London: Cambridge University Press, 1984), p. 134.

43. Lord Scarman, *Scarman Report: The Brixton Disorders, 10–12 April 1981. Report of an Inquiry* (Harmondsworth, England: Penguin, 1982), pp. 167–68.

44. William G. Sumner, cited in R. Preiswerk and D. Perrot, eds. *Ethnocentrism and History, Africa, Asia and Indian America in Western Textbooks* (New York: Nok Publishers International, 1978), p. 14.

45. Preiswerk and Perrot, *Ethnocentrism and History*, p. 17.

46. G. Cornwall Lewis, *Appendix 'G'—Report on the State of the Irish Poor* (no place, no publisher, 1836).

47. Arnold White, "Europe and the Jews—A Typical Alien Report," *Contemporary Review* 73 (February 1898): n.p.

48. Preiswerk and Perrot, *Ethnocentrism and History*, p. 16.

49. Rex and Tomlinson, *Colonial Immigrants*, p. 47.

50. Ibid., p. 65.

51. Herbert G. Gutman, *Work, Culture and Society* (Oxford, England: Basil Blackwell, 1977), p. 69.

52. Ibid., pp. 71–72.

53. Terry Dicks, *Tatler* (February 24, 1989): 35.

54. Fryer, *Staying Power*, p. 382.

55. Arnold Toynbee, *A Study of History: The Prospects of the Western Civilization*, Vol. 9 (London: Oxford University Press, 1963), p. 433.

56. European Parliament, Council, Representatives of the Member States, meeting within the Council and the Commission of the European Community, *Declaration Against Racism and Xenophobia*, signed at Strasbourg, June 11, 1986.

# SELECTED BIBLIOGRAPHY

Bournville Village Trust Research. *When We Build Again: A Study Based on Research into Conditions of Living and Working in Birmingham.* London: George Allen & Unwin, 1941.

Brown, Colin. *Black and White Britain: The Third PSI Survey.* London: Heinemann, 1984.

Castles, S., and G. Kosacks. *Immigrant Workers and Class Structure in Western Europe.* London: Oxford University Press, 1973.

Dicks, Terry. *Tatler* (February 24, 1989): 35.

Duffield, M. *Black Radicalism and the Politics of De-Industrialisation: The Hidden History of Indian Foundry Workers.* Aldershot, England: Gower Publishing, 1988.

Dummett, A. *British Nationality Law: Runnymede Trust's Guide to the Green Paper.* London: Runnymede Trust, 1977.

Eggleston, J. *The Educational and Vocational Experiences of 15–18 Year Old Young People of Minority Ethnic Groups.* Keele, England: Department of Education and Science, University of Keele, 1984.

Fryer, P. *Staying Power, Black People in Britain since 1504.* Atlantic Highlands, England: Humanities Press, 1984.

Gutman, Herbert. *Work, Culture and Society.* Oxford, England: Basil Blackwell, 1977.

Karn, V., J. Kemeny, and P. Williams. *Home Ownership in the Inner City: Salvation or Despair? Studies in Urban & Regional Policy, 3.* Aldershot, England: Gower Publishing, 1985.

Labour Party. *The Housing Programme for England and Wales.* White Paper. London: Her Majesty's Stationery Office, 1966.

Lambeth Council. *Forty Winters On.* London: Author, 1988.

Mabogunje, Akin L. *The Development Process, A Spatial Perspective.* London: Hutchinson, 1980.

Manley, Douglas, and Clarence Senior. *A Report on Jamaican Migration to Great Britain.* Kingston: The Government Printer, 1955.

Manley, Norman W. *Ministry Paper No. 33, Appendix No. LXXVII, Restriction of Immigration to the United Kingdom.* Kingston: The Government Printer, 1961.

Miles, R. *Racism and Migrant Labour.* London: Routledge & Kegan Paul, 1982.

Mishan, E. J. *Economic Issues in Immigration: An Exploration of the Liberal Approach to Public Policy in Immigration.* London: The Institute of Economic Affairs, 1970.

Peach, Ceri. *West Indian Migration to Britain: A Social Geography.* London: Oxford University Press, 1968.

Preiswerk, R., and D. Perrot, eds. *Ethnocentrism and History, Africa, Asia and Indian America in Western Textbooks.* New York: Nok Publishers International, 1978.

Rex, J., and S. Tomlinson. *Colonial Immigrants in a British City.* London: Routledge & Kegan Paul, 1979.

Scarman, Lord. *Scarman Report: The Brixton Disorders, 10–12 April 1981.* Report of an Inquiry. Harmondsworth, England: Penguin, 1982.

Sherwood, M. *Many Struggles—West Indian Workers and Service Personnel in Britain (1939–45).* London: Karia Press, 1985.

South East Region Trades Union Congress Race Working Party. *Black Workers and Trade Unions.* London: Caledonian Press, 1986.

Swann, Lord. *Swann Report: Education for All: Great Britain, Committee of Inquiry into the Education of Children from Ethic Minority Groups.* London: Her Majesty's Stationery Office, 1985.

Toynbee, Arnold. *A Study of History: The Prospects of the Western Civilization.* Vol. 9. London: Oxford University Press, 1963.

Ward, R., and F. Reeves. "West Indian Business in Britain." In R. Ward and R. Jenkins, eds. *Ethnic Communities in Business.* London: Cambridge University Press, 1984.

Wilson, Des. *I Know It Was the Places Fault.* London: Oliphants, 1970.

Wrench, John. *Unequal Comrades: Trade Unions, Equal Opportunity and Racism.* Policy Papers in Ethnic Relations No. 5. Coventry, England: Centre for Research in Ethnic Relations, Warwick University, 1986.

# II

## Settlement and Adaptation

# 4

# Education and Qualifications of Caribbean Immigrants and Their Children in Britain and Canada

ANTHONY H. RICHMOND and ALOMA MENDOZA

Education is a key factor in facilitating the economic and social integration of immigrants in advanced industrial societies. It is of instrumental value in a highly competitive labor market in which literacy, numerical ability, and specific skills are required. It is also of symbolic value, conferring status and promoting social acceptance. The experiences of Caribbean immigrants in Britain and Canada exhibit certain important differences that are partly a result of institutional and policy factors in the receiving countries but are also a consequence of demographic, economic, and social factors influencing the characteristics of the immigrants themselves.[1] This chapter examines the education and qualifications of immigrants entering Britain and Canada during the years 1951 to 1981 and considers some of the obstacles to educational attainment experienced by those of Caribbean ancestry who were born or raised in these two countries.

Caribbean immigration to Britain began to increase after World War II, reaching a peak in 1962. By 1981, there were an estimated 295,000 West Indian-born persons living in Britain, together with an additional quarter of a million—or more—born in Britain of Caribbean parentage. (In both Britain and Canada, the term "Caribbean" includes the Guyanese-born population because of its association with the Commonwealth. The Caribbean population in Canada also includes Haitians and

This chapter was prepared with the assistance of a minor research grant from the · Faculty of Arts, York University. Thanks are due to the various officials and expert informants who contributed information and comments based on their experience in the Metropolitan Toronto school system.

some people from Spanish-speaking as well as other parts of the Caribbean.) Of the combined West Indian ethnic origin category, 1 in 3 was 15 years of age or younger in 1981. Their residences were concentrated, particularly in the central London and West Midland conurbations.[2] In Canada, 211,205 Caribbean-born people were counted in 1981. The West Indian/black population also included a Canadian-born group, which was approximately 50,000 in number. (We may note that in the Canadian census of 1981, only 40 percent of the Caribbean-born respondents described their "ethnic origin" [based on ancestry] as black, negro, Caribbean, Afro-Caribbean, or related terminology, but this does not mean that the others would not be categorized as members of a "visible minority" in Canada. The remaining descriptions include "British," "French," and "Asian," with percentages given as 35 percent, 6 percent, and 10 percent, respectively.) Although there has been a small black population in Canada since early in the nineteenth century, Caribbean immigration was not significant until after 1962 and reached a peak in 1974. In 1981, approximately 14 percent of the Caribbean population in Canada was under 16 years of age. There was a francophone group from Haiti, resident in Montreal, but metropolitan Toronto has the largest proportion—58 percent—of all West Indians. Although there was some residential concentration, it was not as marked in Canadian cities as in Britain.[3]

## WEST INDIAN IMMIGRANTS IN BRITAIN

The Caribbean immigrants who came to Britain in the 1950s included some with higher education and professional qualifications, but these were a minority. There were a few doctors, teachers, social workers, and nurses, some of whom obtained further qualifications in Britain. However, the majority of West Indian immigrants at this time were the product of a colonial education system modeled on British prewar schools, in which access to secondary and tertiary education depended on the ability to pay. Up until 1961, immigrants to Britain tended to be clerical, skilled manual, or unskilled workers with average levels of education. R. B. Davison showed that, in the Greater London area in 1961, West Indian and Asian immigrants were, on average, more likely than the English to have left school after the age of 15.[4] However, this is explained by the younger age of the immigrants. Older United Kingdom-born persons would have been educated in Britain at a time when the minimum age for leaving school was 14.

The census data for 1961 reveal that Caribbean immigrants were not as well educated as Indian and Pakistani immigrants (both male and female), as measured by the age at which education was terminated. Davison's data show that only 2 percent of Jamaican males and 4 percent of other Caribbean immigrants left full-time schooling at 20 years or over, compared with 30 percent of Indian and Pakistani males, and with 12 percent of Indian women and 25 percent of Pakistani women. These figures compared with 4 percent of English men and 2 percent of English women. It is clear that the early Asian immigrants were a well-educated group, although it does not follow that their education and qualifications were fully recognized and accepted in Britain. Language differences and a metropolitan skepticism concerning the quality of "colonial" educational institutions probably resulted in a discounting of the overseas educational experience. However, Davison also showed that a small proportion of the population 15 years of age and over, were still in full-time education in Britain in 1961. With respect to males, this was true of 3 percent of the English, 1.3 percent of the Jamaicans, 5 percent of the other Caribbean nationals, 12 percent of the Indians, and 9 percent of the Pakistanis. A somewhat smaller proportion of women of all nationalities were still in full-time education, with the exception of Jamaican women, 6.5 percent of whom were still full-time students.[5] (The interpretation of 1961 census data for Britain is further complicated by the fact that some persons, born in India and other Commonwealth countries, were of "white," i.e., United Kingdom-born, parentage. However, even allowing for this, it seems certain that the Asian-born population in Britain at that time was better educated than the Caribbean-born.)

Census data for 1971 and 1981 concerning the education and qualifications of immigrant populations in Britain have not been published. However, survey data throw some light on the educational experience of West Indian migrants and their children in England and Wales. A large sample, representative of the West Indian, Asian, and "white" populations, was interviewed in 1982. The sample included persons 16 years and over born in the New Commonwealth and Pakistan and those born in Britain of NCWP−New Commonwealth and Pakistan−parentage. The study indicated that 56 percent of the "white" male respondents left school at the age of 15 or younger; corresponding figures for other groups were 36 percent of the West Indian males and 31 percent of the Asian males. "White" and West Indian women exhibited a similar pattern, but Asian women were less well educated, almost half leaving school by age 15. The data suggest that later cohorts of Asian immigrants were not as well educated as those who were already in Britain in 1961, although there was still an above-average proportion−23 percent of the males and 12 percent of the females−whose age on completing their full-time education was 20 years or over. This compared with only 2 percent of the West Indian men and 3 percent of the women.[6]

Of the West Indians 25 years and older, 97 percent were born overseas, whereas 80 percent of those 16–24 years were born in Britain. Therefore, an analysis of the highest academic or vocational qualification, broken down by the age group of the respondent, provides a basis for comparing the educational experience of the immigrants with those of the second generation.[7] Among men over the age of 44, 87 percent of the West Indian respondents had no qualifications, compared to 64 percent of the "white." In the group aged 25–44, the proportions were 64 percent and 38 percent, respectively. In the youngest—mainly British-born—cohort, 35 percent of the West Indians and 27 percent of the "white" were without academic or vocational qualifications. In all age groups, West Indian women were more likely than men to have some qualification. Among Asians, men over age 25 were better qualified than West Indians, but Asian women were much less likely to have any qualifications or training. In the youngest group, ethnic differentials were reduced. A university degree or some postsecondary "vocational" qualification was held by 18 percent of the West Indian males and 27 percent of the females in the 16–24 age group, and by 25 percent of the males and 30 percent of the females aged 25–44. For those over 44, the figures were 9 percent for males and 12 percent for females.

A later survey, conducted under government auspices, provides a similar profile. This confirms that the younger generation is better educated than the older one and that women are more likely than men to have higher qualifications, which, for the purposes of the survey, were defined as a university degree, member of a professional institute, teaching or nursing qualifications, and possession of the Higher National Diploma/Higher National Certificate (HND/HNC).[8] (Nursing is one of the most common qualifications obtained by West Indian women in Britain.)

## WEST INDIAN IMMIGRANTS IN CANADA

Following the 1967 introduction of selection according to "units of assessment," which were heavily weighted toward educational achievement, immigration from the Caribbean was initially in the nature of a "brain drain," although there was also a continuing flow of female domestic workers (some of them overqualified for service occupations) and others who were less well qualified. The possibility of visitors to Canada applying for landed immigrant status between 1968 and 1972 encouraged many less qualified immigrants to apply. They were admitted on relaxed criteria between 1972 and 1974, although some of those "landed" during this period had already been in Canada for several years. Subsequently, "family re-union" provision applicants, nominated immigrants, and political refugees were admitted without the stringent qualifications required of independent immigrants.

Table 4.1 shows the distribution of the Caribbean-born in Canada by

**Table 4.1**

**Percentage Distribution of Educational Levels of Caribbean-born by Sex and Age Group in Canada, 1981**

| Education | 15-24 | 25-34 | 35-44 | 45-54 | 55-64 | 65+ | 15-65+ |
|---|---|---|---|---|---|---|---|
| | | | | Males | | | |
| University | 9.7 | 18.5 | 20.0 | 23.1 | 17.6 | 12.9 | 17.2 |
| Other Post-secondary | 20.2 | 45.3 | 40.4 | 32.2 | 24.5 | 16.7 | 34.8 |
| Secondary | 63.5 | 30.8 | 30.4 | 32.6 | 38.1 | 41.0 | 39.1 |
| Elementary | 6.7 | 5.4 | 9.2 | 12.1 | 19.6 | 29.8 | 9.0 |
| Total | 100.1 | 100.0 | 100.0 | 100.0 | 99.8 | 100.4 | 100.1 |
| N='000 | 19.1 | 25.3 | 22.4 | 10.3 | 3.8 | 2.6 | 83.4 |
| | | | | Females | | | |
| University | 9.0 | 10.4 | 10.9 | 10.5 | 4.0 | 2.7 | 9.5 |
| Other Post-secondary | 24.9 | 46.5 | 43.4 | 31.0 | 17.6 | 10.4 | 35.6 |
| Secondary | 60.3 | 35.5 | 34.9 | 39.6 | 41.3 | 43.8 | 41.9 |
| Elementary | 5.7 | 7.6 | 11.8 | 19.0 | 37.1 | 42.9 | 13.0 |
| Total | 99.9 | 100.0 | 101.0 | 100.1 | 100.0 | 99.8 | 100.0 |
| N='000 | 21.9 | 32.6 | 25.0 | 11.4 | 6.0 | 5.1 | 102.0 |

Source: Statistics Canada, 1981 Census of Canada, Special Tabulations (Ottawa: Supply and Services, 1981).

education. More than half the Caribbean males aged 15–65 and 45 percent of the women had some university or other postsecondary education in 1981. This was considerably above the average for other immigrants or the Canadian-born. (Of the latter, 36 percent of the males and 34 percent of the females were similarly qualified.) The highest level of qualification was evident in the age groups 35–54 years and, contrary to the British experience, men were better qualified than women. However, later arrivals were less well educated than those who came in the decade 1960–69. In this group, 17 percent of the males and almost 10 percent of the females had some university training, but the proportion fell to 11 percent of the males and 6 percent of the females among those arriving during the period 1975–79. The proportion having only elementary education increased over the same period. The average educational level of males, even among those who arrived toward the end of the decade, remained above the Canadian average, whereas the proportion of Caribbean women with only elementary education approximated that of the Canadian population. This probably reflected the growing number of sponsored "family class" immigrants and others—some of whom originally entered Canada on temporary employment visas—who had obtained landed immigrant status by the time of the 1981 census. (Regulations were changed in 1981 to permit the award of landed immigrant status to foreign domestic workers, resident in Canada for several years, who could show that they had taken education and training to upgrade qualifications.)

A more detailed examination of educational achievement by age group reveals that Caribbean-born persons who immigrated to Canada before 1969 and who were under age 24 at the time of the 1981 census had particularly high levels of attainment.[9] Since this cohort would have arrived in Canada as infants, or under 12 years of age, some or all of their education would have been obtained in the receiving country. Of the small number of males who arrived before 1960, 43 percent had some university education, compared to 22 percent of this cohort of Caribbean women. In the next category—those who arrived in 1960–69—the proportions were 18 percent for the males and 16 percent for the females, which is still above the national average for the Canadian-born (9 percent). In part, these levels of education reflect the metropolitan concentration of immigrants in general and the Caribbean-born in particular. The larger urban areas provided ready access to secondary and postsecondary educational opportunities for those who arrived as children or young adults. Many West Indian immigrants who arrived in Canada while still of school age did take advantage of the opportunities available. Indeed, some of them may have come originally as students and subsequently obtained landed immigrant status, a process that was still legally possible prior to 1973.

There were differences in educational attainment between the Caribbean immigrants resident in Quebec and Ontario. On average, West Indians in Quebec were more likely to have university degrees, or some university training, than their counterparts in Ontario, possibly reflecting the traditional flow of Caribbean students to McGill and Sir George Williams' Universities. Twenty-one percent of the men, compared to 10 percent of the women, in Quebec had some university education (with or without a degree), and there was no difference by language. In Ontario, 14 percent of the Caribbean men, compared to 8 percent of the women, had some university training. Overall, 11 percent of the Caribbean immigrants had only an elementary education. As in the case of Britain, Asian immigrants in Canada tended to be better educated than those from the Caribbean, although there was a good deal of variation by country of origin. In fact, as many as 14 percent of the Asian-born males and 25 percent of the females had only elementary education.[10]

## WEST INDIAN "UNDERACHIEVEMENT"

Much concern has been expressed by educationalists in Britain regarding the apparent "underachievement" of West Indian children in schools. Britain is a "credentialist" society, perhaps more so than most advanced industrial societies. Notwithstanding the move away from segregated "grammar" schools for academically inclined pupils at age 11 toward more "comprehensive" secondary schools, great emphasis is placed on the results of examinations between the ages of 15 and 18. These are hierarchically rated in status from the best marks in the so-called General Certificate of Education (GCE) "A" levels through GCE "O" level results to performance in the less-prestigious Certificate of Secondary Education (CSE) examinations. Entry into postsecondary education is predicated upon good "A" level results, sometimes supplemented by special college entrance and scholarship examinations. Employers also regard these examination results as a basis for selection, particularly when the number of job applicants far exceeds the positions available.

In the 1950s and 1960s, the focus tended to be on the integration of immigrant children into a school system that was not well adapted to the needs of ethnic minorities. The linguistic, cultural, and previous educational backgrounds of the latter were very different from those of the indigenous working class families in those areas in which West Indian and Asian families settled. Often children were left abroad, in the care of relatives, while the parent or parents sought work and accommodation in Britain. There was sometimes a gap of several years before children rejoined their families in Britain. An official policy of "dispersal" of black and Asian children was adopted at this time, in the belief that their social integration would be enhanced if they were not segregated. There was also a feeling that white parents would be less likely to object to the presence of immigrant children in the classroom, if the numbers were small. In 1963, the minister of education stated in the House of Commons that no one school should have more than 30 percent immigrant children.[11]

From the mid-1960s onward, there was an awareness of the problems immigrant children were facing in school and the inadequacy of the response by teachers. Communication difficulties, disciplinary problems, and differing expectations of teachers and parents often led to a situation where a West Indian child was classified as "educationally sub-normal" (ESN) and sent to a special school. By 1972, West Indian children constituted 1.1 percent of all pupils in maintained primary and secondary schools but 4 percent of those in ESN (mild) schools.[12] Although this represented only 2.9 percent of all West Indian children in schools, parents were alarmed, and the North London West Indian Association lodged a complaint of racial discrimination with the Race Relations Board.

As primary West Indian immigration declined, there was a growing proportion of British-born Afro-Caribbean children in schools. The handicaps faced by those born and partly educated abroad were numerically less in evidence, and the ESN question diminished in importance. Nevertheless, it became increasingly evident that children of West Indian parentage were not performing as well in the British examination system as their white or, in some cases, their Asian peers. Care must be taken in the interpretation of evidence in this respect, for a number of reasons. When 14 percent of *all* school leavers have no graded results in any subject, and only 13 percent achieve one or more "A" level passes, there is clearly a wide range of achievement in the majority population. If a particular subpopulation, however defined, differs in the overall distribution of results, the mean and median variations may be less important than the range and standard deviation. No studies comparing the results of West Indian children with others have succeeded in controlling for all the factors known to influence educational performance. These include parental education and socioeconomic status, home background, including family size, neighborhood, and school environment, together with religious and cultural factors influencing aspirations and achievement orientation, which may differ by sex. To these factors, which influence all students, must be added the question of racial prejudice and discrimination, both within schools and in the community at large.[13]

The situation of West Indian children in schools was investigated by a government appointed "Committee of Inquiry into the Education of Children from Ethnic Minority Groups." An interim report was published in 1981[14] and was followed by further investigations culminating in a final report, "Education for All," otherwise known as the Swann Report.[15] Using data from various sources, including children who left school from five local education authority areas with a high proportion of "ethnic minority" students, the Swann Committee concluded that there had been an improvement in the performance of British-born West Indian children between 1978–79 and 1981–82, but that they still lagged behind Asian and other leavers in the number of higher graded "O" and "A" level passes. Although West Indian girls tended to stay in school longer than average and to seek some further education, both boys and girls obtained a lower general level of academic achievement as measured by these examinations. The committee categorically rejected genetically determined IQ as a cause but was unable to determine the precise effects of socioeconomic factors on performance and the influence of racism, either in the classroom or the community.[16] Some studies have gone so far as to suggest that, when local environmental influences are held constant, West Indian pupils may actually do better than their peers.[17] For example, a survey covering inner city neighborhoods in London, Liverpool, Manchester, and Wolverhampton noted "overall our black respondents had left school better qualified than the whites."[18] They also noted that black girls were better qualified than boys and that black respondents generally were more ambitious than white ones.

A somewhat different view of the apparent West Indian underachievement in schools is possible if relative rather than absolute levels of attainment are considered, using intergenerational educational mobility as the criterion. There is always a very high correlation between parental education and that of the child. Better-educated parents are a resource the child can call on to supplement instruction in school. Furthermore, educated parents provide role models and are likely to encourage their children to succeed in school, if only to protect their own self-esteem and social status. As educational opportunity in the younger generation expanded after the Second World War, many children had opportunities for secondary and tertiary education that had been denied their parents. However, for a poorer child from a working class home to obtain good examination results and to go on to obtain formal qualifications can properly be regarded as more of an "achievement" than for a privileged child from an affluent middle-class home. Regarded in this light, the upward educational mobility of West Indian children in Britain must be seen as a remarkable achievement in the face of very real obstacles, including the stereotypical view of their potential "underachievement."

The evidence for the *relatively* higher achievement of young West Indians is obtained in the Policy Studies Institute survey of 1982. The intergenerational comparisons for white, West Indian, and Asian respondents in the survey are summarized in Table 4.2. It is reasonable to assume that the age group 45 and over is representative of the parents of those aged 16–24. For white male respondents, there was a decline of 37 percentage points in the proportion reporting no qualification and an increase of 17 points in the percent reporting GCE "O" levels or better. This compared with the West Indian respondents' 42 point decline in the proportion with no qualification and a 33 point increase in those with "O" levels. Asian males showed greater improvement than whites but less than that of West Indians. There was a 53 percentage point decline among white women for those with no qualifications and a 42 point increase in those with "O" levels. West Indian women showed greater upward mobility, measured by the decline in the proportion with no qualifications but appear to have opted to a greater extent for vocational qualifications rather than academic. Younger Asian women improved their educational standing compared to the older ones, but to a lesser extent than either white or West Indian women. More detailed information, distinguishing the experience of Muslim girls from others, might throw light on this cultural difference.

## EDUCATIONAL EXPERIENCE IN CANADA

Notwithstanding the more selective nature of immigration to Canada and the higher levels of education and qualifications of the adult immigrants, there has been a similar concern expressed in Canada concerning the opportunities and achievement of West Indian and other black children in schools. Despite the achievements of earlier cohorts, some studies and recent interviews with teachers in Metropolitan Toronto suggest that there is growing evidence of some underachievement among black students presently in the school system.

In May, 1975, the *Draft Report of the Work Group on Multicultural Programs* of the Toronto Board of Education stated that "the influx of immigrant students from English speaking countries (e.g., West Indies, Pakistan, Guyana, and Trinidad) is a source of increasing concern."[19] Because of this influx, the integration of new Canadians was not occurring as smoothly as in previous years with white minority groups. A report of the *Consultative Committee on the Education of Black Students in Toronto Schools* identified a high dropout rate, low self-esteem, lack of black teachers as role models, and a need for "black studies" as part of the curriculum as issues requiring further investigation and action.[20] Previous studies noted that black/Caribbean students were being streamed into level three in secondary schools. They were certainly underrepresented in the level five and level six programs.[21] Other studies showed that the teaching staff and administrators appeared to harbor low expectations of students, and these were in turn quickly reflect-

**Table 4.2**
**Intergenerational Educational Mobility by Ethnic Group and Age**

| Ethnic Origin | Decline in Percentage of Whites, West Indians, and Asians Having No Qualification | | |
|---|---|---|---|
| | Oldest | Youngest | Difference |
| | Males | | |
| White | 64 | 27 | -37 |
| West Indian | 87 | 35 | -42 |
| Asian | 74 | 35 | -39 |
| | Females | | |
| White | 75 | 22 | -53 |
| West Indian | 84 | 21 | -63 |
| Asian | 86 | 50 | -36 |

| | Increase in Percentage of Whites, West Indians, and Asians with GCE "O" Level or Better | | |
|---|---|---|---|
| | Males | | |
| White | 16 | 33 | +17 |
| West Indian | 5 | 38 | +33 |
| Asian | 19 | 47 | +28 |
| | Females | | |
| White | 11 | 53 | +42 |
| West Indian | 7 | 41 | +34 |
| Asian | 13 | 37 | +24 |

*Source:* Adapted from Colin Brown, *Black and White Britain: The PSI Survey* (London: Heinemann, 1984), pp. 145–47.

ed in the educational and social experiences of black/Caribbean students. Researchers identified social and home circumstances as major factors that impinged on the academic performances and social adjustment of black/Caribbean students in the schools. Various authors found that students from low occupational status homes were less likely to be in level five of secondary schools and more likely to be from the Caribbean.[22] Others faulted the separation of parents and children during the migratory process as being partly responsible for low academic achievement.[23] The psychological stresses associated with students' adjustment into a new school system and society also affect their academic performances.

Interviews with a cross-section of teachers and others (18 teachers, 2 principals, 1 administrator, and 3 community workers) associated with the Metropolitan Toronto school system conducted in the summer of 1986 confirmed the findings of previous research. Among the adjustment problems identified as common among recent West Indian arrivals in the school system were those relating to family reunion following separation from parents (some of whom had acquired new partners, leading to a change of name); stresses related to unfamiliarity with the new school; language and communication problems; disciplinary conflicts; and difficulty in adjusting to the mother's employment outside the home. It was generally considered that students needed at least six months to adapt to the new environment.

In due course after migration, other problems surface. Questions of identity confusion and low self-esteem are evident and appear to be related to stereotypical attitudes on the part of teachers and white peers. Achievement in athletics is seen as more appropriate than academic goals, and many Caribbean students are streamed into vocational programs that limit future prospects of higher education. Selection procedures and tests are seen as culturally biased against Caribbean children, and insufficient attention is given to "Black Studies." A disproportionate number of West Indian children are in special education classes, where they may be diagnosed as mentally handicapped or as having personality disorders, rather than as suffering from cultural disorientation or poor self-esteem induced by perceived prejudice and discrimination.

Although it may be hard to determine whether the degree and extent of racism in Canada is as serious as it is in Britain, there is little doubt that West Indians in Canada have been among its victims.[24] Racism in Ontario schools remains a serious obstacle to full integration, although most informants thought the situation was improving. A number of schools have adopted explicit policies designed to combat prejudice and discrimination, but some white parents withdraw their children from schools where "visible minorities" predominate. Name calling, racist jokes, graffiti, and some interethnic fighting occur, but there is little serious violence. Nevertheless, there was evidence of underlying feelings of resentment and anger among Caribbean students. The source of the frustration seems to be connected to their own experiences in the community and at school and their perception of the status of blacks in the society at large. Much of the racial discrimination may not be experienced by them directly, but it is indirectly communicated to them by way of their family members, neighbors, friends, and the media. This leads to a general disenchantment and to low expectations of achievement. Black anglophone students in Quebec appear to have faced similar problems to those in Ontario.[25]

A survey of all secondary students in the Toronto City area in 1987 showed that students born in the Caribbean constituted 5.8 percent of the population and that Canadian-born blacks constituted an additional 1.7 percent. Jamaica, Trinidad and Tobago, and Guyana were the main countries of origin. Although black students born in Canada performed at about the average level, those born outside Canada were significantly more likely than Asian and white students to be in basic level programs, to obtain lower marks in English and mathematics, and to achieve fewer credits at age 15. The poorer performance persisted even when the socioeconomic status of the parent or parents was controlled. However, there was evidence of a slight improvement in performance compared to a similar study conducted in 1983.[26]

## CONCLUSION

In Britain, the Swann Report on the *Education of Children from Ethnic Minority Groups* explicitly rejected the view that genetic factors or measured intelligence were responsible for any of the observed differences in educational attainment between racial and ethnic groups. They placed much emphasis on adverse environmental circumstances and social deprivation. The report identified a complex of factors, including socioeconomic status and region of residence, which account for West Indian underachievement. The authors noted that

> all of them involve the interaction of the school and society at large with the West Indian child, the West Indian family and the West Indian community, with, running through the whole complex, the influences of prejudice and discrimination in one form or another.[27]

The report recognized that racism in Britain, which it considered an "insidious evil," may take various forms: individual, institutional, racist attacks, and a pervading "climate" of racism that has a "direct and acute bearing . . . on what goes on in the classroom."[28] The same may be fairly said of Canada also, although the extent of racial violence has been less than in Britain.

Caribbean immigrants in Canada are more recent arrivals than those in Britain. On average, the former are much better educated and qualified than the latter. In Britain, West Indian women are more likely to have more qualification than men, but this is not the case in Canada. In both countries, those born and/or educated in the receiving society appear to exhibit some signs of "underachievement." However, in Britain, the younger generation of West Indian ethnic origin is clearly achieving a higher level of education than the first generation of immigrants. It remains to be seen whether this will be the case in Canada as the numbers in the second generation, proceeding through the education system, increase in the future. The earlier experience of the second generation of largely European origin, resident in the metropolitan Toronto area, was favorable in this respect.[29] Further research is needed to determine what obstacles impede fulfillment of the potential educational capability of black students. Specifically, systematic studies controlling for the socioeconomic status and educational achievement of parents will be required before the relative importance of race and ethnic origin can be compared with the effects of demographic, social, structural, and institutional determinants in the two countries.

## NOTES

1. See J. G. Reitz, *The Institutional Structure of Immigration as a Determinant of Inter-racial Competition* (Toronto: Centre for Industrial Relations, University of Toronto, 1986); Anthony H. Richmond, "Caribbean Immigrants in Britain and Canada: Socio-demographic Aspects," paper presented at the Meetings of the Canadian Population Society, McMaster University, Hamilton, Ontario, June 1987; Richmond, "Caribbean Immigrants in Britain and Canada: Socioeconomic Adjustment," paper presented at the Conference on the Caribbean Diaspora, Institute of Commonwealth Studies, University of London, June 1987; and Richmond, *Immigration and Ethnic Conflict* (London: The Macmillan Press, Ltd., 1988).

2. Commission for Racial Equality (CRE), *Ethnic Minorities in Britain* (London: CRE, 1985).

3. See John Kralt, *Atlas of Residential Concentration for the Census Metropolitan Areas of Montreal, Toronto, and Vancouver*, 3 vols. (Ottawa: Supply and Services, 1986).

4. R. B. Davison, *Black British: Immigrants to England* (London: Oxford University Press, 1966), p. 35.

5. Ibid., Table 15.

6. Colin Brown, *Black and White Britain: The Third PSI Survey* (London: Heinemann, 1984).

7. Ibid., pp. 144–47.

8. Statistics Canada, *Labour Force Survey* (Ottawa: Supply and Services, 1985).

9. See Richmond, *Immigration.*

10. Statistics Canada, *Census of Canada, Special Tabulations* (Ottawa: Supply and Services, 1981).

11. Nicholas Deakin, *Colour, Citizenship and British Society* (London: Panther, 1970), p. 173.

12. Sally Tomlinson, "West Indian Children and ESN Schooling," *New Community* 6:3 (1978): 238.

13. Sally Tomlinson, "The Educational Performance of Ethnic Minority Children," *New Community* 8:3 (1980): 213-34, and *Ethnic Minorities in British Schools* (London: Heinemann, 1983); and G. K. Verma and B. Ashworth, *Ethnicity and Educational Achievement in British Schools* (London: Macmillan, 1986).

14. See Anthony Rampton, *West Indian Children in Our Schools. Interim Report of the Committee of Inquiry into the Education of Children from Ethnic Minority Groups* (London: Her Majesty's Stationery Office, 1981).

15. See Lord Swann, *Education for All: Report of the Committee of Inquiry into the Education of Children from Ethnic Minority Groups* (London: Her Majesty's Stationery Office, 1985).

16. Ibid., pp. 81-84.

17. G. Driver, *Beyond Underachievement* (London: CRE, 1980).

18. K. Roberts, et al., *Unregistered Youth Unemployment and Outreach Careers Work*, Research Papers 31/32 (London: Department of Employment, 1981), p. 16.

19. Toronto Board of Education, *Draft Report of the Work Group on Multicultural Programs* (Toronto: Board of Education for the City of Toronto, 1975), p. 30.

20. See Toronto Board of Education, *Consultative Committee on the Education of Black Students in Toronto Schools* (Toronto: Board of Education for the City of Toronto, 1987).

21. See E. N. Wright, *Programme Placement Related to Selected Countries of Birth and Selected Languages* (Toronto: Board of Education for the City of Toronto, Research Department, 1971); R. Deosaran, E. N. Wright, et al., *The 1975 Every Student Survey: Students' Background and Its Relationship to Program Placement* (Toronto: Board of Education for the City of Toronto, Research Department, 1976); J. Gershman, *The 1975 Every Student Survey: The Background of Students in Special Education and New Canadian Programmes* (Toronto: Board of Education for the City of Toronto, Research Department, 1976); E. N. Wright and A. S. Dhanota, *The Grade Nine Student Survey: Fall 1980* (Toronto: Board of Education for the City of Toronto, Research Department, 1982); and E. N. Wright and G. K. Tsuji, *The Grade Nine Student Survey: Fall 1983* (Toronto: Board of Education for the City of Toronto, Research Department, 1984).

22. See E. N. Wright, *Program Placement*; Subhas Ramcharan, "Special Problems of Immigrant Children in the Toronto School System," in A. Wolfgang, ed., *Education of Immigrant Students* (Toronto: OISE, 1975); Deosaran and Wright, *The 1975 Every Student Survey*; and Wright and Dhanota, *The Grade Nine Student Survey Fall 1980* (Toronto: Board of Education for the City of Toronto, Research Department, 1982).

23. Christopher Beserve, *West Indian Children: A Study of Some Problems of Adjustment* (Toronto: University of Toronto, 1973); Inez Elliston, *Some Learning Needs of English Speaking West Indian Children in Canada* (Scarborough, Ontario: Scarborough Board of Education, 1976); and Deborah Kiladze, "The West

Indian Immigrant in the Canadian School," in G. W. Bancroft, ed., *The Novice and the Newcomer: Student Teachers' Perspectives on Multiculturalism and Education* (London, Ontario: Third Eye Publications, 1982).

24. Frances Henry, "West Indians in Canada: The Victims of Racism?" paper presented at the Conference on the Caribbean Diaspora, Institute of Commonwealth Studies, University of London, June 17–19, 1987.

25. Michel Laferriere, "The Education of Black Students in Montreal Schools: An Emerging Anglophone Problem, A Non-existent Francophone Preoccupation," in M. L. Kovacs, ed., *Ethnic Canadians: Culture and Education* (Regina, Saskatchewan: Canadian Plains Research Center, University of Regina, 1978).

26. M. Cheng, G. Tsuji, M. Yau, and S. Ziegler, *The Every Student Survey: Fall, 1987* (Toronto: Board of Education for the City of Toronto, Research Section, Library Services Department, 1989).

27. Lord Swann, *Education for All*, p. 85.

28. Ibid., p. 30.

29. See Richmond, *Immigration*.

## SELECTED BIBLIOGRAPHY

Beserve, Christopher. *West Indian Children: A Study of Some Problems of Adjustment*. Toronto: University of Toronto, 1973.

Brown, Colin. *Black and White Britain: The Third PSI Survey*. London: Heinemann, 1984.

Cheng, M., G. Tsuji, M. Yau, and S. Ziegler. *The Every Student Survey: Fall, 1987*. Toronto: Board of Education for the City of Toronto, Research Section, Library Services Department, 1989.

Commission for Racial Equality. *Ethnic Minorities in Britain*. London: CRE, 1985.

Davison, R. B. *Black British: Immigrants to England*. London: Oxford University Press, 1966.

Deakin, Nicholas. *Colour, Citizenship and British Society*. London: Panther, 1970.

Deosaran, R., E. N. Wright, et al. *The 1975 Every Student Survey: Students' Background and Its Relationship to Program Placement*. Toronto: Board of Education for the City of Toronto, Research Department, 1976.

Driver, G. *Beyond Underachievement*. London: CRE, 1980.

Elliston, Inez. *Some Learning Needs of English Speaking West Indian Children in Canada*. Scarborough, Ontario: Scarborough Board of Education, 1976.

Gershman, J. *The 1975 Every Student Survey: The Background of Students in Special Education and New Canadian Programmes*. Toronto: Board of Education for the City of Toronto, Research Department, 1976.

Henry, Frances. "West Indians in Canada: The Victims of Racism?" Paper presented at the Conference on the Caribbean Diaspora, Institute of Commonwealth Studies, University of London, June 17–19, 1987.

Kiladze, Deborah. "The West Indian Immigrant in the Canadian School." In G. W. Bancroft, ed. *The Novice and the Newcomer: Student Teachers' Perspec-*

*tives on Multiculturalism and Education.* London, Ontario: Third Eye Publications, 1982.

Kralt, John. *Atlas of Residential Concentration for the Census of Metropolitan Areas of Montreal, Toronto, and Vancouver.* 3 vols. Ottawa: Supply and Services, 1986.

Laferriere, Michel. "The Education of Black Students in Montreal Schools: An Emerging Anglophone Problem, A Non-existent Francophone Preoccupation." In M. L. Kovacs, ed. *Ethnic Canadians: Culture and Education.* Regina, Saskatchewan: Canadian Plains Research Center, University of Regina, 1978.

Ramcharan, Subhas. "Special Problems of Immigrant Children in the Toronto School System." In A. Wolfgang, ed. *Education of Immigrant Students.* Toronto: Office of Immigrant Student Education, 1975.

Rampton, Anthony. *West Indian Children in Our Schools. Interim Report of the Committee of Inquiry into the Education of Children from Ethnic Minority Groups.* London: Her Majesty's Stationery Office, 1981.

Reitz, J. G. *The Institutional Structure of Immigration as a Determinant of Interracial Competition.* Toronto: Centre for Industrial Relations, University of Toronto, 1986.

Richmond, Anthony H. "Caribbean Immigrants in Britain and Canada: Sociodemographic Aspects." Paper presented at the Meetings of the Canadian Population Society, McMaster University, Hamilton, Ontario, June 1987.

_____. "Caribbean Immigrants in Britain and Canada: Socio-economic Adjustment." Paper presented at the Conference on the Caribbean Diaspora, Institute of Commonwealth Studies, University of London, June 1987.

_____. *Immigration and Ethnic Conflict.* London: The Macmillan Press, Ltd., 1988.

Roberts, K., et al. *Unregistered Youth Unemployment and Outreach Careers Work.* Research Papers 31/32. London: Department of Employment, 1981.

Statistics Canada. *1981 Census of Canada, Special Tabulations.* Ottawa: Supply and Services, 1981.

_____. *Labour Force Survey.* Ottawa: Supply and Services, 1985.

Swann, Lord. *Education for All: Report of the Committee of Inquiry into the Education of Children from Ethnic Minority Groups.* London: Her Majesty's Stationery Office, 1985.

Tomlinson, Sally. "The Educational Performance of Ethnic Minority Children." *New Community* 8:3 (1980): 213–34.

_____. *Ethnic Minorities in British Schools.* London: Heinemann, 1983.

_____. "West Indian Children and ESN Schooling." *New Community* 6:3 (1978): 235–42.

Toronto Board of Education. *Consultative Committee on the Education of Black Students in Toronto Schools.* Toronto: Board of Education for the City of Toronto, 1987.

_____. *Draft Report of the Work Group on Multicultural Programs.* Toronto: Board of Education for the City of Toronto, 1975.

Wright, E. N. *Programme Placement Related to Selected Countries of Birth and Selected Languages.* Toronto: Board of Education for the City of Toronto, Research Department, 1971.

Wright, E. N., and A. S. Dhanota. *The Grade Nine Student Survey: Fall 1980.* Toronto: Board of Education for the City of Toronto, Research Department, 1982.

Wright, E. N., and G. K. Tsuji. *The Grade Nine Student Survey: Fall 1983.* Toronto: Board of Education for the City of Toronto, Research Department, 1984.

# 5

## Dominican International Migration: The Role of Households and Social Networks

### PATRICIA R. PESSAR

## INTRODUCTION

This chapter describes and analyzes two important features of Dominican immigration—settlement in the United States and return to the Dominican Republic. In examining these two features, I seek to make the description and analysis of settlement and return more complex and authentic than our simple demographic labels of "temporary migrant," "permanent migrant," and "return migrant" would suggest. How do we describe settlement and return as processes rather than as conditions? How do we ensure that the actors, social relations, institutions, and cultural elements that influence settlement and return are included in our analyses? And how do we measure the extent to which permanently settled immigrants or return migrants attain the characteristics conventionally associated with settlement and return, i.e., total social and economic integration in the host or source society? In this author's opinion, ethnographic research that includes the household and social networks as key analytical units is a way of addressing many of these important issues.

Recently several migration scholars have proposed that focusing on the household rather than the individual migrant when attempting to elucidate why and how the migrant decides to migrate is more sound both empirically and conceptually.[1] The migrant household, they argue, is the actual locus of decision making as well as the social unit for the accumulation of the resources required to sponsor an individual's migration. In previous works, I have argued that to understand the genesis and evolution of an individual's migration experience, the researcher must consider the internal dynamics of the migrant household (its own political economy) as well as how its members interact with the larger political and economic environment.[2] In this chapter, I will argue that women's improved status in migrant households underlies in large part the transition in Dominican households' orientation to migration from a temporary to a long-term or permanent stay.[3]

Social networks are another concept that enables researchers to study migration as a sociocultural process.[4] While this concept has been defined and put into operation in research in different ways, for our purpose here, the migrant social network will be conceived as a web of reciprocal relations among individuals in a migrant source community and other migrant host communities. Migrant social networks are conduits for the transfer of people, services, funds, goods, and information across geographical and economic space. I refer to "economic space," because several authors have stressed the importance of social networks for providing individuals and households with information about and access to diverse loci of production (e.g., agricultural and urban wage labor markets and petty commodity production markets). As Kenneth Roberts argues in the case of rural Mexico and Jorge Dandler and Carmen Medeiros propose for Bolivia, income diversification is a strategy that many households in underdeveloped countries pursue in order to minimize risk;[5] migration becomes an important agency for such income diversification. Inasmuch as the construct of migrant social networks facilitates the study of exchanges of people, services, and other economic values between "economic spaces," social network analysis can help clarify whether migration benefits or hampers labor exporting societies.[6]

In this chapter, I will use the migrant social network as an analytical unit in order to describe and account for: (1) the fragile, conditional nature of the Dominican migrants' return to their home country and (2) the negligible impact return migration has had on Dominican economic development. The discussions of Dominican settlement in the United States and return migration to the Dominican Republic are preceded by a brief characterization of Dominican immigrants in the United States.

## DOMINICAN IMMIGRANTS IN THE UNITED STATES

According to the 1980 census, 169,100 persons of Dominican birth were residing in the United States, with 127,700 of them (76 percent) in the New York metropolitan area.[7] In a more recent demographic study, Eric Larson and Wolfgang Opitz concluded that, as of 1988, approximately 300,000 Dominicans were residing in the United States.[8]

Economic motivation predominates in Dominican emigration:[9] many aim to bolster a precarious middle-class standing in the Dominican

Republic by accumulating savings to invest back home. Nonetheless, the experience of or fear of political repression has also been an explosive factor, and there were major increases in the numbers of Dominicans emigrating after the overthrow of President Juan Bosch in 1963 and the election years of 1974 and 1978.[10] At least Dominicans have been able to leave in recent years. During the Trujillo era (1930–60), restrictive emigration policies made it extremely difficult for Dominicans to move to the United States. It was only after the dictator's death in 1961 that migration to the United States became significant.[11] The 1980 census shows that more than three-quarters of the Dominicans in the United States arrived after 1970.[12]

Contrary to conventional wisdom, as well as early ethnographic accounts of Dominican emigration,[13] the immigrant population is neither predominantly rural nor from the ranks of the chronically unemployed or underemployed. According to the *Diagnos* national survey conducted in 1974 in the Dominican Republic[14] and the 1981 Hispanic Settlement survey in Queens and northern Manhattan,[15] the migration stream is predominantly urban and middle class. The *Diagnos* survey found that about three-quarters of the migrants were from urban areas, and nearly three-quarters of these urban migrants were middle class. While this survey did not provide information on class differences among the rural population, research conducted in the Dominican Republic and the United States documents that migrants from rural areas come mainly from fairly prosperous households. These are middle-sized and large landowning households that engaged in petty commodity production using household labor and/or paid agricultural workers.[16]

New York City census data for 1980 provide us with additional information on the Dominican population. Women outnumber men, with approximately 56 percent of the population being female. The population is youthful: the median age for males is 23.3, for females, 27.1. The percentage of married-couple households among Dominicans is significantly below the New York City level: 52 percent compared to 69 percent. On the other hand, approximately 42 percent of Dominican households had female heads. As reported in the 1980 census, the median incomes of married-couple and female-headed households were $12,156 and $5,933, respectively.[17] These are clearly below the citywide median average of $20,625 for married-couple households and $8,516 for female-headed units.[18] The Dominicans' relatively low household incomes can partially be attributed to the fact that over 23 percent of these households drew public assistance income, as compared to the city's 14 percent average for such recipiency.[19]

On the whole, Dominicans demonstrate relatively high rates of labor force participation; the figure is 75.4 percent for Dominican men and 46.6 percent for Dominican women, according to the 1980 census. The men's labor force participation rates exceeded the overall male rate for New York City of 69.2 percent, while the women's was slightly below the overall female rate of 47.1 percent.[20] Table 5.1 shows the occupational distribution of this Dominican population.

The high levels of labor force participation are consistent with this population's goal of social mobility. In many cases, Dominicans intend to enjoy this social mobility at home rather than in the United States. In survey research on Dominicans in New York conducted by Sherri Grasmuck and myself, as well as in the Hispanic settlement in New York City survey, the majority of the respondents reported their intention to return home rather than settle permanently in the United States. Based on census data for the 1970–80 period, Robert Warren estimates that approximately one-third of the Dominicans resident in the United States eventually return to the island.[21] In the following two sections, I will describe how households and migrant social networks mediate the process by which Dominicans come to settle in the United States or return home.

## FROM TEMPORARY TO PERMANENT MIGRANT

While an earlier body of literature on U.S. immigration focused on settlement due to the authors' concern over the immigrants' abilities to adapt to American society and culture,[22] contemporary studies rarely address this concern. Indeed, the issues of settlement and adjustment are secondary to a concern with the role immigrant labor plays in advanced industrial economies. Consequently, researchers have focused on degrees of the vulnerability of immigrant labor vis-a-vis the labor market and the workplace. And here degrees of vulnerability are usually equated with differences in legal status—e.g., temporary guest workers, illegal aliens, temporary residents—rather than degrees of permanence.[23]

In one important study, however, the author does relate the settlement process to the contemporary concern over the role of immigrant labor in the U.S. economy. In his model of immigrant settlement, Michael Piore asserts that the majority of Latin and Caribbean immigrants begin their migration stay in the United States with the intention of returning home after a relatively short period of time.[24] According to Piore, this temporary orientation to migration makes these immigrants especially well-suited to the dead-end, low-paying, insecure jobs for which they are recruited. That the immigrants are willing to take demeaning jobs most American citizens would eschew is linked by Piore to the fact that temporary immigration creates a sharp dichotomy between work and social identity. As the following attests, for Piore the temporary immigrant's social identity is rooted in the place of origin:

**Table 5.1**
**Percentage Distribution of Occupations of**
**Dominican Males and Females 16 and Over,**
**New York City, 1980**

| Occupation | Males | Females |
|---|---|---|
| Professional | 2.8 | 2.0 |
| Semi-Professional/ | | |
| Technical | 0.9 | 0.5 |
| Managerial | 6.4 | 1.6 |
| Clerical | 10.6 | 18.6 |
| Sales | 3.4 | 3.0 |
| Crafts | 13.2 | 6.1 |
| Operatives | 32.6 | 55.1 |
| Service | 23.5 | 11.5 |
| Labor | 6.2 | 1.4 |
| Farm Labor | 0.2 | 0.0 |

Source: Adapted from Gurak and Falcón-Rodríguez, 1987.

Work performed in the receiving society is purely instrumental: a means to gather income, income that can be taken back to his or her home community and used to fulfill or enhance his or her role within that social structure. From the perspective of the migrant, work is essentially asocial.[25]

According to Piore, for many recent immigrants, this temporary commitment to immigration is itself transitory. Due to the general instability of the jobs in which the migrant is employed, he or she is unable to accumulate sufficient savings to return after a short duration, as initially intended. As the migrant prolongs the stay, he or she develops social attachments, and demands are made upon the individual from within the migrant community. This change in the locus of social attachments from source community to migrant community is the linchpin of Piore's model of settlement. It should be noted that his argument is compatible with social network analysis. He does not, however, explicitly refer to migrant social networks, nor does he substantiate his argument concerning settlement by documenting changes in the types, frequency, and quantity of exchanges occurring between individuals in the source and host communities.

Once the settlement process begins, Piore claims, the migrant begins to share the native worker's concerns for job security, career advancement, and the social status attached to the job. As such, the more settled immigrant worker loses the unique value he or she initially afforded employers.

While Piore should be commended for drawing our attention to the fact that settlement is a social process that does not follow reflexively from the original intentions of the immigrants, his model lacks key analytical elements. Not only does his model neglect a consideration of gender, but it also moves from a consideration of the individual to the community without a thought to how the household may mediate the settlement process. As we shall see, these are serious omissions in the case of Dominican settlement in the United States.

## THE SETTLEMENT OF DOMINICAN IMMIGRANTS

Taking Piore's model as a starting point, one can ask whether, as he claims, the community of origin is the primary social referent for Dominican male and female immigrants during the initial phase of their migration. Ethnographic research has shown that, in the case of male immigrants, the two significant social arenas in which migrant status initially gains definition and purpose are the home community and the household in the host society. The meanings, values, and social relations associated with these two arenas may at times be contradictory and antithetical. For men, the tension between these two domains must be managed throughout the period of migration.

Piore is correct when he observes that the immigrant's first jobs tend to be at the lowest rung of the prestige hierarchy and that the meanings and values associated with these may contradict the immigrant's identity and sense of worth. This is particularly true for Dominican men whose premigration employment placed them in the ranks of the lower-middle class. Although men experience a personal decline in status as measured against their premigration position, they are urged by others in the household and immigrant community to subsume their individual identities and goals within a larger sphere, the household. (In an exploration of changing gender relations among Dominican immigrants in a small New England city, Andrew Gordon comes to a similar conclusion. He notes that men's social relations have become "atomized, making the household, rather than the kin or friend network, the primary unit of social relations."[26])

Herein lies the tension of the migrant experience for many Dominican men. The purpose for migrating, according to most Dominicans— economic and social progress—may not be realized at the level of the individual but is often achieved collectively. The wages the migrants receive and the level of consumption this income makes possible permit the domestic unit to enjoy what is by the standards of its members a middle-class lifestyle. Notwithstanding the social mobility realized at the household level, Dominican men in the United States, because of their low occupational status, may become frustrated by their inability to translate these household gains into publicly recognized prestige. This observation underscores what is for men an uneasy balance between becoming first among equals in the immigrant household and the prevailing gender ideology and sex roles in the Dominican Republic that promote patriarchy in the home and prestige and privilege for men in the public sphere.

With this tension as a major catalyst, some men choose to pursue financial strategies in which frugal living and savings are emphasized to ensure that the household will eventually return to the Dominican Republic. For example, many men told me that they spend far less money in New York than they had back home in socializing with male friends in bars and clubs. As one man expressed this decision:

> Yes, it is lonely to go from home to work and then home again without stopping for a few drinks and conversation with buddies. But one comes to New York to work, not enjoy life. If one tries to mix the two, a man ends up wasting his salary and he can never really enjoy life in New York. It is better to sacrifice here and then go home to enjoy the respect, companionship, and good life that your hard work earns you.

In line with this quote, interviews with returned migrants and immigrants soon to depart for the Dominican Republic revealed that men anticipated not only a rise in occupational status but, equally important, the recognition of the man's social and material achievements among peers and others in the wider community. In fact, upon return to the Dominican Republic, the household and community become realigned from the man's perspective. It is his work in the Dominican Republic and the value it is accorded by the larger community that brings a higher status to the household he represents and maintains.

In contrast to men, Dominican women's identity is firmly rooted in the household. Even as a "bird of passage," the woman may be metaphorically compared to an actual bird, which carries in its genetic makeup the capacity and proclivity to construct a nest wherever it goes. As part of her "cultural programming," the Dominican woman transports the values and roles associated with the home wherever she settles. The tension that migrant men experience between the demands and goals of their household in the United States on the one hand, and the meanings and values of the home community on the other, are much less pronounced for women. The household was the locus of female social identity prior to migration and continues as that after migration. Indeed, the household gains salience in the United States for all members, regardless of gender. These facts prove beneficial to women and have profound consequences for the orientation of women to migration and settlement. In marked contrast to Piore's assertion that temporary migrants dichotomize between themselves as social beings on the one hand and workers on the other, the data presented in this chapter show that very real negotiations over gender ideology and the sexual division of labor within the household are possible precisely because Dominican women do not dichotomize between the home and the workplace. Consideration of how these negotiations affect Dominican settlement in the United States will follow a preliminary discussion of how Dominican women's status has improved within migrant households.

## DOMINICAN WOMEN'S IMPROVED STATUS IN THE HOUSEHOLD

Observers of the family in the Dominican Republic have distinguished two basic forms of domestic organization—the single-mate and the multiple-mate patterns—each associated with specific forms of authority.[27] In the single-mate household, authority resides largely with the senior male; in the multiple-mate unit, women tend to command authority.[28] With Dominican settlement in New York, a third pattern of domestic authority has emerged in many immigrant households. There has been a movement away from the hegemony of one sex over decision making and control of domestic resources to a more egalitarian division of labor and distribution of authority.

Since the single-mate pattern predominates among the middle-economic strata in the Dominican Republic, and since most Dominican immigrants come from this strata, changes in domestic authority in immigrant households generally involve a movement away from patriarchal relations and values toward greater egalitarianism. These changes have been most evident in three areas: beliefs about household authority, household decision making, and the allocation of household members to housework tasks.

For most Dominicans, the status of household head is equated with the concept of "defending the family" (quien defienda la familia). This "defense" is conceived of largely in material terms. Now that women contribute a larger share of the household income in New York, they begin to expect to be partners in "heading" the household. Thus, when I asked a sample of 55 immigrant women to state who headed their household now and who headed it before they emigrated, the majority— 70 percent—echoed the words of one woman:

> We are both the heads. If both husband and wife are earning salaries, then they should equally rule in the household. In the Dominican Republic it is always the husband who gives the orders in the household [manda en la casa]. But here when the two are working, the woman feels herself equal

to the man in ruling the home [*se siente capacitada de mandar igual al hombre*].

In his study of Dominican immigrants in a small New England city, Gordon also found a change toward greater equality between working husbands and wives.[29] In the words of one of his male informants, "[In the Dominican Republic women] had to accept whatever the man did. In the U.S., the woman says, *Yo poncho la tarjeta* (I punch the card; i.e., clock in the factory). She says, 'I contribute too.' She says what she wants."[30]

Interviews and participant observation revealed that women's claims to copartnership in heading the household have brought them increased authority in decision making about budgeting, the education of children, and control over their own social life outside the household. Let us begin with a consideration of changes in decision making over household budgeting.

Interviews with the 55 immigrant women showed that in the Dominican Republic, before emigration, men controlled the household budget in 69 percent of their households, even though women, either as wives or daughters, contributed income in many of these households on a regular or semiregular basis. Of the 38 households where men controlled the budget, 26 percent were characterized by the traditional, patriarchal form in which members gave all or part of their wages or profits to the senior male who, in turn, oversaw the payment of household expenses; 74 percent operated with the household allowance pattern, i.e., the wife was given a housekeeping allowance to cover basic expenditures such as food and clothing. When women in households with the household allowance pattern generated income, it was most commonly used for household rather than personal items of consumption. And these household purchases tended to be "luxuries," rather than staples. Both objectively and symbolically, the direction of these women's savings to nonessential prestige items reinforced the image of the man as the breadwinner and the woman, at best, as the bestower of modern status goods and, at worst, as the purchaser of *tonterias* (frivolities). Finally, 31 percent of these 55 premigration households were characterized by what I term a "pooled household income pattern." All but two of these 17 households were headed by a woman, with no senior male present, so that pooling of income occurred among a female head and her dependents.

In the United States, there has been a profound change in budgetary allocation for Dominican households. Far fewer households have a patriarchal form of budget control, and many more pool their income. Not only is pooling more common in the United States, but it is increasingly found in households with a senior male present. Thus, only 2 of the 55 migrant households in New York follow the traditional patriarchal pattern of budgetary control. And in most of the households where women received a household allowance, the wife was either not employed or was engaged in industrial homework. The dominant pattern, found in 69 percent of the 55 households in New York was to pool income; of these 38 domestic units, 58 percent were nuclear and 42 percent were female-headed. When nuclear families pool income, the husband, wife, and working children pool a specific amount of their wages or profits for shared household expenses such as food, rent, and electricity. Sometimes they also pool the rest of their salaries; in other cases, household members keep the rest of their income for personal expenses and savings.

Income pooling within nuclear households brings women advantages that were unknown in the Dominican Republic. Responsibility for meeting the household's basic subsistence costs is distributed among members regardless of gender, thus mitigating the invidious comparison between "essential" male contributions and the "supplementary" female inputs. Moreover, according to informants, men's greater participation in domestic tasks generally assigned to women in the Dominican Republic, such as developing strategies for stretching the food budget, has led them to appreciate more fully the experience and skills women bring to these activities.

In addition to improvements in control over budgeting, Dominican immigrant women have also increased their authority over decision making concerning education of children and the social life of women outside the home. As with budgeting, there has been a change from the dominance of men over these decisions to greater parity.

Most of my informants reported having an equal voice to men with regard to their children's education. Women observed that this change has been especially beneficial for daughters. According to informants, it is the wife, far more than the husband, who realizes that both daughters and sons will likely have to work after marriage. Consequently, women insist that both have equal access to household funds to underwrite this education.

In the Dominican Republic, men were given the liberty to decide when they would leave the home for socializing and where they would go. It was the man's discretion to decide whether he would consult his wife on this decision. In contrast, in the Dominican Republic, the majority of my female informants felt obligated to discuss their social plans with husbands and some even required the latter's permission before departing their homes. This situation has changed in the United States. Here, most informants reported increased parity between the sexes, with both spouses advising the other of individual plans for social activities, without permission being solicited or demanded.

The following quotes are representative of the ways in which women helped to bring about greater equity in decisionmaking:

> Now I advise him if I am going to visit a friend after work. But it is merely a sign of respect, or maybe more of a courtesy. I expect the same from him. . . . When we were first in New York, I just went along with the old style of asking his permission to go visit my friends and family. I did it at first, but one day my sister took me aside and said, "Look, Carmen, you're not his slave; you pay the rent just like him. Stop acting like a slave by asking his permission for everything." After that I spoke to Tonito and he was very understanding.

> When we came to New York, Ramón was over-protective of our teenage daughters. He wanted to keep them like little nuns. He had always been strict with them at home [in the Dominican Republic], but now it was too much. One day I sat down with him and explained that someday soon, like me, they would be going out of the house to work. If he didn't let them gain experience in the outside world, they would be too innocent and likely to fall prey to unscrupulous people. I just kept talking to Ramón that way. . . . Little by little he asked my advice when I told him that the girls wanted to go out with friends to a school dance or movie, and when I told him that the eldest [a daughter] wanted to go to college. I guess you would say he is no longer the patriarch of the house.

The problem of the double burden is also an area in which immigrant women report significant changes in men's willingness to accept the need for change. Women complain that it is unjust if they alone are forced to toil in the home after work and on weekends when they, like their husbands, are generating an income by working outside the home—something that is much more common in New York than in the Dominican Republic. The "compromise" reached in the households of most women I interviewed involves the husband's minor participation in housework. The degree of his participation usually depends on the domestic cycle and gender composition of the household. The man's contribution is greatest when his children are young and decreases once daughters are old enough to help their mothers. The most commonly shared domestic tasks are cooking and weekly shopping.

Because wage work has brought immigrant women many personal gains, including greater household authority and self-esteem, they are much more active agents than men in prolonging the household's stay in the United States. Despite original intentions to return home quickly, many women come to realize that if they return to the Dominican Republic, they may well end up cloistered in the home once again. This is the case because the sexual division of labor in the Dominican economy militates against productive employment for women of their limited training and class background. (According to the 1980 census, Dominican women in New York City have an average education of 8.2 years. Given such low levels of education, return migrant women could not compete for the limited professional and clerical jobs that would be "socially acceptable" to these women and their families.)

While the data indicate that the modification in status for migrant women from temporary to semipermanent or permanent migrant unfolds within the interdependent settings of the household or workplace, this finding requires further specification, for there are several types of Dominican immigrant households, and women toil in different work contexts. As we will see, a woman's job and the specific type of household in which she resides contribute to differences in the way women view settlement in the United States. Furthermore, despite the common reluctance of women to return to the Dominican Republic, many households do eventually relocate. This phenomenon also requires explanation.

As we have noted, two major household forms exist within the Dominican immigrant community—nuclear households and female-headed households. These two forms can be further subdivided, however. The nuclear form can be broken down into those units in which the wife engages in both wage work and housework (type one), and those in which she works solely in the home or in a family business (type two). The female-headed household can be divided into those units where the majority of income comes from wages (type three) and households that subsist mainly on public assistance payments (type four).

My research in return migrant neighborhoods in the Dominican Republic and in immigrant communities in the United States shows that type two nuclear households are those most likely to return to the Dominican Republic. There are several factors that contribute to this development. Of the 35 return migrant households interviewed, 20 owned their own business in the United States and, of these, 80 percent of the wives were working full- or part-time in the family business at least one year prior to the return. These households were characterized by the combination of sufficient savings to establish a business and middle-class lifestyle in the Dominican Republic, with the wife's positive orientation toward relocating. The renegotiation of the woman's influence in the household, which informants who worked until their departure cited as one of the most feared aspects of readjustment, was already confronted and managed by the first groups of returnees while in the United States. These female returnees had accepted the traditional bourgeois model in which the removal of the wife from the labor market symbolizes the household's material and social achievements. In most cases, the wife's decision to return to the Dominican Republic was motivated by the desire to hire a domestic employee to relieve her of

many housekeeping chores, to increase her social contacts, and to provide the children with a healthier (más sana) social and home environment.

In cases of dual wage-earning households in which couples relocated
to the Dominican Republic, all of the women expressed reservations
about the return. In most cases, the decision was the husband's, after he
convinced the wife that they had accumulated sufficient property and
savings to replicate or improve their standard of living. The second, and
often more powerful inducement from the wife's perspective was the
husband's claim that the children would receive a better upbringing in
the Dominican Republic. Reflected in women's acquiescence to these
arguments is the tension that many women experience between their
roles as wage earners and as mothers. The critical question is whether
they are meeting their children's needs most effectively by working to
acquire necessary commodities and savings for a good education, or
whether they are gambling with their children's futures by not remaining at home to oversee their socialization. When the wife's income is
needed to sustain the household in the United States, this role conflict
must be relegated to a secondary concern. However, if the savings realized from the couple's combined income do not make it necessary for
the wife to work, she is often prodded by the husband to weigh the
personal gains derived from her work and salary against her responsibilities as a mother. When the children actively oppose the return, this
fortifies the woman's belief that she is being a good mother by working.
In these instances, the weight of the wife-mother/child coalition diminishes the husband-father's ability to insist on the household's relocation.

In all but the type two household, one finds an orientation on the part
of women to postpone the family's return to the Dominican Republic.
Let us consider the strategies by which women delay the return and
relate the motives behind this reorientation to the particular situation
found in each household type. In the case of nuclear households where
both wife and husband are employed, I found that many women begin to
use their income to create a household type that resembles, in several
features, the domestic form that Louise Tilly and Joan Scott have termed
"the family consumer economy."[31] This domestic category refers to a
change for working families from a previous state of acquiring sufficient
income to subsist, to a condition in which members toil to meet new
and increasing family consumption needs, which are often defined and
managed by the wife.

In the Dominican household context, this is manifested in the insis-
tence of women that part of the pooled household income be used to
purchase expensive durable goods, such as new appliances and home
furnishings, rather than deposited in a joint savings account. Such be-

havior can be attributed, in part, to women's greater identification with the household and their desire to have it represent the struggle of all members to acquire a middle-class lifestyle. There is, however, another fundamental issue operating, and it is captured in the complaint by men that, "Five dollars wasted today means five more years of postponement of the return to the Dominican Republic." Most employed married women who were interviewed sought to delay the family's return to the Dominican Republic. A common strategy is to spend money to root the family securely and comfortably in the United States. In the terms of network analysis, these women chose to direct valuable household resources (income) to locally purchased goods and services (e.g., private parochial schools for children). Such a strategy at once ties the household to the United States and serves to deplete the funds available both to maintain social relations in the Dominican Republic via gifts and remittances and to finance investments back home.

Female heads of households were even more adamant in their interviews than were married women about the unlikelihood of their return to the Dominican Republic. One of the contrasts that helps to explain the difference between these two categories of female migrants is that female household heads do not have to contend with a husband's proclivities to return to the Dominican Republic. There is a second reason that reinforces the desires of women to remain in the United States. For female-headed households, the original motive for settling temporarily in the United States—to progress economically and socially—is rendered highly problematic by the fact that they are women. For example, the average Dominican woman earns approximately $2,500 less per year than a man.[32] Furthermore, women are employed in segments of the economy, such as the garment industry, that experience tremendous instability in employment and sometimes operate illegally. This means that women may not have access to unemployment insurance when they are laid off and must use their savings to sustain themselves and their families. When these funds are dissipated, women may be forced to obtain welfare. In many cases, then, the incomes of female heads of households are insufficient to permit a return to the Dominican Republic with adequate savings to sustain the quality of life associated with a successful migratory experience.

In this section, we have seen how Dominican immigrants' settlement is a social process influenced by changing gender relations within immigrant households.[33] We have also observed that some immigrants do return home and this return is also mediated by household composition, domestic social relations, and modes of income generation. In the next section we will examine, with the assistance of social network analysis, why return to the Dominican Republic by immigrant households is often a fragile and contingent phenomenon.

## RETURN MIGRATION TO THE DOMINICAN REPUBLIC[34]

In analyzing international migration from the perspective of social networks, we can observe the transfer of economic value from labor-exporting countries, such as the Dominican Republic, to labor-importing countries.[35] By economic value, I refer to the workers whose socialization, formal education, and job training were assumed by the source country.[36] In many cases, too, the dependents of the immigrant worker are being cared for by household members in the source country.[37] As a result, employers in the host society need not pay immigrant workers a true family wage.

If outmigration often represents a transfer of economic value from less-developed to more-developed countries, can it be said that return migration represents a redirection and rebalancing of this unequal exchange? This might be the case if return migrants brought home superior education and training acquired abroad, as well as savings that were invested in productive enterprises. Another way in which the previous unequal exchange might be recalibrated would be if return migrants maintained their social and economic ties with the host community in order to underwrite entrepreneurial activities in both locations.[38] If these conditions existed, return migration would benefit the development efforts of the source society. This positive view of return migration is shared by two Dominican researchers, who state that returnees have helped solidify the Dominican middle class.[39]

On the other hand, return migration would present the illusion of middle-class stability and have negligible, if any, positive impacts on local development, if return migrant households remained materially dependent on the host society for periodic employment and transfer payments. Ethnographic research conducted in Dominican return migrant neighborhoods in the city of Santiago reveals that such dependency is the norm. (The findings must be viewed with some reservation, pending more representative survey research aimed at testing the validity of making generalizations based upon them.)

Of the 35 return migrant households studied, the majority were unable to meet their consumption needs through exploiting *local* income-generating activities. Nearly two-thirds (62.9 percent) obtained all or the majority of their income from U.S. sources. These sources included savings, transfer payments from estranged family members, and salaries acquired from temporary U.S. employment. (The latter source reflects the existence of a pattern of circulating migration that characterized almost one-fourth (22.8 percent) of the returnees.) Only 22.8 percent of the households relied totally on local sources of income, with 14.3 percent existing on income from both the United States and the Dominican Republic.

The question arises as to whether this economic dependency is temporary. Is it an outcome of the fact that the majority of the return households are in an initial reconsolidation phase? In such a case, the return households would either be missing primary providers who still reside in the United States or could have recently resettled and be in the process of exploring investments or new employment. Closer scrutiny of the family situations of the households dependent on U.S. sources of income, however, does not confirm this idea of a temporary dependence to be soon overcome. Six cases uncovered in our ethnography of households that are missing primary providers and subsist largely on remittances from these absent members illustrate the point. Three of these return migrants were separated or divorced from the spouse who was providing alimony and/or child support in U.S. dollars. These are instances of economically dependent, divided households that are unlikely to become socially and materially reunited in the Dominican Republic. In the case of the remaining three divided households, one woman, aged 35, was planning, after a five-year separation, to rejoin her husband in the United States; another 27-year-old woman, resident in the Dominican Republic for less than one year, planned to return to her family in the United States after a prolonged, unsuccessful job search. The last woman with a resident spouse in the United States had already lived apart from him for four years and intended to wait another four years until her husband retires and returns home. There is little reason to believe that these divided return migrant households will evolve into households that are no longer dependent on U.S.-acquired income.

A further indication that a few years of social and economic reconsolidation do not generally lead to a solution to the pattern of U.S. economic dependence was found among those domestic units that have resided in the Dominican Republic for one to two years and were living solely on U.S.-earned savings. These households uniformly expressed an intention to return shortly to the United States. Moreover, the already noted high incidence of circulating migration among the returnees appears to be a relatively "permanent" solution to the lack of employment opportunities in the home country and not a temporary strategy of a readjustment period. The following two ethnographic cases further exemplify this pattern:

Matilde, 50-years old at the time of our interview, emigrated to New York in 1962. A year earlier, she had left an abusive husband and had moved back to her parents' home with her small child. Matilde did not want to strain the limited resources of her parents who had 11 other children, so she left her daughter behind and joined a sister in New York. Nine years later, Matilde was able to bring her daughter to New York, and shortly afterwards Matilde remarried. In 1977, Matilde, her husband, and daughter returned to the Dominican Republic. Matilde was tired of working so hard and wanted to return to her country. Since the return, Carlos, Matilde's husband, has worked in the United States for half of every year. Carlos works in a country club which is only in operation six months of the year. So, according to Matilde, "It is perfect. Carlos is home half of the year and then goes to New York where he lives and works in the country club." Matilde has not been employed since her return and claims that, "A woman should not work if the husband provides for her and their children."

Carmen is 40, and her husband is 35. They emigrated in 1965 and returned to the Dominican Republic the last time with their two children in 1979. The previous attempts at return—lasting one and a half and two years, respectively—had proved abortive. In both cases, the small business Simon invested in had failed to provide the income the family required. Since the household's return three years ago, Carmen has returned to work in New York for a period of five months each year. When in New York, Carmen lives with a sister. Simon, who has established himself as a money lender in Santiago, also works approximately one month a year in New York in a cousin's store.

Both of these cases are creative solutions to the difficulty of surviving on local sources of income. These solutions are possible because the returnees have continued to maintain strong social networks with individuals and workplaces in the United States to ensure access to information, housing, and work.

While the majority of the returnees were dependent on foreign income, a relatively small number returned to establish their own businesses. As mentioned previously, the introduction of new skills and ideas acquired abroad and the initiation of new investments that lead to increased employment and capital accumulation would represent positive contributions on the part of return migrants. Judging from the ethnographic data, however, there is scant evidence that the exposure to new ideas and opportunities, assuming this occurs, translates into usable skills or widens the range of entrepreneurial activities returnees entertain. First, there is a tremendous redundancy in the types of businesses Dominican returnees establish. The majority of my entrepreneurial informants had established themselves as money lenders and owners of groceries, restaurants, and gas stations. Several key informants attributed what they perceived as high rates of business failure and reemigration by returnees to such redundant activities. Second, many of the "new businesses" established by return migrants represented skills or interests which they had prior to emigration. For example, of the 11 male returnees who were currently merchants, 7 had been either shop owners or employed in sales prior to emigration. Third, the experiences of Dominican women in the United States, in particular in the garment industry, typically translated into unemployment on return to Santiago. While approximately one-half of the 35 female return migrants had worked in the United States, with one exception, all these women were unemployed in the Dominican Republic after their return.[40] The following case illustrates a perception among some return migrants that they are often taken advantage of in the Dominican Republic:

Rosario, who had been a floor lady in a U.S. garment shop, said that she had learned "how to run a factory." In fact when she returned to the Dominican Republic, she brought five sewing machines with her. She had intended to start her own shop in Santiago. Nonetheless, she soon abandoned the plan because, in her own words, "Electricity and rent are high and arbitrary. The company is hard up and charges exorbitant rates to those people it thinks can afford it. Consequently, the company takes special advantage of returnees. . . . I wasn't going to subsidize the electric company with my hard-earned income."

Finally, there is little evidence of educational attainment in the United States among returnees. Only 2 of 30 male return migrants in our ethnographic sample had completed some formal education in the United States, and the formal training of women was almost exclusively restricted to beautician classes.

The ethnography did reveal, however, some minimal employment generation among the return migrant enterprises. That is, a total of 35 workers were employed in the 15 enterprises established by the return migrants. In a country of high unemployment, even modest increases in jobs are important. However, it should be recalled that more than half of the entrepreneurs were reestablishing the same type of business they had owned prior to emigration. Thus it is highly likely that many of these jobs were not actually new ones but reestablished ones. Further, the expectation that returnees would be entrepreneurs who would be able to multiply their U.S. savings through diversified investments at home also proved illusory. Of the 12 return migrant households that had businesses in Santiago at the time of the research, only 2 had been able to expand and diversify by reinvesting profits obtained in the Dominican Republic.

Return migration involves not only a counterflow of people, capital, and goods. It also involves the repatriation of new ideas, values, and consumption patterns. As I have alluded to earlier and described elsewhere in detail,[41] Dominican emigration is fueled by the inability of Dominicans to attain a middle-class lifestyle. Paradoxically, this lifestyle is defined in large part in the Dominican Republic by advertisements and mass media financed by U.S. investors. While Dominicans reside in the United States, it is middle-class identity and aspirations which give meaning and motive to their struggles abroad. It should come as no surprise then that returnees invest much of their savings and income in commodities and memberships that symbolize a middle-class standard of living, including owning an American car, sending children to private schools, and belonging to prestigious social clubs. Unfortunately, for many return households, the acquisition of these markers of social mobility carries with it the risk of undermining the economic foundation for sustaining such a comfortable lifestyle. In other words, the pursuit of upper–middle-class consumption patterns in the Dominican Republic threatens their own economic stability. Many returnees attributed their previous unsuccessful attempts to reestablish themselves at home to an inability to control their consumption at levels that reflected the limited income they were accumulating.

In this section on return migration, I have employed the analytical concept of social networks to examine the counterflow of savings, skills, and values that Dominican returnees bring back home. I have found little evidence to support the optimistic claims that return migration helps to break the pattern of economic dependency of labor-exporting countries through the repatriation of entrepreneurial workers who invest in new businesses that create jobs and expand investment capital. Rather, my research has documented that most return households continue to rely predominantly on income earned abroad, either in the form of savings, remittances, or wages earned through periodic shuttle migration. Indeed, due to economic constraints in the Dominican Republic, many return households have been able to maintain a middle-class standard of living only by retaining such social and economic ties to the United States. It is for this reason, a return most fragile and conditional.

## NOTES

1. See Charles Wood, "Equilibrium and Historical-Structural Perspectives on Migration," *International Migration Review* 16:2 (1982): 298–319; Robert Bach and Lisa Schraml, "Migration, Crisis and Theoretical Conflict," *International Migration Review* 16:2 (1982): 320–41; Patricia Pessar, "The Role of International Migration and the Case of U.S.-Bound Migration from the Dominican Republic," *International Migration Review* 16:2 (1982): 342–64; and Patricia Pessar, "The Constraints Upon and Release of Female Labor Power," in D. Dwyer and J. Bruce, eds., *Women, Income, and Poverty* (Palo Alto, California: Stanford University Press, 1988).

2. See Pessar, "The Constraints"; and Sherri Grasmuck and Patricia Pessar, *Between Two Islands: Dominican International Migration* (Berkeley, California: University of California, forthcoming.)

3. Earlier discussions by this author of the mediating role households play in Dominican settlement have appeared elsewhere; see Patricia Pessar, "The Role of Gender in Dominican Settlement in the United States," in J. Nash and Helen Safa, eds., *Women and Change in Latin America* (South Hadley, Massachusetts: Bergin and Garvey Publishers, 1985); "The Dominicans: Women in the Household and in the Garment Industry," in Nancy Foner, ed., *New Immigrants in New York* (New York: Columbia University Press, 1987); and "The Constraints."

4. See Jorge Dandler and Carmen Medeiros, "Temporary Migration from

Cochabamba, Bolivia, to Argentina: Patterns and Impact in Sending Areas," in Patricia Pessar, ed., *When Borders Don't Divide: Labor Markets and Refugee Movements in the Americas* (New York: Center for Migration Studies, 1988); and Michael Kearney, "From the Invisible Hand to Visible Feet: Anthropological Studies of Migration and Development," *Annual Review of Anthropology* 15 (1986): 331–61.

5. See Kenneth Roberts, "Household Labour Mobility in a Modern Agrarian Economy: Mexico," in G. Standing, ed., *Labour Circulation and the Labour Process* (London: Croom Helm, 1985); and Dandler and Medeiros, "Temporary Migration."

6. See Kearney, "From the Invisible Hand."

7. See Ellen Perry Kraly, "U.S. Immigration Policy and the Immigrant Populations of New York," in Nancy Foner, ed., *New Immigrants in New York* (New York: Columbia University Press, 1987).

8. See Eric Larsen and Wolfgang Opitz, "Sex Ratio-Based Estimates of Emigration from the Dominican Republic," paper presented at the Conference on Dominican Migration to the United States, sponsored by the Fundación Friedrich Ebert and the Fondo Para el Avance de las Ciencias Sociales, Santo Domingo, Dominican Republic, 1988.

9. See Pessar, "The Role of International Migration"; "The Constraints"; Sherri Grasmuck, "The Impact of Emigration on National Development: Three Sending Communities in the Dominican Republic," *Development and Change* 15 (1984): 381–403; and David Bray, "Economic Development: The Middle Class and International Migration in the Dominican Republic," *International Migration Review* 18 (1984): 217–36.

10. See Bray, "Economic Development"; and Eugenia Georges, *New Immigrants in the Political Process: Dominicans in New York*, Occasional Paper No. 45 (New York: New York University Center for Latin American and Caribbean Studies, 1984).

11. Ibid.

12. See Kraly, "U.S. Immigration Policy."

13. See Glenn Hendricks, *The Dominican Diaspora: From the Dominican Republic to New York City—Villagers in Transition* (New York: Teachers College Press, Columbia University, 1974); Nancie González, "Peasants' Progress: Dominicans in New York," *Caribbean Studies* 10:3 (1970): 154–71; and Nancie González, "Multiple Migratory Experiences of Dominican Women," *Anthropological Quarterly* 49:1 (1976): 36–43.

14. See Antonio Ugalde, Frank Bean, and Gil Cardenas, "International Migration from the Dominican Republic: Findings from a National Survey," *International Migration Review* 13:2 (1979): 235–54.

15. See Douglas Gurak and Mary Kritz, "Women in New York City: Household Structure and Employment Patterns," *Migration Today* 10:3/4 (1982): 15–21.

16. See Bray, "Economic Development"; Pessar, "The Role of International Migration"; and Grasmuck and Pessar, *Between Two Islands*.

17. See Evelyn Mann and Joseph Salvo, "Characteristics of New Hispanic Immigrants to New York City: A Comparison of Puerto Rican and Non-Puerto Rican Hispanics," paper presented at the Annual Meeting of the Population Association of America, Minneapolis, Minnesota, 1984.

18. Elizabeth Bogen, *Immigration in New York* (New York: Praeger, 1987), p. 48.

19. Mann and Salvo, "Characteristics of New Hispanic Immigrants," p. 19.

20. Ibid., p. 18.

21. Robert Warren, personal communication, 1988.

22. See Oscar Handlin, *The Uprooted: The Epic History of the Great Migrations That Made the American People* (Boston: Little, Brown, 1951); and Milton Gordon, *Assimilation in American Life: The Role of Race, Religion, and National Origin* (New York: Oxford University Press, 1964).

23. See Alejandro Portes, "Toward a Structural Analysis of Illegal (Undocumented) Immigration," *International Migration Review* 12 (1978): 469–84; Saskia Sassen-Koob, "Immigrant and Minority Workers in the Organization of the Labor Process," *Journal of Ethnic Studies* 1 (1980): 1–34; and Grasmuck, "The Impact of Immigration."

24. Michael Piore, *Birds of Passage: Migrant Labor and Industrial Societies* (Cambridge: Cambridge University Press, 1979).

25. Ibid., p. 54.

26. Andrew Gordon, "Hispanic Drinking after Migration: The Case of Dominicans," *Medical Anthropology* 2:4 (1978), p. 80.

27. See Susan Brown, "Coping with Poverty in the Dominican Republic: Women and Their Mates," Ph.D. dissertation, University of Michigan, 1972; Fernando Ferrán, "La familia nuclear de la subcultura de la probreza dominicana," *Estudios Sociales* 27 (1984): 137–85; Instituto Dominicano de Estudios Aplicados, "La condición de la campesina dominicana y su participación en la economía," Secretaria de Estado de Agricultura, Santa Domingo, Dominican Republic; Nancie González, "Peasants' Progress" and "Multiple Migratory Experiences"; and Shosona Tancer, "La Quesqueyana: The Dominican Women, 1940–1970," in A. Pescatello, ed., *Female and Male in Latin America* (Pittsburgh: University of Pittsburgh Press, 1973).

28. See Brown, "Coping with Poverty"; and Ferrán, "La familia nuclear."

29. Andrew Gordon, "Hispanic Drinking," p. 80.

30. Ibid., p. 66.

31. See Louise Tilly and Joan Scott, *Women, Work and Family* (New York: Holt, Rinehart and Winston, 1978).

32. See Gurak and Kritz, "Women in New York City."

33. See Pessar, "The Constraints."

34. Several of the ideas in this section were developed by Dr. Sherri Grasmuck and myself in collaboration.

35. See Kearney, "From the Invisible Hand."

36. See Dawn Marshall, "Migration and Development in the Eastern Caribbean," in R. Pastor, ed., *Migration and Development in the Caribbean* (Boulder, Colorado: Westview Press, 1985); and Alejandro Portes, "Modes of Structural Incorporation and Present Theories of Labor Immigration," in Mary Kritz, Charles B. Keely, and Silvano M. Tomasi, eds., *Global Trends in Migration: Theory and Research on International Population Movements* (New York: Center for Migration Studies, 1981).

37. See Claude Meillassoux, *Maidens, Meal, and Money: Capitalism and the Domestic Community* (New York: Cambridge University Press, 1981); and Mi-

chael Buravoy, "The Functions and Reproduction of Migrant Labor: Comparative Material from South Africa and the United States," *American Journal of Sociology* 81 (1971): 1050–87.

38. See Elizabeth Thomas-Hope, "Return Migration and Its Implications for Caribbean Development," in R. Pastor, ed., *Migration and Development in the Caribbean* (Boulder, Colorado: Westview Press, 1985).

39. See Franc Baez-Evertsz and Frank D'Oleo Ramirez, "La emigracion de dominicanos a Estados Unidos: Determinantes socioeconómicos y consequencias," Documento Base Fundación Friedrich Ebert, Santo Domingo, Dominican Republic, 1985.

40. See Grasmuck and Pessar, *Between Two Islands*.

41. Ibid.

## SELECTED BIBLIOGRAPHY

Bach, Robert, and Lisa Schraml. "Migration, Crisis and Theoretical Conflict," *International Migration Review* 16:2 (1982): 320–41.

Baez-Evertsz, Franc, and Frank D'Oleo Ramirez. "La emigracion de dominicanos a Estados Unidos: Determinantes socioeconómicos y consequencias," Documento Base Fundación Friedrich Ebert, Santo Domingo, Dominican Republic, 1985.

Bogen, Elizabeth. *Immigration in New York*. New York: Praeger, 1987.

Bray, David. "Economic Development: The Middle Class and International Migration in the Dominican Republic," *International Migration Review* 18 (1984): 217–36.

Brown, Susan. "Coping with Poverty in the Dominican Republic: Women and Their Mates." Unpublished Ph.D. dissertation, University of Michigan, 1972.

Buravoy, Michael. "The Functions and Reproduction of Migrant Labor: Comparative Material from South Africa and the United States," *American Journal of Sociology* 81 (1971): 1050–87.

Dandler, Jorge, and Carmen Medeiros. "Temporary Migration from Cochabamba, Bolivia, to Argentina: Patterns and Impact in Sending Areas." In Patricia Pessar, ed. *When Borders Don't Divide: Labor Markets and Refugee Movements in the Americas*. New York: Center for Migration Studies, 1988.

Ferrán, Fernando. "La familia nuclear de la subcultura de la probreza dominicana," *Estudios Sociales* 27 (1984): 137–85.

Georges, Eugenia. *New Immigrants in the Political Process: Dominicans in New York*. Occasional Paper No. 45. New York: New York University Center for Latin American and Caribbean Studies, 1984.

González, Nancie. "Multiple Migratory Experiences of Dominican Women," *Anthropological Quarterly* 49:1 (1976): 36–43.

———. "Peasants' Progress: Dominicans in New York," *Caribbean Studies* 10:3 (1970): 154–71.

Gordon, Andrew. "Hispanic Drinking after Migration: The Case of Dominicans," *Medical Anthropology* 2:4 (1978): 61–84.

Gordon, Milton. *Assimilation in American Life: The Role of Race, Religion, and National Origin*. New York: Oxford University Press, 1964.

Grasmuck, Sherri. "The Impact of Emigration on National Development: Three Sending Communities in the Dominican Republic," *Development and Change* 15 (1984): 381–403.

Grasmuck, Sherri, and Patricia R. Pessar. *Between Two Islands: Dominican International Migration*. Berkeley, California: University of California, forthcoming.

Gurak, Douglas, and Luis Falcón-Rodríguez. "The Social and Economic Situation of Hispanics in the United States and New York City in the 1980's." In Office of Pastoral Research, ed. *Hispanics in New York*. Vol. II. New York: Office of Pastoral Research, 1987.

Gurak, Douglas, and Mary Kritz. "Women in New York City: Household Structure and Employment Patterns," *Migration Today* 10:3/4 (1982): 15–21.

Handlin, Oscar. *The Uprooted: The Epic History of the Great Migrations That Made the American People*. Boston: Little, Brown, 1951.

Hendricks, Glenn. *The Dominican Diaspora: From the Dominican Republic to New York City—Villagers in Transition*. New York: Teachers College Press, Columbia University, 1974.

Kearney, Michael. "From the Invisible Hand to Visible Feet: Anthropological Studies of Migration and Development," *Annual Review of Anthropology* 15 (1986): 331–61.

Kraly, Ellen Perry. "U.S. Immigration Policy and the Immigrant Populations of New York." In Nancy Foner, ed. *New Immigrants in New York*. New York: Columbia University Press, 1987.

Larsen, Eric, and Wolfgang Opitz. "Sex Ratio-Based Estimates of Emigration from the Dominican Republic." Paper presented at the Conference on Dominican Migration to the United States, sponsored by the Fundación Friedrich Ebert and the Fondo Para el Avance de las Ciencias Sociales, Santo Domingo, Dominican Republic, 1988.

Mann, Evelyn, and Joseph Salvo. "Characteristics of New Hispanic Immigrants to New York City: A Comparison of Puerto Rican and Non-Puerto Rican Hispanics." Paper presented at the Annual Meeting of the Population Association of America, Minneapolis, Minnesota, 1984.

Marshall, Dawn. "Migration and Development in the Eastern Caribbean." In R. Pastor, ed. *Migration and Development in the Caribbean*. Boulder, Colorado: Westview Press, 1985.

Meillassoux, Claude. *Maidens, Meal, and Money: Capitalism and the Domestic Community*. New York: Cambridge University Press, 1981.

Pessar, Patricia R. "The Constraints Upon and Release of Female Labor Power." In D. Dwyer and J. Bruce, eds. *Women, Income, and Poverty*. Palo Alto, California: Stanford University Press, 1988.

_____. "The Dominicans: Women in the Households and in the Garment Industry." In Nancy Foner, ed. *New Immigrants in New York*. New York: Columbia University Press, 1987.

_____. "The Role of Gender in Dominican Settlement in the United States." In J. Nash and Helen Safa, eds. *Women and Change in Latin America*. South Hadley, Massachusetts: Bergin and Garvey Publishers, 1985.

_____. "The Role of International Migration and the Case of U.S.-Bound Migration from the Dominican Republic," *International Migration Review* 16:2 (1982): 342–64.

Piore, Michael. *Birds of Passage: Migrant Labor and Industrial Societies.* Cambridge: Cambridge University Press, 1979.

Portes, Alejandro. "Modes of Structural Incorporation and Present Theories of Labor Immigration." In Mary Kritz, Charles B. Keely, and Silvano M. Tomasi, eds. *Global Trends in Migration: Theory and Research on International Population Movements.* New York: Center for Migration Studies, 1981.

_____. "Toward a Structural Analysis of Illegal (Undocumented) Immigration," *International Migration Review* 12 (1978): 469–84.

Roberts, Kenneth. "Household Labour Mobility in a Modern Agrarian Economy: Mexico." In G. Standing, ed. *Labour Circulation and the Labour Process.* London: Croom Helm, 1985.

Sassen-Koob, Saskia. "Immigrant and Minority Workers in the Organization of the Labor Process," *Journal of Ethnic Studies* 1 (1980): 1–34.

Tancer, Shosona. "La Quesqueyana: The Dominican Women, 1940–1970." In A. Pescatello, ed. *Female and Male in Latin America.* Pittsburgh: University of Pittsburgh Press, 1973.

Thomas-Hope, Elizabeth. "Return Migration and Its Implications for Caribbean Development." In R. Pastor, ed. *Migration and Development in the Caribbean.* Boulder, Colorado: Westview Press, 1985.

Tilly, Louise, and Joan Scott. *Women, Work and Family.* New York: Holt, Rinehart and Winston, 1978.

Ugalde, Antonio, Frank Bean, and Gil Cardenas. "International Migration from the Dominican Republic: Findings from a National Survey," *International Migration Review* 13:2 (1979): 235–54.

Wood, Charles. "Equilibrium and Historical-Structural Perspectives on Migration," *International Migration Review* 16:2 (1982): 298–319.

# 6

# Dependents or Independent Workers?: The Status of Caribbean Immigrant Women in the United States

MONICA H. GORDON

## INTRODUCTION

Contemporary international migration is distinguished by its global scope and the extensive regulatory and control mechanisms that govern crossing international boundaries. These regulations allow states to define the characteristics of the immigrants they let in, their national origin, the number allowed to enter any particular country, and their statuses and privileges in those countries. The United States, a major receiving country, has a long history of regulations that restricted entry on the basis of race and national origin, starting in the late 1800s. Northern European countries were the principal beneficiaries of the race/national origin restrictions that remained in effect until Congress modified the immigration laws to eliminate the race and national origin preferences in 1965 (Public Law 89-236). The new law, at least in theory, opened the possibility to all persons who qualify, regardless of race or national origin.

Since the 1960s, migration from Europe has declined steadily and significantly while, correspondingly, the migration from Asia and the Americas, including the Caribbean, has increased rapidly and significantly. Mexico and the Caribbean have supplied the majority of immigrants from the Americas or Western Hemisphere. Thus, by eliminating racial preference from immigration policy, the United States has changed the racial composition of the immigrant population.[1]

One other feature of the recent immigration is the significant number of women who have been identified as "principal aliens"—those persons from whom other aliens derive privilege or status under immigration regulation. The "principal alien" is an immigrant worker under the immigration law within a specific or delineated labor force capacity. It is this status that activates other provisions in the migration network of family members.

The recent migration from the Caribbean to the United States includes a significant proportion of women with the status of principal alien. Women were the overwhelming majority between 1967 and 1970 and remained a majority in 1980, according to the U.S. Census. These women entered occupational areas approved by the U.S. Department of Labor, based on their skills.

This chapter looks at Caribbean immigrant women in the United States with a primary focus on their economic roles. I will argue that these women participate significantly in the labor force, regardless of their marital status and the circumstances of their entry into the United States and that they are part of an identifiable "female sector" of the labor force whose experiences are shaped not only by gender but also by race. This chapter also discusses the role of gender in the context of the immigration experience, the characteristics of immigrant women, and the special implications of the migration experience for Caribbean women. The principal data source is the 1980 United States Decennial Census.

## GENDER MIGRATION: CONTEXT AND THEORIES

There has been no immigration policy specific to the sex of potential immigrants. However, there has been a general assumption that immigrants are men and that women and children are the dependents of those men. The development of feminist scholarship provides the incentive to examine such commonly held assumptions about women. Women's roles and the general social contexts of their experiences as immigrants can then be analyzed without the imposition of preconceived gender-assigned categories.

No feminist discourse, or even the women's movement, can be held accountable for women's migration or their newly defined roles in the labor market. Goulda Kosack very eloquently argues that emigration is an economic necessity and that women do not migrate to escape second-class status or patriarchal dominance. She also points out the long-ignored fact that there have always been two categories of immigrant women: those who joined spouses and those who migrated, independently, to find employment. Kosack's observations were made of immigrants in Europe, but it is even more obvious in the United States, where employment became central to selecting immigrants.[2]

This shift in perception of women as "immigrant women" instead of "immigrant wives" represents more than a change in terminology. It reflects a rejection of the assumption, stated or implied, that immigrants are men and dependents are women and children. This change in perception can be credited to the women's movement and the internationalization of women's discontent with their social, political, and legal statuses. It is feminist scholarship that most effectively articulated a framework for understanding women's experiences in migration. There is a three-stage development in the perception and categorization of women: (1) as immigrants, (2) as women, and (3) as workers.[3] Each category, if taken separately, reveals its own characteristics. Combined, they represent a particular labor force component—immigrant women workers. Because Caribbean and other immigrants of color in the United States become part of the "racial minorities" category, which has definitions and disadvantages that preceded their entry into the country, it is expected that gender and race will have a significant impact on Caribbean immigrant women workers.

Most contemporary immigrants, regardless of their status at the time of entry, become economically active. The focus of theorists on economic roles and labor relations is not unwarranted. There has been much concern about the impact of immigrant labor on the market value of the native workers. Immigrants are supposed to fill the gaps in the labor force, especially in areas where it is difficult to attract native workers. (Under U.S. immigration policy, the Sixth Preference requires that visas be issued in occupations in which workers are in short supply.) The presence of immigrant labor, therefore, should be positive, but the perception is that immigrants exercise downward pressure on working class wages while effectively reducing the bargaining power of the native workers, according to Edna Bonacich, S. Castles and G. Kosack, A. Portes, and Saskia Sassen-Koob.[4] None of these authors examined gender differentiation, although John Salt noted that the high labor force participation rate of immigrant women in Europe was comparable to that of native women.[5] This pattern has also been demonstrated by Caribbean immigrant women relative to native-born women in the United States.

Another omission of labor theorists that has been challenged is what Portes refers to as the unconditional structuring of immigrants at the bottom of the labor pool.[6] He argues that immigrants are employed in the primary or secondary labor markets depending on qualifications. Primary labor markets, he argues, are those sectors in government and private industry where workers are highly trained and regulated by bureaucratic norms and that provide extensive career opportunities and mobility. Secondary markets, on the other hand, are those sectors where jobs require little or no training, where wages tend to be low, where there is little opportunity for mobility, and where there is a rapid turnover.

Low status and low wages are not automatically assigned to contemporary immigrants. Those in the primary markets have the same opportunities for starting salaries and promotions as natives. To support his argument, Portes refers to a study of foreign medical graduates in U.S. hospitals where no evidence was found that foreign interns and residents were paid less or worked longer hours than U.S. medical graduates.[7] He noted, however, that these doctors were disproportionally concentrated in the less-prestigious hospitals.[8]

Primary sector immigrant workers, according to Portes, are hired on the basis of ability rather than ethnicity; their mobility chances are comparable to those of the native workers; and they give elasticity to the domestic supply of labor. In the secondary sector, the most desirable characteristic of the workers is cheapness, not formal skills, and there is little job stability and opportunity for mobility.[9]

Gender differences were not discussed by Portes in this context, but in another study, he locates women in the secondary labor markets.[10] M. Morokvasic elaborates on this placement, arguing that cheap female labor has been the cornerstone of the survival of industrial economies.[11] The theory here is that as industrial economies mature, the cost of labor tends to increase. The search for less expensive workers is usually directed at new categories of workers to whom employers can, according to human capital theorists, justifiably pay lower wages. Women and minorities are the principal victims of this perspective, which explains labor market practices and wage differentials in terms of individual attributes and ignores gender and racial discrimination as human capital attributes.

For this reason, the present system of female migrant labor is more attractive to the capitalist sectors than male workers. Such women enter traditionally female sectors with low-wage rates based on the concept of women's secondary function as earners. Also, Morokvasic argues, immigrant women bear, disproportionately, the burden of racism and insecure political and legal statuses. He concludes that "[it] is the articulation between the process of gender discrimination of migrant workers and class exploitation as working class that makes their position particularly vulnerable."[12]

Caribbean women in the United States have not been placed unconditionally in low-wage, low-status employment, although they have experienced gender stratification. One study shows that consciousness of racism among these immigrants is likely to be more acute in the primary sector.[13]

The classification of female immigrant workers as secondary-sector employees corresponds with the position of women workers generally. The characteristics of such workers are low wages, short or nonexistent promotion ladders, less work stability, poor working conditions, arbitrary work rules, and several points of entry. In contrast, primary-sector employment is dominated by white males; hierarchical in structure, with extensive opportunities for promotion, good working conditions, and job security.[14]

Some theorists developed, more explicitly, a world economy perspective on the international migration of labor in which they classified migratory labor movements in the same context as capital and other commodities. This approach locates labor as primarily the movement from the periphery (or developing regions of the world) to areas of capital accumulation (or core countries).[15] It also accommodates the conditions for the selection of the immigrants, the regulations that govern boundary crossings, and other variables operative in the international movement of immigrants. And it is also sociohistorical and comparative, as in the framework developed by Watson for the Caribbean.[16]

Gender analysis has only recently begun to receive attention from scholars in the field of migration studies. Consequently, gender is not an integrated part of the discourse on migration issues. And while the presence of women in the migration milieu has not been ignored, the implications of the shift from males as preferred immigrants to a more differentiated gender selection, based on occupational categories, has not been given comprehensive treatment in migration theory. A few studies have initiated analyses of gender issues.[17] Castro's comment on the nature of many studies of the female immigrant experience is worth noting, "Their analysis is often limited to descriptions of female immigrant characteristics and experiences focusing on women's living and working conditions, cultural and psychological profiles, and individual effects of participation in migration."[18]

While these aspects are necessary for understanding the complexities of immigrant women's lives, they tend to overgeneralize situations that are often particular in nature. Castro's framework for the analysis of women and migration is a link between the "logic of gender" and the "logic of capitalism" in a Marxist context.[19] Sassen-Koob used such a perspective and applied the concept "feminization of migration" to explain the preference for females in contemporary migration.[20] The feminization concept evolved to explain the circumstances of women who were experiencing unaccustomed conditions, such as poverty. Thus the "feminization of poverty" concept was developed around the circumstances of white middle-class women who had become poor as a consequence of divorce or some other situation that separated them from previous means of economic support. Immigrant women generally have different economic histories and different patterns of economic activities in the host countries. If they are poor, their poverty has different origins and articulation. As Linda Burnham explains:

> This "theory" [feminization of poverty] is not simply an identification of demographic shifts in the poverty population; it also projects a reconceptualization of the social factors that generate and regenerate poverty and the sectors of the population who are most vulnerable to impoverishment. This reconceptualization incorrectly shifts the focal point of analysis from class and race to gender, betraying a superficial understanding of the relationship between women's oppression, class exploitation and racism.[21]

Immigrant women tend to see migration as a means to improve their economic and social status. The wage differential between the sending and receiving countries ensures that this expectation is realized, at least from the immigrants' perspective. The "feminization of migration," to the extent that it has occurred, has positive economic outcomes even if social and cultural outcomes of the migration are less positive. (We may note that although women featured significantly as "principal aliens" in the migration to the United States, as well as being in the majority, M. R. Houston and coresearchers found that this was not true internationally. Female immigrant labor seems to be in demand only in advanced service-oriented economies.)[22]

The integration of migration theories around themes of differentials or selectivity, causal factors, patterns of migration flow, consequences of migration, and political aspects has been urged.[23] The world economy theoretical perspective can accommodate all these themes, as well as incorporating gender and its social implications.

## SOME CHARACTERISTICS OF CARIBBEAN IMMIGRANT WOMEN

The data used in this paper have been extracted from the 1980 U.S. decennial census microdata prepared for public use. This source provides the most comprehensive social demographic survey of immigrants as of 1980. Statistical data from the annual reports of the Immigration and Naturalization Service have been used in conjunction with the census data, where expedient, to identify shifts and changes in occupational and other characteristics of the immigrants.

Four countries from the English-speaking Caribbean were selected for analysis—Barbados, Guyana, Jamaica, and Trinidad and Tobago—from which the vast majority of Caribbean immigrants come. An overview of the data reveals that the English-speaking Caribbean immigrants share characteristics common to all immigrants, regardless of country of origin.

One factor has remained constant since the acceleration of Caribbean migration to the United States in the 1960s: women have been in the majority. In 1980, the male to female ratio of immigrants was 85.8 for the entire Caribbean region. The ratio for the countries selected for analysis is shown in Table 6.1. No specific meaning can be given to the sex ratio imbalance in 1980. Between 1967 and 1969, the ratio of women to men was approximately 2 : 1, with the vast majority women in their prime working years 20–49.[24]

The majority of the women were married, although numerically there were more married men than married women. More women than men fell into the categories of divorced, separated, or widowed, as Tables 6.2 and 6.3 show. Marital status has implications for a woman's socioeconomic status. Although single status does not necessarily equate with poverty, the majority of poor people in the United States are single women with children. It is impossible to determine the source of poverty among Caribbean immigrant women. The majority of those aged 15–24 years were registered in educational institutions, according to the 1980 Census. They were, therefore, not primarily workers. Newer arrivals also tended to be at the lower end of the income scale. A more detailed analysis is needed to determine the relationship between poverty and marital status in this population.

Households headed by single women—either never married, divorced, widowed, or separated—made up approximately 22 percent of all households with dependent children (see Table 6.4). There is a built-in elasticity in Caribbean immigrant households and in the family structure that can be attributed partly to continuing migration but also to social patterns that predate migration. Statistically, the Caribbean immigrant household fell between those of African-Americans and white Americans. About 68 percent of all Caribbean immigrant households were married couples with families, compared with 85.7 percent for white Americans and 55.5 percent for African-Americans. Twenty-two percent of the immigrant women were heads of households, compared to

**Table 6.1**
**Sex Ratio of Immigrants from Selected Caribbean Countries, 1980**

| Country | Total | Male | Female | Ratio (M/F) |
|---------|-------|------|--------|-------------|
| Barbados | 26,847 | 12,230 | 14,617 | 83.7 |
| Guyana | 48,608 | 22,562 | 26,046 | 86.6 |
| Jamaica | 196,811 | 87,264 | 109,547 | 79.7 |
| Trinidad & Tobago | 65,907 | 29,752 | 36,155 | 82.3 |

Source: U.S. Department of Commerce, Bureau of the Census, *Statistical Abstract of the United States, 1980* (Washington, D.C.: Government Printing Office, 1980).

**Table 6.2**
**Marital Status of Caribbean Immigrants 15 Years
and Over, 1980**

| Marital Status | Male | Female |
|---|---|---|
| | Barbados | |
| Single | 3,109 | 4,650 |
| Married | 6,639 | 5,668 |
| Divorced, Widowed, or Separated | 1,548 | 3,399 |
| | Guyana | |
| Single | 6,119 | 6,898 |
| Married | 11,213 | 10,897 |
| Divorced, Widowed, or Separated | 1,511 | 4,497 |
| | Jamaica | |
| Single | 25,323 | 34,737 |
| Married | 43,438 | 42,449 |
| Divorced, Widowed, or Separated | 7,934 | 21,883 |
| | Trinidad & Tobago | |
| Single | 9,698 | 11,428 |
| Married | 14,340 | 14,457 |
| Divorced, Widowed, or Separated | 2,701 | 7,036 |

Source: U.S. Department of Commerce, Bureau of the Census,
Statistical Abstract of the United States, 1980 (Washington, D.C.: Government Printing Office, 1980).

11.6 percent and 40.3 percent, respectively, for native white women and
African-American women.[25]

The single-parent household is not a migration phenomenon, but a
highly integrated part of the premigration experience. However, the
social organization of the extended family system in the sending country, which provides a variety of services to family members (including
nurturing and protecting children of working mothers), is absent in the

**Table 6.3**
**Percentage Distribution of the Marital Status of Caribbean Immigrants 15 Years and Over, 1980**

| Country | Married | | Divorced or Separated | |
|---|---|---|---|---|
| | Male | Female | Male | Female |
| Barbados | 59.0 | 42.0 | 13.3 | 25.0 |
| Guyana | 60.0 | 50.0 | 6.8 | 20.0 |
| Jamaica | 56.0 | 43.0 | 10.0 | 22.0 |
| Trinidad & Tobago | 54.0 | 44.0 | 10.0 | 21.0 |
| Average | 57.3 | 44.8 | 10.0 | 22.0 |

Source: Calculated from U.S. Department of Commerce, Bureau of the Census, *Statistical Abstract of the United States, 1980* (Washington, D.C.: Government Printing Office, 1980).

host country. That is not to say that, in the absence of empirical data, such services may not have evolved in the years since migration began. Observations indicate an existence of family networks providing a variety of services in accordance with the circumstances and needs in the host country. These observations require systematic research. Whether or not such assistance exists, the impact on family organization and relations when women migrate cannot be determined from census data. However, the seemingly high rate of disrupted marriages may be viewed as one possible result.

In 1980, households composed of married couples had a higher me-

**Table 6.4**
**Caribbean Immigrant Single Women Heads of Households with Children, 1980**

| Country | Never Married | Divorced or Separated | Percentage |
|---|---|---|---|
| Barbados | 1,281 | 2,820 | 26.0 |
| Guyana | 1,557 | 3,825 | 17.0 |
| Jamaica | 10,916 | 18,413 | 22.0 |
| Trinidad & Tobago | 3,153 | 5,959 | 23.0 |

Source: Calculated from U.S. Department of Commerce, Bureau of the Census, *Statistical Abstract of the United States, 1980* (Washington, D.C.: Government Printing Office, 1980).

dian income that the single-women households. While the median household/family income of Caribbean immigrants was below the national average, households in which Caribbean women were married to American-born spouses had a higher median income than those in which they were married to other immigrants (see Table 6.5). The median family income of Caribbean immigrants in 1980 was $14,672, compared with a national median of $21,042. For white American families, it was $21,768 and for black families, $15,232. In families headed by females, the median income of black women was $9,976; for white women, $13,202. In New York City, where the majority of English-speaking Caribbean immigrants (West Indians) are concentrated, the median family income for 1980 was estimated at $15,645 for the entire population and $10,971 for female-headed families. In comparison, the median family income for native New Yorkers was $17,361 and $7,625 for families with female heads.[26]

Caribbean immigrant families had a poverty level of 14.7 percent in 1980, compared with the national average of 13 percent. The rates for selected countries with a poverty line of $8,414 were Barbados, 10.9 percent, Guyana, 14.4 percent, Trinidad and Tobago, 14.3 percent, and Jamaica, 12.4 percent.

Comparable figures for white Americans and black Americans were 8 percent and 28.9 percent, respectively. The pattern of poverty in female-headed households was significantly higher than that in male-headed households with no spouse present. Figures for 1980 were black American females, 49.4 percent, white American females, 25.7 percent, black males, 17.7 percent, and white males, 9.4 percent. Unfortunately, the data for Caribbean immigrants are not so specific. However, to the ex-

**Table 6.5**
**Median Income of Caribbean Immigrants by Household and Family, 1980**

| Countries | Caribbean-born Head | | American-born Head with Caribbean Spouse | |
|---|---|---|---|---|
| | Household | Family | Household | Family |
| Barbados | $ 14,290 | 17,020 | 21,545 | 20,969 |
| Guyana | 15,913 | 17,415 | 22,088 | 22,049 |
| Jamaica | 15,290 | 17,323 | 22,156 | 21,944 |
| Trinidad & Tobago | 14,733 | 16,915 | 21,248 | 21,193 |

Source: U.S. Department of Commerce, Bureau of the Census, *Statistical Abstract of the United States, 1980* (Washington, D.C.: Government Printing Office, 1980).

tent that aggregate data can indicate socioeconomic status, Caribbean immigrants are closer to black Americans in median family income and to white Americans in poverty status.

It has been demonstrated that the economic position of the family is related to its composition, regardless of race. Families headed by women with no husband present have much lower incomes than men in similar situations or married couples.[27] Clearly, gender is operative in the status of women but, as Margaret Andersen argues, "The likelihood of a family being poor is complicated not only by the sex of the head of the household, but by the person's marital and racial status. Caribbean women's situation is further complicated by their 'immigrant status'."[28] These immigrant women, as individual earners, were several times more likely to be in the lower-income bracket (under $5,000), while immigrant men were most likely to be in the $5,000 and over category. It is quite probable that the high rate of labor participation by Caribbean immigrant women depressed the median wage for that entire population. Neither education nor occupation can wholly account for income variance between these immigrant men and women. Sex, on the other hand, seems to account for much of the difference.

Of Caribbean immigrants 25 years and older, 55.3 percent completed a minimum of 4 years of high school and 13.1 percent had 4 or more years of college in 1980. For the selected countries, 67 percent completed high school, and 13 percent completed 4 or more years of college. Compared with native-born Americans of the same age cohort, the percentages for both high school and college education were about four and five points lower, respectively, than for whites; measured against blacks, the figures were higher by about 15 and 5 points, again respectively. Overall, Caribbean immigrants had levels of education comparable to those of the native population.

The pattern of female and male education, as shown in Table 6.6, varied by country. When the region is taken as a whole, women seem to lag behind men. There were, however, variations from country to country. Women from Jamaica and Trinidad and Tobago have larger numbers completing all levels of education, while Guyana had an advantage only at the high school level. In general, the greater the share of women in the immigrant population, the larger the number of immigrants with high school and college diplomas.

Labor force participation is high among immigrants. The average rate for persons 16 years and over was 77.6 percent for Caribbean immigrants, 78.3 percent for white Americans, and 70.8 for black Americans (see Table 6.7). The labor participation rate of Caribbean immigrant women was decidedly lower than that of Caribbean immigrant men. However, it was much higher than that of native American women, which was 54.9 percent for blacks and 50.6 percent for whites. This

**Table 6.6**
**Educational Achievement of Caribbean Immigrants 25 Years and Over by Sex, 1980**

| Country | 4 Years High School | | 1-3 Years College | | 4+ Years College | | High School and Above |
|---|---|---|---|---|---|---|---|
| | Males | Females | Males | Females | Males | Females | |
| Barbados | 4,414 | 5,158 | 1,471 | 1,789 | 1,002 | 814 | 14,675 |
| Guyana | 5,534 | 8,070 | 3,657 | 3,608 | 3,178 | 1,672 | 25,719 |
| Jamaica | 23,633 | 32,585 | 11,629 | 15,911 | 7,731 | 8,180 | 131,538 |
| Trinidad & Tobago | 8,983 | 12,079 | 4,600 | 5,829 | 2,374 | 2,666 | 37,531 |

*Source:* U.S. Department of Commerce, Bureau of the Census, *Statistical Abstract of the United States, 1980* (Washington, D.C.: Government Printing Office, 1980).

**Table 6.7**
**Labor Force Participation of Caribbean Immigrants 16 Years and Over by Sex, 1980**

| Country | Males | % | Females | % | Total |
|---------|-------|------|---------|------|-------|
| Barbados | 8,529 | 74.5 | 8,720 | 64.3 | 17,249 |
| Guyana | 14,685 | 78.4 | 13,730 | 62.9 | 28,415 |
| Jamaica | 75,720 | 75.9 | 96,882 | 68.6 | 125,620 |
| Trinidad & Tobago | 21,543 | 72.1 | 22,597 | 65.1 | 44,140 |

Source: U.S. Department of Commerce, Bureau of the Census, *Statistical Abstract of the United States, 1980* (Washington, D.C.: Government Printing Office, 1980).

pattern reinforces Kosack's and Morokvasic's observation concerning cheap immigrant female labor in Europe.[29]

Although women are dispersed in a variety of occupations, the data point to heavy concentration in a few employment areas. This concentration is consistent with declared occupation at the time of entry. Whatever shifts in employment may have occurred, the wider employment areas into which these immigrants were initially recruited remained relatively stable in 1980. Table 6.8 provides a comparison of occupations listed at the time of entry for the period 1967–77 with those reported in the 1980 Census for selected countries. Data in this table are not separated by sex because the original Immigration and Naturalization Service data were not separated by sex. Employment categories are the most reliable—although not absolute—indicators of sex.

Table 6.9 shows the occupational distribution of Caribbean immigrants by sex and country of origin. Together, Tables 6.8 and 6.9 indicate that there was substantial gain in the administrative, executive, and managerial occupations compared to a rather modest increase in the professional occupations. Private household employment decreased sharply, by approximately 80 percent, while the "other service" category increased equally sharply, by about 75 percent. There was an almost three-fold increase in the clerical area, compared to a 30 percent increase in the crafts and operatives category. (Although "crafts," representing skilled workers, and "operatives" [excluding transportation], representing semiskilled workers, appear as separate categories in the 1980 Census, they have been combined into a joint category for this chapter. The occupational areas represented in this chapter are those in which the immigrants are significantly concentrated, rather than encompassing all areas of employment.)

**Table 6.8**
**Occupational Distribution of Caribbean Immigrants
at Time of Entry, 1967–77 and 1980**

| Occupation | 1967-1977 | 1980 |
|---|---|---|
| Administrative, Executive, and Managerial | 4,476 | 11,275 |
| Professional | 19,307 | 20,324 |
| Clerical | 20,155 | 57,545 |
| Crafts and Operatives | 46,366 | 60,418 |
| Private Household Service | 36,646 | 7,357 |
| Other Service | 10,971 | 42,477 |

Source: U.S. Department of Justice, Immigration and Naturalization Service, *Annual Reports, 1965–1982* (Washington, D.C.: Government Printing Office, 1965–82); and
U.S. Department of Commerce, Bureau of the Census,
*Statistical Abstract of the United States, 1980* (Washington, D.C.: Government Printing Office, 1980).

Private household employment remains the almost exclusive province
of women with clerical and "other service" only a little less so. Numerically, women were better represented in the professions than men. This
is partly due to the large number of Caribbean immigrant women in the
nursing profession. Men, however, had a more than a 2 : 1 ratio repre-
sentation in the administrative, executive, and managerial areas. Only
in the crafts/operatives areas were men concentrated in impressive
numbers. Women in that category were more likely to be operatives
rather than crafts workers.

The data, although lacking in refinement, strongly indicate that Caribbean immigrant women's employment is structurally different from that
of Caribbean immigrant men. This is consistent with the pattern of
female employment, in general, in the United States. Data for New York
City non-Hispanic Caribbean immigrants show that women were heavily concentrated in a few occupations. For employed workers, 16 years
and over, 75 percent of the females were classified under 15 job titles.
Approximately 20 percent were nurses' aides; 12 percent, maids, ser-
vant/cleaners, or housekeepers; 10 percent, nurses; and 7 percent, sec-
retaries. Only 25 percent of the males fell under these 15 job titles, and
there was no clustering similar to that of the females.

The pattern of clustering of immigrant women in specific industries
is emphasized by Walter Stafford's study of labor markets in New York

**Table 6.9**
**Occupational Distribution of Caribbean Immigrants 16 Years and Over by Sex and Country of Origin, 1980**

| Occupation | Sex | Barbados | Guyana | Jamaica | Trinidad & Tobago |
|---|---|---|---|---|---|
| Administrative, Executive, and Managerial | M | 570 | 1,352 | 4,070 | 1,535 |
| | F | 248 | 534 | 2,277 | 689 |
| Professionl | M | 516 | 1,542 | 3,652 | 1,607 |
| | F | 1,026 | 1,636 | 8,107 | 2,238 |
| Clerical | M | 1,144 | 2,435 | 6,213 | 2,704 |
| | F | 2,132 | 4,087 | 16,507 | 7,028 |
| Crafts and Operatives | M | 3,230 | 4,676 | 23,582 | 7,722 |
| | F | 606 | 1,568 | 5,009 | 1,332 |
| Private Household Service | M | 15 | 18 | 107 | 44 |
| | F | 922 | 651 | 4,535 | 1,065 |
| Other Service | M | 1,222 | 1,075 | 8,041 | 1,065 |
| | F | 2,479 | 2,795 | 10,765 | 4,931 |

Source: U.S. Department of Commerce, Bureau of the Census, *Statistical Abstract of the United States, 1980* (Washington, D.C.: Government Printing Office, 1980).

City. After extensive analysis, he concludes that blacks, Hispanics, and women were underrepresented in New York City's core industries and jobs. These groups, he argues, were concentrated in lower-level jobs in peripheral industries, many of which were declining. With the exception of banks, insurance companies, telephone communications, and department stores, blacks and Hispanics remained concentrated in their traditional bases of employment. Blacks were confined largely to the health and social services industries and Hispanics in low-paying, nondurable goods and services. Black females, he further argued, were concentrated more than any other group in the health industry, with even those in the professional category found there. White females, on the other hand, made gains in all the major industries, both as managers and professionals and in nonsupervisory positions.[30]

Stafford's findings and arguments are supported by J. Malveaux's analysis of national data, which confirmed employment patterns for women. She argues that black women's occupational patterns were more similar to those of white women than to those of any other race-sex group. However, she maintains

> black women differ from white women when the proportional occupational representations are compared. There are proportionally fewer black female managers than managers from any other race-sex group.

> Proportionally half as many black women as white women workers are employed as retail sales workers. . . . The largest portion of black women are employed as clerical workers, as the largest portion of white women are. But black women lag behind white women in this area. More black women than white women work in non-white collar jobs—the second highest concentration of women is in service occupations, and a significant proportion of black women work as operatives in private household work. Black women's occupational similarity to white women's is less indicative of occupational parity than it is illustrative of the impact of sex stratification on occupational attainment.[31]

Malveaux also notes that there were clear parallels between black male and black female occupational status. Black men were less represented in white collar and skilled job categories than white males. It seems, then, that race and sex operate in ways that affect immigrant women differently than immigrant men. Neither Stafford nor Malveaux differentiates between native and immigrant blacks. However, the data on Caribbean immigrants correspond with their analyses and findings, especially those of Stafford, whose data represent the area of New York City with the highest black immigrant concentration.

## IMMIGRATION AND THE STATUS OF WOMEN

Caribbean people migrated to the United States in response to the demand for certain categories of workers. In 1980, approximately 12 percent of the Caribbean immigrants in the United States arrived prior to the passage of the 1965 Immigration Act and the amendments to this act; female workers were well represented among these earlier immigrants, and their employment was mostly in non-white collar occupations. Those who came after the 1965 Act differed from earlier arrivals by virtue of their selection and integration into the labor force. While earlier immigration consisted largely of undifferentiated lower-status workers (regardless of skills or level of education), contemporary immigration is made up of workers with skills and the relatives of people already in the United States. Thus, contemporary migration must be seen not only in the context of the transfer of labor but also as a social class phenomenon, as Portes suggests.[32] To fully understand this phenomenon, we must consider the meaning and implications of gender in this latter migration.

During the 1960s and into the 1970s, the United States experienced labor shortages, especially in the health industry and in private households, both traditional areas of employment for women. (These shortages existed despite the entrance of women into the paid labor force in increasing numbers.) Caribbean women and those from other Third World countries were recruited to fill the gaps when the women who usually work in these occupations moved to other employment. The majority of Caribbean women who had "principal alien" status and could, under immigration provisions, extend immigration privileges to others, were absorbed by these traditional employment areas.

It is the "principal alien" classification that underscores the importance of gender in migration. Kosack, with specific reference to Europe, argues that women develop social and political consciousness as a consequence of their economic roles as immigrant workers. Even those who migrated as dependent wives and children became politicized through participation in the "immigrant labor market."[33] Caribbean women with principal alien status migrated as independent workers in identifiable employment categories. This position gave women a subtle kind of power, a kind of gender reversal, whereby they became status givers.

Migration confers not only economic opportunities but also opens new options for social growth and self-definition, which may have unanticipated consequences for familial and other relationships existing prior to their migration. As we pointed out earlier, the category "immigrant wives" assumed that all women were dependents of men. For several years, "housewives, children, and others with no occupation" defined the category under which husbands, sponsored by wives who were principal aliens, were admitted to the United States. Did these husbands acquire the subordinate, dependent status of housewives because of the organization of the sponsorship?

From the time of their entry into the U.S. labor force, Caribbean women earned more than they did prior to migration, purely on the basis of wage differential between the sending and the receiving countries, even when they were in low-status employment. They also possessed the options of changing jobs and upgrading their education and skills in the receiving country. Changing jobs, as evidenced in the category of private household workers, often involves occupational upgrading, better working conditions, and benefits such as educational opportunities, health coverage, paid vacations and holidays, and greater job security through unionization. Women also often change jobs for family reasons.

Nurses represent the largest professional category among Caribbean immigrant women. Upgrading skills in this area is necessary to maintain professional status as well as for promotion. In order to move into administrative positions, nurses are often required to have academic degrees. Some Caribbean women have followed this path to job mobility. This may partially account for the increase in the number of these women in the administrative, executive, and managerial occupations category. Stafford noted that black women were overly represented in the health field, although they were not as well represented at the administrative level as white women.[34] Personal conversations with nurses over several years have revealed a strong resentment against the system of placing inexperienced nurses with degrees in supervisory positions over experienced nurses without academic degrees. In all, the pattern suggests a racial stratification system of white administrators and black nurses. Yet the options, benefits, and potential professional advancement and earnings open to Caribbean nurses define them as "better off" than they were before they migrated.

The clerical area incorporates an amalgam of immigrants with varying levels of skills. The 1980 Census showed clustering around younger workers in this category, which suggests that the children of immigrants with no stated occupations at the time of arrival have moved primarily into this area when they entered the labor force. This area may also have absorbed those skilled workers who classify themselves as unskilled workers for the purpose of obtaining visas. It is much more difficult to comprehend the advantages or disadvantages of workers in the category, especially since the skills and experience levels vary considerably. Again, the reference point for immigrants is how well they perceive themselves as doing in relation to their home country situation. Younger immigrants with no prior work experience before migrating have only their native American peers, white and black, with whom to compare themselves.

If immigration improves the economic status of Caribbean immigrant women vis-à-vis their status prior to migration, are they doing as well or better than other categories of workers in the United States? How do sex, race, and immigrant status affect these women workers? The level of analysis of the data does not allow for definitive answers, but there are some indicators. Ransford W. Palmer, using 1980 Census data, concludes from his analysis of labor force participation of Caribbean immigrants that they did not receive comparable economic returns on educational investments, either in terms of income or occupation. After isolating industries on the assumption that they could depress overall wages of the entire group, Palmer found that, even when the higher employment categories are isolated, the income disparities remained.[35] Gender difference was not specified in Palmer's study. However, for the United States as a whole, the income/occupation hierarchy has been, and was in 1980, as follows: white males, black males, white women, black women.[36] Family and individual median incomes of Caribbean immigrant women were below the median of all other groups. They were also below the median income of Caribbean immigrant men with comparable education and occupations.

In conclusion, immigrant status, gender, and race have been demonstrated to be significant constraints on the occupation and income of women. Yet there is some indication that, over time, education and training will overcome those constraints associated with their immigrant status. While Caribbean immigrant women on the average seem not to be doing as well as other women in the United States, their relatively low level of poverty and their even lower rate of dependency on social welfare augur well for the future. Whether their labor force participation will make them more socially and politically conscious of race/gender inequities requires another type of investigation.

## NOTES

1. United States Department of Justice, Immigration and Naturalization Service, *Annual Reports, 1965-1982* (Washington, D.C.: Government Printing Office, 1965-82).

2. Goulda Kosack, "Migrant Women: The Move to Western Europe—A Step Toward Emancipation," *Race and Class* 17:4 (1976): 370-79.

3. W. A. Dumon, "The Situation of Migrant Women Workers," *International Migration* 12:2/1 (1981): 190-209.

4. Edna Bonacich, "Advanced Capitalism and Black/White Relations in the United States: A Split Labor Market Interpretation," *American Sociological Review* 41:1 (1976): 34-51; S. Castles and G. Kosack, *Immigrant Workers and Class Structure in Western Europe* (London: Oxford University Press, 1973); A. Portes, "Modes of Structural Incorporation and Present Theories of Labor Immigration," in Mary Kritz, Charles B. Keely, and Silvano M. Tomasi, eds., *Global Trends in Migration* (New York: Center for Migration Studies, 1983); Saskia Sassen-Koob, "The International Circulation of Resources and Development: The Case of Labor Migration," *Development and Change* 9 (1978): 509-45.

5. John Salt, "International Labor Migration in Western Europe: A Geographical Review," in Mary Kritz, Charles B. Keely, and Silvano M. Tomasi, eds., *Global Trends in Migration* (New York: Center for Migration Studies, 1983).

6. A. Portes, "The Labor Function of Illegal Aliens," *Society* 14 (September–October 1977): 31-37.

7. R. Stevens, L. Goodman, and S. Mick, *The Alien Doctors: Foreign Medical Graduates in American Hospitals* (New York: Wiley, 1978).

8. Portes, "Modes," pp. 281-84.

9. Ibid., pp. 282-87.

10. A. Portes and R. Bach, "Immigrant Earnings: Cuban and Mexican Immigrants in the United States," *International Migration Review* 14:3 (1978): 319.

11. M. Morokvasic, "Birds of Passage Are Also Women . . . ," *International Migration Review* 18:4 (1984): 886-907.

12. Ibid., p. 891.

13. Monica H. Gordon, "Identification and Adaptation: A Study of Two Groups of Jamaican Immigrants in New York City," unpublished Ph.D. dissertation, City University of New York, 1979, p. 191.

14. F. Blau and C. L. Jusenius, "Economists' Approaches to Sex Segregation in the Labor Market: An Appraisal," *Signs* 1 (Spring 1976): 181-91; E. Beck, P. Horan, and C. M. Tolbert II, "Stratification in a Dual Economy," *American Sociological Review* 43:5 (1978): 704-20.

15. E. Petras, "The Global Labor Market in the Modern World Economy," in Mary Kritz, Charles B. Keely, and Silvano M. Tomasi, eds., *Global Trends in Migration* (New York: Center for Migration Studies, 1983); H. Watson, "International Migration and the Political Economy of Underdevelopment: Aspects of the Commonwealth Caribbean Situation," in Roy S. Bryce-Laporte, ed., *Caribbean Immigration to the United States* (Washington, D.C.: Smithsonian Institution Research Institute on Immigration and Ethnic Studies, 1976); see also Sassen-Koob, "International Circulation."

16. See Watson, "International Migration."

17. M. G. Castro, J. Gearing, and M. Gill, *Women and Migration—Latin America and the Caribbean: A Selected Annotated Bibliography* (Gainesville, Florida: Center for Latin American Studies, University of Florida, 1984); M. Houston, R. Kramer, J. M. Barrett, "Female Predominance in Immigration to the United States Since 1930: A First Look," *International Migration Review* 18:4 (1984): 908–58; Delores M. Mortimer and Roy S. Bryce-Laporte, eds., *Female Immigrants to the United States: Caribbean, Latin American, and African Experiences* (Washington, D.C.: Smithsonian Institution Research Institute on Immigration and Ethnic Studies, 1981); M. Tienda, "Immigration, Gender and the Process of Occupational Change in the U.S., 1970–1980," *International Migration Review* 18:4 (1984): 1021–44; see also Morokvasic, "Birds of Passage."

18. Castro, et al., *Women and Migration*, p. 4.

19. Ibid., p. 5.

20. Saskia Sassen-Koob, "Notes on the Incorporation of Third World Women into Wage Labor Through Immigration and Off-Shore Production," *International Migration Review* 18:4 (1984): 1144–67.

21. Linda Burnham, "Has Poverty Been Feminized in America?" *Black Scholar* (March/April 1985): 14–15.

22. See M. Houston, et al., "Female Predominance."

23. R. Pryor, "Integrating International and Internal Migration Theories," in Mary Kritz, Charles B. Keely, and Silvano M. Thomasi, eds., *Global Trends in Migration* (New York: Center for Migration Studies, 1983), pp. 110–29.

24. See United States Department of Justice, Immigration and Naturalization Service, *Annual Reports, 1965–1982.*

25. United States Department of Commerce, Bureau of the Census, *Statistical Abstract of the United States, 1980–1986* (Washington, D.C.: Government Printing Office, 1980–86).

26. New York City, Office of Immigration Affairs, *West Indian Immigrants in New York City* (1985). Unpublished paper.

27. M. Simms, "Black Women Who Head Families: An Economic Struggle," *Review of Black Political Economy* (Summer 1985): 141–51.

28. Margaret Andersen, *Thinking about Women: Sociological and Feminist Perspectives* (New York: Macmillan, 1983).

29. See Kosack, "Migrant Women," and Morokvasic, "Birds of Passage."

30. Walter Stafford, *Closed Labor Markets: Underrepresentation of Blacks, Hispanics and Women in New York City's Core Industries and Jobs* (New York: Community Services of New York, 1985).

31. J. Malveaux, "The Economic Interests of Black and White Women: Are They Similar?" *The Review of Black Political Economy* (Summer 1985): 15–16.

32. See Portes, "Modes of Structural Incorporation."
33. See Kosack, "Migrant Women."
34. See Stafford, *Closed Labor Markets.*
35. Ransford W. Palmer, "Making It in the First World: Caribbean Immigrants in the United States," paper presented at the North American Economics and Finance Association—Allied Social Science Associations Annual Meeting, New York City, December, 1985.
36. See Andersen, *Thinking about Women*, pp. 94–95.

## SELECTED BIBLIOGRAPHY

Andersen, Margaret. *Thinking about Women: Sociological and Feminist Perspectives.* New York: Macmillan, 1983.

Beck, E., P. Horan, and C. M. Tolbert II. "Stratification in a Dual Economy," *American Sociological Review* 43:5 (1978): 704–720.

Blau, F., and C. L. Jusenius. "Economists' Approaches to Sex Segregation in the Labor Market: An Appraisal," *Signs* 1 (Spring 1976): 181–91.

Bonacich, Edna. "Advanced Capitalism and Black/White Relations in the United States: A Split Labor Market Interpretation," *American Sociological Review* 41:1 (1976): 34–51.

Boyd, Monica. "At a Disadvantage: The Occupational Attainments of Foreign Born Women in Canada," *International Migration Review* 18:4 (1984): 1091–1119.

_____. "Immigration Policies and Trends: A Comparison of Canada and the U.S.," *Demography* 13:1 (1976): 83–104.

Bryce-Laporte, Roy S., ed. *Caribbean Immigration to the United States.* Washington, D.C.: Smithsonian Institution, Research Institute on Immigration and Ethnic Studies, 1976.

Burnham, Linda. "Has Poverty Been Feminized in America?" *Black Scholar* (March/April 1985): 14–15.

Castles, S., and G. Kosack. *Immigrant Workers and Class Structure in Western Europe.* London: Oxford University Press, 1973.

Castro, M. G., J. Gearing, and M. Gill. *Women and Migration—Latin America and the Caribbean: A Selected Annotated Bibliography.* Gainesville, Florida: Center for Latin American Studies, University of Florida, 1984.

Cooper, Dereck. "Migration from Jamaica in the 1970s: Political Protest or Economic Pull?" *International Migration Review* 19:4 (1985): 728–45.

Dumon, W. A. "The Situation of Migrant Women Workers," *International Migration* 12:2/1 (1981): 190–209.

Gordon, Monica H. "Caribbean Migration: A Perspective on Women." In Delores M. Mortimer and Roy S. Bryce-Laporte, eds. *Female Immigrants to the United States: Caribbean, Latin American and African Experiences.* Washington, D.C.: Smithsonian Institution Research Institute on Immigration and Ethnic Studies, 1981.

_____. "Identification and Adaptation: A Study of Two Groups of Jamaican Immigrants in New York City." Unpublished Ph.D. dissertation, City University of New York, 1979.

Houston, M., R. Kramer, and J. M. Barrett. "Female Predominance in Immigration to the United States Since 1930: A First Look," *International Migration Review* 18:4 (1984): 908–58.

Kosack, Goulda. "Migrant Women: The Move to Western Europe—A Step Toward Emancipation," *Race and Class* 17:4 (1976): 370–79.

Kritz, Mary, Charles B. Keely, and Silvano M. Tomasi, eds. *Global Trends in Migration.* New York: Center for Migration Studies, 1983.

Ley, K. "Migrant Women. Is Migration a Blessing or a Handicap?: Situation of Migrant Women in Switzerland," *International Migration* 19:1–2 (1981): 75–82.

McLaughlin, Megan. "West Indian Immigrants: Their Social Networks and Ethnic Identification." Unpublished Ph.D. dissertation, Columbia University, 1981.

Malveaux, J. "The Economic Interests of Black and White Women: Are They Similar?" *The Review of Black Political Economy* (Summer 1985): 5–27.

Morokvasic, M. "Birds of Passage Are Also Women . . . ," *International Migration Review* 18:4 (1984): 886–907.

Mortimer, Delores M., and Roy S. Bryce-Laporte, eds. *Female Immigrants to the United States: Caribbean, Latin American and African Experiences.* Washington, D.C.: Smithsonian Institution Research Institute on Immigration and Ethnic Studies, 1981.

New York City, Office of Immigrant Affairs. *West Indian Immigrants in New York City.* Unpublished paper. 1985.

Palmer, Ransford W. "Making It in the First World: Caribbean Immigrants in the United States." Paper presented at the North American Economics and Finance Association—Allied Social Science Associations Annual Meeting, New York City, December 1985.

Petras, E. "The Global Labor Market in the Modern World Economy." In Mary Kritz, Charles B. Keely, and Silvano M. Tomasi, eds. *Global Trends in Migration.* New York: Center for Migration Studies, 1983.

Portes, A. "The Labour Function of Illegal Aliens." *Society* 14 (September–October 1977): 31–37.

_____. "Modes of Structural Incorporation and Present Theories of Labor Immigration." In Mary Kritz, Charles B. Keely, and Silvano M. Tomasi, eds. *Global Trends in Migration.* New York: Center for Migration Studies, 1983.

Portes, A., and R. Bach. "Immigrant Earnings: Cuban and Mexican Immigrants in the United States," *International Migration Review* 14:3 (1978): 315–39.

Pryor, R. "Integrating International and Internal Migration Theories." In Mary Kritz, Charles B. Keely, and Silvano M. Tomasi, eds. *Global Trends in Migration.* New York: Center for Migration Studies, 1983, pp. 110–29.

Salt, John. "International Labor Migration in Western Europe: A Geographical Review." In Mary Kritz, Charles B. Keely, and Silvano M. Tomasi, eds. *Global Trends in Migration.* New York: Center for Migration Studies, 1983.

Sassen-Koob, Saskia. "The International Circulation of Resources and Development: The Case of Labor Migration," *Development and Change* 9 (1978): 509–45.

_____. "Notes on the Incorporation of Third World Women into Wage Labor

Through Immigration and Off-Shore Production," *International Migration Review* 18:4 (1984): 1144–67.

Simms, M. "Black Women Who Head Families: An Economic Struggle," *Review of Black Political Economy* (Summer 1985): 141–51.

Stafford, Walter. *Closed Labor Markets: Underrepresentation of Blacks, Hispanics and Women in New York City's Core Industries and Jobs.* New York: Community Services of New York, 1985.

Stevens, R., L. Goodman, and S. Mick. *The Alien Doctors: Foreign Medical Graduates in American Hospitals.* New York: Wiley, 1978.

Tienda, M. "Immigration, Gender and the Process of Occupational Change in the U.S., 1970–1980," *International Migration Review* 18:4 (1984): 1021–44.

United States Department of Commerce, Bureau of the Census. *Statistical Abstract of the United States, 1980–1986.* Washington, D.C.: Government Printing Office, 1980–86.

United States Department of Justice, Immigration and Naturalization Service. *Annual Reports, 1965–1982.* Washington, D.C.: Government Printing Office, 1965–82.

Watson, H. "International Migration and the Political Economy of Underdevelopment: Aspects of the Commonwealth Caribbean Situation." In Roy S. Bryce-Laporte, ed. *Caribbean Immigration to the United States.* Washington, D.C.: Smithsonian Institution Research Institute on Immigration and Ethnic Studies, 1976.

# 7

# The *New* Female West Indian Immigrant: Dilemmas of Coping in the Host Society

AUBREY W. BONNETT

## INTRODUCTION

West Indian immigrants have been described as the prototypical American success story and are often used to refute the presence of U.S. racism toward blacks.[1] Further, many conservative black and white scholars—among the more notable are Walter Williams, an economist at George Mason University, and Glenn Loury, a political economist at Harvard University's Kennedy School of Government—continue to assert that the success of past generations of these immigrants would serve as a role model to current immigrants in their quest for ascendancy to a middle class in a relatively short period of time.

I have contended elsewhere that this portrayal depicts only part of the picture and that current structural shifts in the U.S. economy are presenting this cohort of "new immigrants" with totally different problems, which are forcing them to suffer, even more, the harsher effects of the sociopsychological experiences of migration.[2] Further, unlike previous immigrations, especially those entering in 1952 and 1965, when preference was given to professionals and highly trained and skilled individuals, this immigration is different. The current group is composed primarily of women, often from the working class or rural peasantry, who lack much formal education and clearly defined employment histories.[3] With the reduction of manufacturing and blue collar industries (especially along the Northeastern seaboard) and with a decline in employment in the state sector, the job and career opportunities for this group—both parents and children—are at best limited.[4]

As a result, these new immigrants, and later their children, have become exploitable labor in our highly segmented labor market.[5] Roy S. Bryce-Laporte, in writing of the important changes and adaptations the immigrants must make, states:

> The international or transitional family is quite common today among new immigrants either because both spouses, and perhaps children, are of different nationalities or cultures, or because family members are dispersed across national boundaries while the unit tries to remain operational and intact. This often means that family affairs and ties must be attended to over great distances and with all the added difficulties of time and international complications.[6]

This chapter attempts to analyze this female-skewed immigration and to assess the stressors inherent in the process, which cause tremendous social and psychological trauma. Although it focuses on female adjustment, it also looks at the sometimes peripheral, sometimes pivotal, role of both male immigrants and children in this odyssey—this complex web of social phenomena.

## THE FEMALE SKEW

Between 1972–79, at least 51 percent of the immigrants from Trinidad and Tobago, Barbados, Guyana, Jamaica, St. Kitts/Nevis, and Antigua were women.[7] Typically, the West Indian immigrant pattern has been for the male to seasonally migrate to cut sugar cane in other islands or the mainland and then return home. Migration to England and the United States followed this sojourner pattern, which continued up to the late 1960s.[8] In the early 1970s, we began to see the female skew first emerging, and this coincided with the large number of West Indian nurses who began to migrate from the islands and from an increasingly impoverished and societally hostile United Kingdom. This increasing hostility toward its nonwhite citizens from the Commonwealth, fed by a changing and constricting economy with shrinking state resources, pitted West Indians against Britain's working class whites. The resultant conflict acted as a catalyst to force West Indians to join their kin in the United States.

Not only is this migration predominantly female but invariably the women come alone—with ambitions for their children and themselves—leaving their offspring and, at times, their spouses, with surrogates. Inherent in this process are the stressors which lead to separation anxieties, at times their own physical neglect, and certainly the emergence of psychosomatic disorders.[9] It is to these issues that we now turn.

## THE MALE CONNECTION:
## CONSORTS, LOVERS, OR WHAT?

Many of these female immigrants are found in the lowest paying sectors of the U.S. economy. They work as domestics in suburban homes where many "live-in" and become parent surrogates to the children who often do not relate positively to their highly mobile professional parents. Some immigrants work as hospital aides, beauticians, or seamstresses in the garment district, to name a few occupations—all are jobs that require long hours for little pay.

Initially in this period of adjustment to the host society, their relationships with men are few and spasmodic, often revolving around sexual contact. One female indicated to me in an interview in the early 1980s that "sometimes I need a man to squeeze, somebody to satisfy my [physical] needs for awhile. But I'm scared of getting too close to these West Indian men. You never know when dey two-timing yuh."[10]

Indeed, there is tremendous ambiguity among these immigrants, for while they say they fear social intimacy, yet sexual intimacy solely can lead to consort relationships that are prone to exploitative patterns on the part of the male. It is for this reason that some of these women engage in relationships with southern Afro-American males who are truck drivers or in some other way transient to the area in which the women live. In this instance, the relationship tends to be both instrumental and expressive, since both parties tend to be mutually supportive to each other.

But there is another option, and that is for these immigrants to establish relationships with second-generation male migrants who are married. In these relationships, the norms and expectations are clearly defined, with each partner setting clear guide lines as to what is expected from the "affair." In some instances, children have resulted from these unions, and the males are expected to help arrange for child care, often with members of their extended network. Recently, in the last 7 to 10 years, naturalized West Indian females who are professionals and single have begun—like their Afro-American counterparts—to initiate and cement relationships with married males who are also their professional peers. Invariably this results because of the unavailability of "suitable" partners and the reluctance of the females to interact with men they consider to be crass and unsophisticated.

Finally, there are those immigrants who avoid social relationships at all costs. They work endlessly—double shifts, triple shifts—to amass money to send remittances back to the islands—back home—or to make a down payment on a brownstone in Brooklyn or Queens or a house in Fort Myers, Florida. They have few friends and are devoid of "significant others" and the social networks so prevalent in earlier migrations.[11]

But many of these immigrants are also mothers who have left their children and, at times, their spouses or lovers, in the islands. A large percentage of this group are the "undocumented" workers who have overstayed their stay and must seek employment to legalize their status. Shellee Colen describes their plight:

> Like their relatives and friends before them, these West Indian women migrate to "better themselves." In New York they seek opportunities in employment and in education, for themselves and their children. They are drawn, as well, by the availability of basic consumer goods unaffordable at home and especially important to them as mothers.[12]

She continues:

> While to be a good mother means to leave one's children and migrate, ironically, taking care of someone else's children is often their first job in New York, especially for those without permanent residence status, the green card.[13]

It is to the children of these immigrants and the stressors revolving about them that we now turn.

## COPING WITH CHILDREN AND
## THE PROBLEMS OF CHILDREN

As we stated earlier, an individual's decision to migrate was often made with deep anguish but with some certainty that it was the only good decision and that it would be short lived. In many instances, arrangements had to be made to leave the children with relatives—often grandparents—and to send remittances back on a frequent basis. In addition to the financial arrangements, parents (the immigrants) would often send "barrels" of clothing and food several times a year, this to be shared not only with the children but with the extended kin—cousins, uncles, aunts, and so on.

These arrangements worked in many instances, but at times there were conflicting situations. Problems surrounding the use and abuse of money and the mistreatment of children often led to tremendous strain for the immigrant parents. Exorbitant sums of money for telephone bills in an attempt to employ corrective action would result. Joyce Toney describes the situation aptly:

> Although the financial questions sometimes strained the relationship, it very rarely led to a complete break. Complete severance of ties was likely to occur only when the migrants suspected that the children were mistreated. In such cases the children were taken away and handed over to another caretaker. This rarely happened, if only because the caretakers were afraid that the remittance they received for the children would be

taken away. On the contrary the migrant children were more likely to be spoiled, and pampered. . . . The migrants [parents] themselves compensate materially for their physical absence. Migrant children were often better dressed, had more money, and were more likely to attend secondary schools than their peers.[14]

When the children do arrive in the United States, other problems and stressors come into play. As Toney notes, the adjustment can initially be very demanding:

The parents sometimes left a baby behind, and were reunited with a teenager or young adult. They often found that they did not like or understand each other. Some children stayed with parents in New York only a few months after arrival, before they moved in with friends or other relatives.[15]

The problems of this reunion can be compounded if the parent has remarried or has a "live-in" lover. And even further difficulties arise if there are siblings arising from the new relationship. The children must adapt to new and different sociocultural patterns, which their parents are often unable to help them define.[16] This often results in the youngsters having minimal contact with their parents.

If the children are of school age, additional stressors exist. Often the schools they attend are located in close proximity to some of the most disadvantaged and violent black urban areas and suffer from severe staff shortages, large classes, the threat of violence, and drug trafficking. The immigrant students may find few peers with whom to associate.[17]

For many West Indian immigrant children, entrance into, and coping with, public education systems can be a nightmare. I describe their plight in this manner:

Sometimes their heavy accents make it difficult for them to be understood by their peers and at times even expose them to ridicule and jeering. Teachers often exhibit the same intolerance, often "passing over" these kids during question and answer periods in the interest of expediency. The net result is that the student develops a poor self-image, refuses or is unable to learn, finds himself or herself segregated from his or her "peers" and ultimately develops negative attitudes about school and learning.[18]

Some children try desperately to hide their differences and to lose their accents as they confront this crisis of identity. Other families have adapted to this crisis by working overtime shifts, and by sending their children to parochial schools or to private academies, staffed predominantly by West Indian teachers and populated only by other West Indian children.[19] The sad fact is that few families can readily afford to do this and, moreover, using this option further stultifies the children's acculturation to American norms and helps perpetuate the "sojourner" mindset.

Some commentators have observed that in cases where the parents appear to be denied acceptance and economic opportunity in their adopted country, the children develop a sense of hopelessness, which turns to rebellion from their parents and from the host country's norms.[20] Often the children reach the point of joining with other youths and becoming antisocial delinquents. Suzanne Michael pointedly sets out the dilemma:

> Unlike their parents, they do not see themselves as sojourners. They do not look as much to the West Indian community to gain a sense of orientation and identity. Instead they often resent their West Indian upbringing. They want to assimilate, to become American, and begin the process with acculturation, their role models being the stars of T.V. and the movies, and their peers on the streets and in the school.[21]

Michael continues her description of the migrant child as remaining marginal to four cultural and social contacts: (1) his or her island home, (2) his or her "new" family and the West Indian community in New York City, (3) the black and minority community, and (4) the larger American society.[22]

The immigrant child experiences a cognitive dissonance between expectation and opportunity and is left with anomie.[23] But, as Michael contends, the parents of these children do continue to have ambitions for them—ambitions defined by the American dream, the histories of past generations of immigrants, and the West Indian folk belief of profound success.[24] In actuality, many of these children do not succeed, and it is this dilemma—indeed, the profound disappointment—that still continues to plague these immigrants with visions of an unfulfilled American dream.[25]

Finally, let us now turn to another stressor of some importance: the relationship between the female immigrants and their spouses.

## FEMALE AND MALE IMMIGRANTS: ROLE DIFFERENTIATION AND ROLE STRAIN

For many female immigrants, the time does come when their spouses join them in the United States. This movement to the host society presents counterpressures posed by the more egalitarian nature of sex roles in this country and the patriarchal traditional male-female relationship found in many Third World societies—a classic Catch-22. For the male, the dilemma is even more profound. Should he enforce his predominant traditional "old country" male identity and risk losing his spouse, or should he succumb to this role reversal and thus lose the respect of his male peers who still retain, and subscribe to, the "old country" role?

The females' problems are somewhat similar, and often these stressors lead to marital disharmony and disruption. Gordon observes:

> Men who do not usually perform household chores prior to migration, find that they must contribute in this area as well as to the usual tasks of income earning. But the women are also income earners. Immigrant males reported that they found immigrant women more demanding of their men in domestic and interpersonal relationships.[26]

In some instances, the male spouse feels pressures emerging from children. His own biological children are often reluctant to follow his dictates, and he has to constantly reassert his authority. This causes tremendous strain between him and his offspring, at times damaging an already brittle relationship.

When the children are not his own but part of the "new" family that his wife may have started, his problems are even greater. He is often torn between conflict and loyalty to the two groups of children and ends up feeling estranged from both of them. Feeling endless role strain, he minimizes physical and social contact and may abandon the family or seek his own sexual liaison elsewhere. One male migrant described the situation to me in this manner:

> My wife now feel she can tell me what to do 'cause she making more than me . . . can't even speak to my damn kids. . . . Back home I would have whipped their asses but here the cops are on my case. Shit! I can't handle the hassle. I give up.[27]

A small number of second generation West Indian psychiatrists, psychiatric social workers, and clinical psychologists have begun to serve this group. However, they still experience great difficulty because of the immigrants' reluctance to seek help from psychiatrists or psychologists, who are often perceived in the "old country" as only treating, or dealing with, the truly "insane."

A tremendous amount of anxiety and other forms of neuroses and psychiatric disorders lie dormant within this group of immigrants. Some men report the inability to perform sexually, and others report creeping impotence because of their inability to cope with the stressors they face. Caught in a Catch-22 situation, they leave their homes and establish outside sexual relationships with younger women, often to prove their sexual virility. This only compounds their dilemma, for if offspring result, they are faced with supporting even larger networks— for many an impossible task.

## CONCLUSION

What we have tried to show in this chapter is that some of the stressors faced by this new group of female immigrants are formidable. Yet, for many, the choice to immigrate must be made, for the alternative is more dismal. The ethnic community, as I have stated elsewhere, remains the key to alleviating the problems of adaptation. It is a structural shield and as such constitutes a buffer to the larger society.[28] We agree with the comment that these new immigrants tend to be young, resourceful, and adaptable,[29] and that even in difficult circumstances, they will find ways to adjust and contribute to their new society.[30] Finally, we would urge, as the American Jewish Committee has, that professional service providers and mainstream agencies should continue to work to assure the success and competence of new immigrant associations and ethnic mutual aid societies.[31] It is only by empowering professionals from these groups that we can contribute to a lessening of the immigrants' trauma and the formation of a much better ethnic identity on their way to becoming useful American citizens. Indeed, in many of the large urban metropoles—Brooklyn, Boston, and Miami, to mention a few—these organizations are finally emerging. With this element of institutionalization and the help of the more informal networks already in existence, it is hoped that some of the dilemmas discussed in this chapter will be addressed and alleviated.

## NOTES

1. In this connection, see Thomas Sowell, *Essays and Data on American Ethnic Groups* (Washington, D.C.: The Urban Institute, 1978) and *Ethnic America: A History* (New York: Basic Books, 1981); also Nancy Foner, "West Indians in New York City and London: A Comparative Analysis," *International Migration Review* 13 (1979): 284–97.

2. Aubrey W. Bonnett, "Patterns of Accommodation in the West Indian Community in New York," in A. Carrasquillo and E. Sandis, eds., *Schooling, Job Opportunities and Ethnic Mobility Among Caribbean Youth in the United States* (Bronx, New York: Fordham University Press, 1985).

3. See Nancy Foner, *Jamaican Migrants: A Comparative Analysis of the New York and London Experience*, Occasional Paper No. 36, New York Research Program in Inter-American Affairs (New York: New York University Press, 1983); Adrianna Marshall, *Immigration in a Surplus-Worker Market: The Case of New York*, Occasional Paper No. 39, Center for Latin American and Caribbean Studies (New York: New York University, 1983); Suzanne Michael, "Children of the New Wave Immigrations: An Exploration," in Aubrey W. Bonnett and G. L. Watson, eds., *Emerging Perspectives on the Black Diaspora* (Washington, D.C.: University Press of America, forthcoming); and Elsa Chaney, "Women Who Go and the Women Who Stay Behind," *Migration Today* 10:3/4: 6–13.

4. See Michael, "Children of Immigrations"; and Adrianna Marshall, "New

Immigrants in New York's Economy," in Nancy Foner, ed., *New Immigrants in New York* (New York: Columbia University Press, 1987).

5. See Michael, "Children of Immigrations"; and Delores M. Mortimer and Roy S. Bryce-Laporte, eds., *Female Immigrants to the United States: Caribbean, Latin American, and African Experiences*, Research Institute on Immigration and Ethnic Studies, Occasional Paper No. 2 (Washington, D.C.: Smithsonian Institution, 1987) for some excellent articles.

6. Roy S. Bryce-Laporte, *Give Me Your Tired, Your Poor . . . ? Voluntary Black Migration to the United States* (New York: The New York Public Library, Schomburg Center for Research in Black Culture, 1986), p. 18.

7. M. Houston, R. Kramer, and J. M. Barrett, eds., "Female Predominance in Immigration to the United States Since 1930: A First Look," *International Migration Review* 18:4 (Winter 1984): 928–29.

8. Nancy Foner, "Introduction: New Immigrants and Changing Patterns in New York City," in Nancy Foner, ed., *New Immigrants in New York* (New York: Columbia University Press, 1987).

9. See Michael, "Children of Immigrations"; Joyce Toney, "The Perpetuation of a Culture of Migration: West Indian Ties with Home, 1900–1979," paper presented at the Caribbean Studies Association Annual Meeting, Guadeloupe, May, 1988; Aubrey W. Bonnett, *Institutional Adaptation of West Indian Immigrants to America: An Analysis of Rotating Credit Associations* (Washington, D.C.: University Press of America, 1981); and Aubrey W. Bonnett, "Psycho-Social Stressors of West Indian Immigrants and Their Adaptive Behavior," paper presented at the National Medical Association Conference, New York City, August 1985.

10. This was drawn from numerous interviews conducted in barber shops and beauty shops during 1984 for a paper on psychosocial stressors of Caribbean immigrants; see Bonnett, *Psycho-Social Stressors*; see also Charles Green, "Culture, Health Care and the New Caribbean Immigrants: Implication for New Health Policy and Planning," *Migration Today* 12:4/5 (1984): 25–29.

11. See Bonnett, *Institutional Adaptation*. Many West Indian realtors cater to this market in New York, Boston, Los Angeles, and Florida. General Dynamics has also employed many salespersons and supervisory personnel who find this market highly susceptible to the lure of homeownership.

12. Shellee Colen, "With Respect and Feelings: Voices of West Indian Child Care and Domestic Workers in New York City," in Johnetta Cole, ed., *All American Women: Lines that Divide, Ties that Bind* (New York: The Free Press, 1986), pp. 46–48.

13. Ibid.

14. Toney, "The Perpetuation of a Culture," p. 9.

15. Ibid.

16. See Michael, "Children of Immigrations"; and also Monica Gordon, *The Impact of Migration on the Caribbean Family* (unpublished).

17. See Michael, "Children of Immigrations."

18. See Bonnett, "Patterns of Accommodation."

19. Ibid, p. 45.

20. Ibid.; see also Michael, "Children of Immigrations."

21. See Michael, "Children of Immigrations."

22. Ibid.

23. See Michael, "Children of Immigrations"; and Bonnett, "Psycho-Social Stressors."

24. Ibid.; see also Gordon, *The Impact of Migration*.

25. Two recent books stress this dilemma. They are Constance Sutton and Elsa Chaney, eds., *Caribbean Life in New York City: Sociocultural Dimensions* (New York: Center for Migration Studies, 1987), in which the introductory articles by Chaney and Sutton are especially useful; and Nancy Foner, *New Immigrants in New York*. See also Vivienne Walt, "Caught Between Two Worlds! Immigrants Discover Success, Racism in the U.S.," *Newsday*, April 15, 1988, pp. 9 and 26.

26. Gordon, *The Impact of Migration*, p. 13.

27. Bonnett, 1984 interviews (see Note 10).

28. See Bonnett, *Institutional Adaptation*.

29. Genge M. Szabad and Gary Rubin, eds., *The Newest Americans: Report of the American Jewish Committee's Task Force on the Acculturation of Immigrants to American Life* (New York: AJC Institute on Human Relations, 1987), p. 21.

30. Ibid., p. 20.

31. Ibid., p. 21.

## SELECTED BIBLIOGRAPHY

Bonnett, Aubrey W. *Institutional Adaptation of West Indian Immigrants to America: An Analysis of Rotating Credit Associations*. Washington, D.C.: University Press of America, 1981.

_____. "Patterns of Accommodation in the West Indian Community in New York." In A. Carrasquillo and E. Sandis, eds. *Schooling, Job Opportunities and Ethnic Mobility Among Caribbean Youth in the United States*. Bronx, New York: Fordham University Press, 1985.

_____. "Psycho-Social Stressors of West Indian Immigrants and Their Adaptive Behavior." Paper presented at the National Medical Association Conference, New York City, August 1985.

Bryce-Laporte, Roy S. *Give Me Your Tired, Your Poor . . . ? Voluntary Black Migration to the United States*. New York: The New York Public Library, Schomburg Center for Research in Black Culture, 1986.

Chaney, Elsa. "Women Who Go and the Women Who Stay Behind," *Migration Today* 10:3/4: 6–13.

Colen, Shellee. "With Respect and Feelings: Voices of West Indian Child Care and Domestic Workers in New York City," in Johnetta Cole, ed. *All American Women: Lines that Divide, Ties that Bind*. New York: The Free Press, 1986.

Foner, Nancy. *Jamaican Migrants: A Comparative Analysis of the New York and London Experience*. Occasional Paper No. 36, New York Research Program in Inter-American Affairs. New York: New York University Press, 1983.

_____. *New Immigrants in New York*. New York: Columbia University Press, 1987.

_____. "West Indians in New York City and London: A Comparative Analysis," *International Migration Review* 13 (1979): 284–97.

Green, Charles. "Culture, Health Care and the New Caribbean Immigrants: Implication for New Health Policy and Planning," *Migration Today* 12:4/5 (1984): 25–29.

Houston, M., R. Kramer, and J. M. Barrett, eds. "Female Predominance in Immigration to the United States Since 1930: A First Look." *International Migration Review* 18:4 (Winter 1984): 908–58.

Marshall, Adrianna. *Immigration in a Surplus-Worker Market: The Case of New York.* Occasional Paper No. 39. New York: Center for Latin American and Caribbean Studies, New York University, 1983.

_____. "New Immigrants in New York's Economy." In Nancy Foner, ed. *New Immigrants in New York.* New York: Columbia University Press, 1987.

Michael, Suzanne. "Children of the New Wave Immigrations: An Exploration." In Aubrey W. Bonnett and G. L. Watson, eds. *Emerging Perspectives on the Black Diaspora.* Washington, D.C.: University Press of America, forthcoming.

Mortimer, D., and R. S. Bryce-Laporte, eds. *Female Immigrants to the United States: Caribbean, Latin American, and African Experiences.* Research Institute on Immigration and Ethnic Studies, Occasional Paper No. 2. Washington, D.C.: Smithsonian Institution, 1987.

Sowell, Thomas. *Essays and Data on American Ethnic Groups.* Washington, D.C.: The Urban Institute, 1978.

_____. *Ethnic America: A History.* New York: Basic Books, 1981.

Sutton, Constance, and Elsa Chaney, eds. *Caribbean Life in New York City: Sociocultural Dimensions.* New York: Center for Migration Studies, 1987.

Szabad, Genge M., and Gary Rubin, eds. *The Newest Americans: Report of the American Jewish Committee's Task Force on the Acculturation of Immigrants to American Life.* New York: AJC Institute on Human Relations, 1987.

Toney, Joyce. "The Perpetuation of a Culture of Migration: West Indian Ties with Home, 1900–1979." Paper presented at the Caribbean Studies Association Annual Meeting, Guadeloupe, May 1988.

Walt, Vivienne. "Caught Between Two Worlds! Immigrants Discover Success, Racism in the U.S.," *Newsday*, April 15, 1988, pp. 9 and 26.

# III

## Illegal Migration

# 8

# Amnesty for Illegal Aliens from the Caribbean: Implications for Future Immigration Flows

LISA S. RONEY

## BACKGROUND

After nearly a decade of debate of immigration reform, the Immigration Reform and Control Act of 1986 (IRCA) was passed by Congress and signed into law on November 6, 1986. This landmark legislation included several provisions that were collectively designed to address the illegal alien problem in the United States, a problem that had grown progressively larger and more diverse, both in terms of nationality groups and areas of residence, over the previous two decades.

On the one hand, the Immigration Reform and Control Act of 1986 was geared to bring those illegal aliens with a considerable investment in the United States out of the shadows and into a legal status. These provisions created a new legal status through a two-step program for aliens who had resided continuously in the United States prior to January 1, 1982, a similar program for aliens who had worked at least 90 days in qualifying perishable agriculture between May 1985 and May 1986, and permanent resident status for certain entrants from Cuba and Haiti.

On the other hand, the new law provided for major increases in border and interior enforcement and sanctions against employers who hired illegal aliens; the aim is to cut off the primary magnet—U.S. jobs—for illegal migration. The Reform Act authorized a 50 percent increase in the size of the border patrol. It also addressed the expeditious removal of criminal aliens and increased detention space for such aliens awaiting hearings and/or removal from the United States.

Employer sanctions, however, were the keystone to the reform package, for it was geared to reduce substantially—if not eliminate—future illegal flows to the United States. Under employer sanctions, a set of escalating penalties, from civil to criminal, were established for employers who knowingly hired illegal aliens. Protections for workers who believed they were discriminated against because of sanction-related employment practices were also established through the creation of a special counsel within the Department of Justice.

The Reform Act also mandated a series of reporting requirements on employer sanctions-related issues, the legalized population, and the characteristics of immigrant flows and their likely impact in the future.

## PROVISIONS OF THE LEGALIZATION PROGRAMS

The primary program for regularizing the status of aliens living illegally in the United States included those persons residing in illegal status prior to January 1, 1982, and ran from May 5, 1987 through May 4, 1988. To be eligible for legal temporary resident status under this two-step program, the illegal presence had to be continuous, with no more than two absences of up to 45 days each during the qualifying period. Additionally, applicants were required to undergo a medical examination and be in good health, not be excludable from the United States, and be able to demonstrate financial responsibility.

Clarifications of the eligibility policies relating to this program were made later to include persons in situations that met the basic intent of the law but who, because of technicalities in the Immigration and Naturalization Service (INS) regulations, might have been excluded from qualifying. For instance, illegal residents who had temporarily departed from the United States and reentered "legally" with non-immigrant visas in order to return to unrelinquished unlawful U.S. residences, but who were otherwise qualified, were made eligible to apply.

Following 18 months in temporary resident status, legalized aliens have a 12-month period in which to apply for legal permanent residence, which will put them on a track to attain U.S. citizenship after at least 5 years additional residence. The second phase of the legalization program runs for two years, beginning in November 1988 and requires that applicants be able to pass basic tests in everyday English and U.S. history and government or show proof that they are currently enrolled in such classes.

The second program included under IRCA to regularize groups of illegal aliens is the Special Agricultural Worker (SAW) Program. The provisions relating to this group are less stringent in many ways than those for the regular legalization program. To qualify for SAW status, an applicant must have worked in qualifying perishable agriculture for at least 90 days between May 1985 and May 1986 and have applied to INS for this status between June 1, 1987 and November 30, 1988.

Phase Two—permanent residence—under the SAW program is more pro forma in that this benefit is conferred on this group without additional qualifying requirements. For those SAW workers who also worked in perishable agriculture for 90 days during the 1983–84 and 1984–85 periods, permanent residence was conferred on December 1, 1989. For those qualifying based on 90 days' work in only the 1985–86 period, permanent residence status is conferred on December 1, 1990.

The third legalization program provided for under the Reform Act is for nationals of Cuba and Haiti who arrived in the United States before January 1, 1982 and had an INS record established before that date. The application period for this program ran from November 6, 1986 through November 5, 1988. Unlike the other legalization programs, the Cuban-Haitian Entrant program was a one-step program with added benefits. This program conveyed permanent, rather than temporary, status, and for naturalization purposes, the date of admission was rolled back to January 1, 1982. This means that virtually all successful applicants under this program have met the length of residence requirement for naturalization at the time they apply. Also, unlike the other programs, those qualifying under this program retain their eligibility for social service benefits provided under earlier laws.

## THE LEGALIZATION PROCESS

Applicants for the regular legalization and SAW programs applied at 107 INS legalization offices that opened on May 5, 1987. In almost all instances, these were new offices separate from other INS locations, since the existing offices were feared by many who might come forward. Although the actual application process varied somewhat, applicants either came in directly to the INS facilities themselves, in the company of legal or other special representatives, or filed their applications through one of several hundred "qualified designated entities"—QDEs—social, religious, community, or government groups specially authorized and trained to help applicants.

A fee of $185 per person, with a family maximum of $465, was paid to INS when the application and documentation were submitted. At that time, INS opened the file and scheduled an interview. At the interview—the same day to several weeks later, depending upon how busy the office was—the application and supporting materials were reviewed and, if the case appeared approvable, a card authorizing work was given to the applicant.

Subsequently, the case file was sent to an INS contractor for data entry and initiation of background checks and then to one of four INS

Legalization Processing Centers for final review and decision. The notification of that decision was then sent to the applicant. In the high percentage of approval cases, the applicant next returned to the INS legalization office to pick up his or her Temporary Resident Card, the last step in phase one. In the cases of the relatively rare denials, no enforcement action was taken by INS unless document fraud was clearly involved.

It should be noted that substantial demographic information was obtained from applicants for legalization which, stripped of all identifiers and aggregated, can provide substantial information on the legalization and SAW populations.

## STATISTICAL DATA BASES

Statistics on applicants for legalization and SAW status are available from two automated systems, the first a case-taking, fee-receipt system capturing the number of applicants for each program for each legalization office and the second a data base of information on each applicant. Because of the delay inherent between the receipt of the application and the on-site interview and submission of the case for centralized data processing, the total number of cases in the second (data base) system are lower than total case receipts as reported by the case-tracking system. As processing is completed, the total number in both systems should agree.

As of the end of August 1988, over 2,549,000 applicants had applied at INS offices for temporary resident status through the regular legalization and SAW programs. Of these cases, over 72 percent, or 1,843,000 had been entered into the statistical data base. Data discussed in this chapter relate to this latter number, rather than the total number of applications received and should be considered provisional. Although the characteristics data presented as percentages should be similar for either data base, disparate workload volumes in legalization offices across the country resulted in varying case processing times and, therefore, potentially uneven input of cases into the data base. Therefore, in the final analysis, when all data input is complete, there may be some minor shifting of characteristics, especially relating to smaller segments of the legalizing population, such as that from the Caribbean. It should also be noted that the data relate to applications and not to approvals, although approval rates are high.

## TOTAL APPLICATIONS NATIONWIDE

As of the end of August, 1988, 1,762,000 applicants had applied for the regular (pre-1982) legalization program. Of these applicants, 89 percent were from 10 countries: Mexico, El Salvador, Guatemala, the Philippines, Colombia, Haiti, the Dominican Republic, Nicaragua, Poland, and Iran. As would be expected, Mexico accounted for the largest portion of applicants, with 70 percent of the total coming from that country.

Similarly, applicants for legalization were heavily concentrated. Ten states accounted for 94 percent of the applicants nationwide: California, Texas, Illinois, New York, Florida, Arizona, New Jersey, New Mexico, Nevada, and Oklahoma. California and Texas together accounted for almost three-quarters of all applicants. Overall, the legalization population was youthful, with a median age of 30 years, and predominantly— but not overwhelmingly—male (55 percent).

By the end of August 1988, an additional 786,953 persons had applied for special agricultural worker (SAW) status, a program continuing through November 1988. SAW applicants were even more concentrated than legalization applicants in terms of nationality—95 percent were from eight countries, with 83 percent from Mexico alone. SAW applicants were younger and much more predominantly male than those for legalization.

## TOTAL APPLICATIONS FROM THE CARIBBEAN

Between the two programs, legalization and special agricultural workers, applicants from the Caribbean account for about 80,000 persons, or 4.4 percent of the total. As a group, Caribbean nationals were much more evenly divided between the two programs than other groupings of applicants. Of the 80,000 Caribbean applicants, 52 percent were in the legalization program, with the remaining 48 percent applying for SAW status. There were, however, major variations within the Caribbean nationality groups. For instance, 71 percent of the Haitians, which were the largest nationality group represented, applied for SAW status. Other groups applied predominantly for legalization rather than the SAW program: Jamaica (69 percent), Dominican Republic (87 percent), and "other Caribbean" (90 percent).

## CARIBBEAN LEGALIZATION (PRE-1982) APPLICANTS

As mentioned above, about 52 percent (or 42,000) of all Caribbean applicants applied under the general legalization program requiring continuous illegal residence in the United States prior to 1982. Of these applicants from the Caribbean, 31 percent were from Haiti, 27 percent from the Dominican Republic, and 21 percent each from Jamaica and "other Caribbean" countries.

Reflecting the proximity of the Caribbean to the United States (including Puerto Rico), 47 percent of all Caribbean legalization applicants entered illegally, rather than with non-immigrant visas. Reflecting traditional migration patterns of Dominicans to Puerto Rico, 72 percent of the Dominicans reported that they entered without inspection. The other major nationality groups were more likely to have overstayed nonimmigrant visa entries: Haiti (56 percent), Jamaica (65 percent), and "other Caribbean" (78 percent).

Caribbean applicants had a similar age structure to the general legalizing population, with 77 percent of all applicants between the ages of 15 and 44. This trend held for specific countries, with the exception of the Dominican Republic, where 85 percent of the total were in that age group. Unlike the overall population, which was predominantly male, however, Caribbean legalization applicants were evenly divided between men and women. For specific nationality groups, females outnumbered males, with the exception of the Dominican group, where males accounted for 60 percent of the applicants. Similarly, Dominicans were far more likely to have never married (63 percent) than the Caribbean group as a whole (50 percent).

A predominant number of applicants from each of the major Caribbean nationality groups reported they worked in service occupations in the United States. This trend was somewhat higher for Haitians and slightly lower for the "other Caribbean" group. Haitians (24 percent) and Dominicans (27 percent) were most likely to work as operators, fabricators, or laborers, while Jamaicans and the "other Caribbean" group were more likely to be in professional, administrative, managerial, or administrative support occupations, with 22 percent of each of these latter nationality groups falling into this occupational grouping.

Compared with the total legalizing populations, Caribbean applicants were much more concentrated in New York, Florida, and Puerto Rico. Ninety percent of the Caribbean legalization applicants lived in New York (51 percent), Florida (22 percent), Puerto Rico (8 percent), New Jersey (5 percent), and Massachusetts (4 percent). While New York predominated as the state of residence for each of the Caribbean groups, including half of all Haitian and "other Caribbean" applicants, it included 60 percent of the Dominicans but only 44 percent of the Jamaicans. Florida was the second-ranking state of residence for Jamaicans (35 percent), Haitians (27 percent), and "other Caribbean" (27 percent), but only 3 percent of the Dominicans resided there. Puerto Rico, the third-ranking area of residence, included 28 percent of all legalizing Dominicans, a figure that comprised 93 percent of the total legalization applicants in that jurisdiction.

## CARIBBEAN SPECIAL AGRICULTURAL
## WORKER APPLICANTS

While legalization applicants from the Caribbean were relatively evenly spread among the four country areas reviewed, Haitians accounted for

82 percent of the Caribbean special agricultural worker applicants. Jamaicans accounted for another 11 percent, with Dominicans and the "other Caribbean" category accounting for 4 percent and 3 percent, respectively. Most Caribbean SAW applicants sought to qualify on 90 days' work in agriculture during the May 1985 through May 1986 qualifying period. Another 6 percent showed documentation that they had worked at least 90 days in agriculture during the 1984, 1985, and 1986 qualifying periods. (Data are unknown for the remaining 4 percent.)

Compared with the legalization population, the SAW population from the Caribbean was younger (87 percent between the ages of 15 and 44 versus 77 percent), more predominantly male (57 percent versus 50 percent), and more likely to be single (66 percent versus 50 percent). Dominicans were even more concentrated in the 15 to 44 age group, with 94 percent falling into that category, and more likely to be male (74 percent). It should be noted, however, that compared to all SAW applicants, Caribbean SAW applicants were slightly older and included a considerably larger proportion of women (43 percent versus 16 percent).

Caribbean SAW applicants reported qualifying based primarily on work in cash grains (36 percent) and in vegetables and melons (26 percent). Another 13 percent worked in fruits and tree nuts. This pattern clearly reflects the preponderance of Caribbean SAW qualifying work done in Florida, where half of all qualifying agricultural work was performed by Caribbean SAW applicants and contrasts with all SAW qualifying work nationally, where only 7 percent qualified under cash grains and 5 percent through vegetables and melons. Overall, 89 percent of Caribbean SAWs applied in Florida, including most Haitian, Jamaican, and "other Caribbean" SAW applicants. However, only 22 percent of the Dominicans applied in Florida, with another 67 percent applying in Puerto Rico, where that nationality group accounted for virtually all of the SAW applications filed.

## CUBAN-HAITIAN ADJUSTMENT PROGRAM

As discussed earlier, the Immigration Reform and Control Act of 1986 also provided a separate program to regularize the status of certain Cuban and Haitian entrants who entered the United States before January 1, 1982, and had an INS record established prior to that time. Through August 1988 almost 33,000 persons adjusted their status to permanent residence under this provision. Almost all of these adjustments were Haitians, since most of the 1980 Cuban entrants had availed themselves of the Cuban adjustment program in 1985 under the Cuban Adjustment Act of 1966.

## IMPLICATIONS OF THE REFORM ACT FOR FUTURE
## FLOWS OF IMMIGRANTS FROM THE CARIBBEAN

There is, unfortunately, no accurate means of predicting what future flows may derive from legalization and SAW beneficiaries. To help refine estimates, INS is collecting data generated by both applications and a separate sample survey; these data may help refine estimates of the number of persons potentially deriving benefits. There are, however, several considerations that should be taken into account in discussing potential flows of immigrants in the future.

The first factor is timing. The impact of IRCA on future flows of immigrants will not be immediate. As temporary residents, newly legalized aliens cannot petition to bring relatives to the United States. Beginning in late 1988 and lasting through 1990, temporary residents can come to INS and apply for permanent resident ("green-card") status. As permanent residents, these aliens can petition for their spouses and unmarried sons and daughters under the second preference. However, there is already a one and a half year backlog for such visas; this can be expected to get longer as petitions from newly legalized permanent residents increase. U.S. citizenship—which adds at least another five years—is required to petition for other preferences or to bring spouses, children, or parents outside any numerical limitation.

The second factor is attrition. The number of legalized and SAW aliens will decrease over time. Some temporary residents will, for whatever reason, not apply for permanent residence. Others will apply but not qualify. Some will emigrate as either temporary or permanent residents, and some will die before they bring any relatives.

A third factor relates to the numbers involved. Looking at future demand from the Caribbean flowing from the Reform Act, we are not looking at derivatives of a large base population of legalizing aliens. Assuming that up to 100,000 persons from the Caribbean may change their status under the legalization and SAW programs, that level is in the range of one year's immigration from the Caribbean. It is not a flood of new U.S. residents who can petition for relatives.

There is no factor that can be used to estimate the number of persons who will derive benefits and then choose to immigrate for each legalized alien. Many relatives—spouses, children, parents, or siblings—may already be legally resident in the United States. Others, potentially eligible overseas, may not wish to immigrate or, in some cases, may no longer be living. Additionally, there is overlap in families. Finally, a large percentage of legalized aliens from the Caribbean are single and cannot all be expected to marry persons overseas.

The final factor is the rate at which persons naturalize. Based on past experience—which may or may not hold true for legalized aliens—many

Caribbean immigrants either will not naturalize or will delay taking this step. Because U.S. citizenship is required to bring most relatives, including all groups outside the numerical limits, lower naturalization rates or delayed naturalization will further limit "petitioning capacity." If naturalization of Caribbean nationals occurs at relatively low rates, the impact of legalized aliens on derivative immigrants, either on demand or actual immigrant entries, will probably not be large and will not occur until well into the 1990s to the early 2000s.

Derivative flows may be more immediate than just discussed from one group, the Cuban-Haitian adjustees. The provisions of the section of the Reform Act dealing with this group initially confer permanent, rather than temporary, resident status and "roll back" eligibility for naturalization to 1982, making the Cuban-Haitian adjustment group immediately eligible to become U.S. citizens. This group will therefore be able, potentially, to bring immediate relatives and petition for preference relatives in the near future. The Cuban-Haitian adjustees, however, are a much smaller group numerically than either the legalization or SAW populations.

# 9

## Illegal Migration from the Caribbean

RANSFORD W. PALMER

Illegal migration in the Western Hemisphere is, for the most part, the result of wide economic disparities between neighboring countries and the controls imposed on migration by the richer countries. In the United States, the problem of illegal migration is created almost exclusively by the inflow of people from Latin America and the Caribbean. For Caribbean countries, which are separated from the United States by sea, there is obviously greater control over the movement of people across national borders. The cost of border crossing is also greater since it normally entails traveling by air for those who enter the United States legally. Even those who enter illegally by boat must pay for their transportation.

The data indicate that most of the illegal aliens from the English-speaking Caribbean entered the United States legally with temporary visas. The cost of travel and the control over issuing visas suggest that temporary visitors who travel to the United States for business, pleasure, or for study are likely to come from the middle-income strata of the sending countries. This makes illegal migration from the Caribbean more of a middle-class than a lower-class phenomenon, as is the case of illegal migration from Mexico.

The middle class, of course, is not a homogeneous group; it covers a wide range of skills and income. The propensity of temporary visitors from this group to violate the conditions of their temporary visas while in the United States is motivated largely by the prospect of earning higher incomes. High underemployment combined with high open unemployment in the Caribbean, particularly among the unskilled, act as a powerful brake on the growth of income among a wide range of middle-class occupations, especially those requiring low levels of skills. Visitors with these skills are often tempted by job opportunities in the United States, which pay wages higher than those at home.

With the objective of solving the illegal immigration problem, the Immigration Control and Reform Act of 1986 has removed the employment incentive by providing sanctions against those employers who hire illegal aliens. This is likely to be far more effective in controlling the flood of middle-class illegals from the Caribbean, many of whom had jobs at home, than in controlling unemployed Mexicans who walk across the border without inspection or desperate Haitians who come by boat.

While the Immigration Reform and Control Act of 1986 was designed to attack the problem of illegal migration directly, the Caribbean Basin Initiative enacted in 1983 was designed to attack it indirectly by addressing its root cause—poverty generated by inadequate development. In an important way, the success of the direct strategy hinges on the success of the indirect strategy. For even if the United States succeeds in reducing the volume of illegal migration with employer sanctions, the perception of better opportunities in the United States will persist if economic conditions for the majority of the Caribbean population do not improve rapidly. Without this development, the character of illegal Caribbean migration may change from a middle-class phenomenon in which most of the illegals enter legally to a lower-class phenomenon in which most of the illegals are unemployed people who attempt to enter without inspection. Such a development would represent a spreading Haitianization of the illegal migration phenomenon.

## THE CHARACTERISTICS OF ILLEGAL MIGRATION

A full understanding of illegal migration from the English-speaking Caribbean since the beginning of its political independence in 1962 requires an examination of the data provided in the Annual Reports of the U.S. Immigration and Naturalization Service (INS). First we look at the behavior of illegal immigration from the English-speaking Caribbean as a whole (including Belize) and then we focus on Jamaica, the largest English-speaking Caribbean source of migration, both legal and illegal. For the region, we use the INS tabulation of "deportable aliens" as a measure of the behavior of illegal migration and, for Jamaica, we use the INS tabulation of "aliens required to depart." The reason for using the latter is that there is no published tabulation of deportable aliens for individual Caribbean countries up to 1986.

Table 9.1 shows that between 1963 and 1986, 54 percent of all deportable English-speaking Caribbean aliens entered the United States on temporary visitor's visas, while 6 percent entered on student visas. Ta-

**Table 9.1**
**Deportable Aliens from the English Caribbean Located by the U.S.**
**Immigration and Naturalization Service, 1963–86**

| Year | Deportable Aliens | Deportable Aliens by Status of Entry | | Deportable Visitors as % of Total Deportable Aliens | Deportable Students as % of Total Deportable Aliens |
|---|---|---|---|---|---|
| | | Temporary Visitors | Students | | |
| 1963 | 1,875 | 812 | 209 | 43.3 | 11.1 |
| 1964 | 1,907 | 1,088 | 182 | 57.1 | 9.5 |
| 1965 | * | * | * | * | * |
| 1966 | 2,336 | 1,443 | 192 | 61.8 | 8.2 |
| 1967 | 1,970 | 1,237 | 152 | 62.8 | 7.7 |
| 1968 | 2,541 | 1,785 | 145 | 70.2 | 5.7 |
| 1969 | 3,053 | 1,840 | 176 | 60.3 | 5.8 |
| 1970 | 4,074 | 2,723 | 104 | 66.8 | 2.6 |
| 1971 | 9,011 | 5,845 | 200 | 64.9 | 2.2 |
| 1972 | 4,137 | 2,423 | 180 | 58.6 | 4.3 |
| 1973 | 4,457 | 2,799 | 294 | 62.8 | 6.6 |
| 1974 | 5,512 | 3,207 | 303 | 58.2 | 5.5 |
| 1975 | 6,759 | 3,712 | 344 | 54.9 | 5.1 |
| 1976 | 6,652 | 2,847 | 294 | 42.8 | 4.4 |
| 1977 | 3,895 | 1,710 | 180 | 43.9 | 4.6 |
| 1978 | 2,703 | 1,343 | 133 | 49.7 | 4.9 |
| 1979 | 2,267 | 1,062 | 113 | 46.8 | 5.0 |
| 1980 | 1,831 | 920 | 103 | 50.2 | 5.6 |
| 1981 | 2,301 | 1,193 | 112 | 51.8 | 4.9 |
| 1982 | 2,203 | 1,140 | 96 | 51.7 | 4.4 |
| 1983 | 2,106 | 1,073 | 136 | 50.9 | 6.5 |
| 1984 | 1,337 | 613 | 107 | 45.8 | 8.0 |
| 1985 | 1,026 | 434 | 93 | 42.3 | 9.1 |
| 1986 | 1,180 | 580 | 92 | 49.2 | 7.8 |
| | | Average | | 54.2 | 6.1 |

*Not available.

Source: U.S. Department of Justice, Immigration and Naturalization Service, *Annual Reports, 1963–1980* (Washington, D.C.: Government Printing Office, 1963–80).

ble 9.2 shows that over the same period, a far larger share of students (3.1 percent) became deportable aliens than did temporary visitors (0.94 percent). In the 1960s, the student share declined sharply from a high of 9.4 percent in 1963 to a low of 1.2 percent in 1970. It rose to 5.2 percent in the middle of the 1970s and fell steadily to 0.9 percent in 1986. The significant decline in the share of deportable aliens among temporary visitors in the 1980s has been due largely to the sharp increase in the number of temporary visitors. While not all deportable aliens are apprehended by the INS, these numbers nevertheless suggest a low propensi-

**Table 9.2**
**Deportable Aliens from the English Caribbean as a Percentage of Temporary
Visitors and Students, Fiscal Years 1963-86**

| Year | Temporary Visitors | Students | Deportable Aliens by Status | | Deportable Aliens as % of: | |
|------|------|------|------|------|------|------|
| | | | Temporary Visitors | Students | Temporary Visitors | Students |
| 1963 | 63,401 | 2,215 | 812 | 209 | 1.3 | 9.4 |
| 1964 | 78,821 | 2,577 | 1,088 | 182 | 1.4 | 7.1 |
| 1965 | * | * | * | * | * | * |
| 1966 | 114,149 | 3,473 | 1,443 | 192 | 1.3 | 5.5 |
| 1967 | 131,237 | 4.219 | 1,237 | 152 | 0.9 | 3.6 |
| 1968 | 174,866 | 5,310 | 1,785 | 145 | 1.0 | 2.7 |
| 1969 | 194,228 | 6,243 | 1,840 | 176 | 0.9 | 2.8 |
| 1970 | 241,500 | 8,318 | 2,723 | 104 | 1.1 | 1.2 |
| 1971 | 209,676 | 7,881 | 5,845 | 200 | 2.8 | 2.5 |
| 1972 | 209,433 | 7,071 | 2,423 | 180 | 1.2 | 2.5 |
| 1973 | 210,801 | 6,534 | 2,799 | 294 | 1.3 | 4.5 |
| 1974 | 229,676 | 7,189 | 3,207 | 303 | 1.4 | 4.2 |
| 1975 | 197,141 | 6,609 | 3,712 | 344 | 1.9 | 5.2 |
| 1976 | 209,133 | 6,557 | 2,847 | 294 | 1.4 | 4.5 |
| 1977 | 232,006 | 7,196 | 1,710 | 180 | 0.7 | 2.5 |
| 1978 | 268,248 | 7,425 | 1,343 | 133 | 0.5 | 1.8 |
| 1979 | 181,828 | 4,566 | 1,062 | 113 | 0.6 | 2.5 |
| 1980 | * | * | 920 | 103 | * | * |
| 1981 | 421,228 | 9,523 | 1,193 | 112 | 0.3 | 1.2 |
| 1982 | 536,496 | 10,119 | 1,140 | 96 | 0.2 | 0.9 |
| 1983 | 556,129 | 15,537 | 1,073 | 136 | 0.2 | 0.9 |
| 1984 | 446,653 | 10,040 | 613 | 107 | 0.1 | 1.1 |
| 1985 | 472,186 | 10,465 | 434 | 93 | 0.1 | 0.9 |
| 1986 | 535,418 | 10,260 | 580 | 92 | 0.1 | 0.9 |
| | | | Average | | 0.94 | 3.10 |

*Not available.

Source: U.S. Department of Justice, Immigration and Naturalization Service, *Annual Reports,
1963-1980* (Washington, D.C.: Government Printing Office, 1963-80).

ty on the part of visitors to violate the conditions of their temporary
visas, even before employer sanctions were introduced in 1986.

The reason for the apparent higher propensity of students to violate
the conditions of their visas is largely economic. The foreign student
from the Caribbean is far more sensitive to changes in economic conditions at home than the temporary visitor for the simple reason that the
foreign exchange requirement per student is greater than that per temporary visitor on business or on vacation. And because in small open
economies, changes in economic conditions are quickly reflected in the

availability of foreign exchange, a rationing of available foreign exchange usually means that students already in the United States will experience difficulty receiving financial support from home, especially when they are not studying in fields given high priority by their governments. As a result, many drop out of school to work illegally. Others drop out because of academic problems and find it difficult to return home without achieving their objective. Still others, having completed their studies, opt to extend their stay illegally to take advantage of job opportunities.

## THE CASE OF JAMAICA

Because published INS data up until 1986 did not include tabulations of deportable aliens for individual English-speaking Caribbean countries, we use the tabulation for "aliens required to depart" as a substitute in our examination of the behavior of illegal migration from Jamaica over the 1963–86 period. First, a few observations about Table 9.3. While the number of temporary visitors for business or pleasure increased significantly over this period, the sharpest increases occurred during the 1980s, when the pro–private enterprise government of Edward Seaga ran the country. The most dramatic one-year increase occurred between 1982 and 1983, as the number of temporary visitors for business jumped from 9,863 to 52,142. While some of this increase no doubt is the result of a switch in the basis of tabulation from last permanent residence to country of origin, much of it is the result of other factors. One is the introduction in 1983 of the Caribbean Basin Initiative program by the Reagan administration—a program that triggered many visits to the United States by numerous business delegations to explore market opportunities. Another is the explosion of small entrepreneurs in Jamaica. The slimming down of the public sector and the inability of the private sector to absorb a growing labor force into wage employment accelerated the growth of the informal sector, where thousands of small retailers compete with each other. Many of these small retailers commute to Miami and New York to buy merchandise for their businesses. Because many of them do not obtain their foreign exchange through official channels, foreign exchange restrictions are usually no serious barrier to travel. Still another factor contributing to the growth of travel to the United States was the premature liberalization of foreign exchange rules by the Seaga government in the early 1980s. This stimulated greater travel to the United States, not only for business but also for pleasure. In contrast, the growth of the number of foreign students over the 1963–86 period was modest, with virtual stagnation occurring in the 1980s.

Even though the Jamaican economy was struggling in the 1980s, the

**Table 9.3**
**Jamaican Non-Immigrants, Temporary Visitors, and Students Entering the United States and Jamaican Aliens Required to Depart from the United States, 1963–86\***

| Year | Non-immigrants | Students | Temporary Visitors | | Aliens Required to Depart** |
|------|------|------|------|------|------|
| | | | Business | Pleasure | |
| 1963 | 29,340 | 742 | 1,048 | 12,835 | 580 |
| 1964 | 36,851 | 918 | 1,373 | 17,134 | 647 |
| 1965 | † | † | † | † | † |
| 1966 | 46,383 | 975 | 1,978 | 21,915 | 1,078 |
| 1967 | 59,003 | 1,157 | 1,727 | 22,429 | 2,203 |
| 1968 | 49,120 | 1,329 | 2,235 | 28,941 | 2,106 |
| 1969 | 47,825 | 1,398 | 2,675 | 28,788 | 1,572 |
| 1970 | 62,555 | 1,751 | 3,244 | 38,024 | 1,119 |
| 1971 | 58,448 | 1,683 | 4,163 | 36,877 | 1,354 |
| 1972 | 63,384 | 1,600 | 5,082 | 41,843 | 1,315 |
| 1973 | 68,598 | 1,596 | 5,222 | 46,750 | 1,132 |
| 1974 | 72,977 | 1,406 | 6,508 | 49,281 | 1,040 |
| 1975 | 76,645 | 1,512 | 5,938 | 55,055 | 865 |
| 1976 | 90,087 | 1,867 | 6,589 | 67,135 | 530 |
| 1977 | 76,165 | 2,183 | 6,575 | 55,654 | 428 |
| 1978 | 79,842 | 2,090 | 7,070 | 63,654 | 329 |
| 1979 | 54,984 | 1,104 | 4,290 | 45,902 | 299 |
| 1980 | † | † | † | † | † |
| 1981 | 111,572 | 1,855 | 8,059 | 92,961 | 529 |
| 1982 | 136,070 | 2,064 | 9,863 | 113,897 | 662 |
| 1983 | 160,121 | 2,928 | 52,142 | 80,837 | 692 |
| 1984 | 116,000 | 1,715 | 28,488 | 67,692 | 683 |
| 1985 | 127,000 | 1,821 | 30,643 | 76,223 | 872 |
| 1986 | 147,137 | 1,850 | 38,863 | 85,954 | 795 |

*Note:* Data in this table are based on last permanent residence for years 1963–82 and country of birth for 1983–86. The year 1979 includes data for October–June only.
\*Based on country of destination.
†Not available.

*Source:* U.S. Department of Justice, Immigration and Naturalization Service, *Annual Reports, 1963–1980* (Washington, D.C.: Government Printing Office, 1963–80).

liberalization of foreign exchange—much of it coming from international aid and loans—must be seen as ultimately responsible for the reduction in the propensity of temporary visitors to violate their visas. It is also possible that an increase in the share of business visitors among the temporary visitors helped to reduce this propensity; since many business visitors have a proprietary interest back home, they are less likely to be induced by employment incentives to violate the conditions of their visas. Since our measure of the rate of visa violations is dependent upon the data of those apprehended, one additional factor of importance is the effectiveness of the INS in apprehending those who violated their visas. We will return to this subject later.

Since 1986, INS tabulations for individual Caribbean countries have provided further insights into the nature of illegal migration from the region. Table 9.4, for example, shows that for Jamaica and Haiti, roughly 60 percent of those who were apprehended by the INS had been in the United States for over a year. Less than 5 percent were apprehended at entry. In contrast, roughly 22 percent of those from the Dominican Republic were apprehended at entry, and 40 percent within 72 hours. Only 17 percent of the Dominicans apprehended had been in the United States for over one year. (Many Dominicans enter the United States through Puerto Rico.)

The fact that most Jamaican illegals were apprehended after they had been in the United States for over a year suggests that they were more likely to have been engaged in some kind of employment than were the Dominican illegals, since most of them were apprehended at entry or within 72 hours after they entered the country. If this pattern of apprehension prevails, employer sanctions may have a greater impact on Jamaicans and Haitians than on Dominicans.[1]

Table 9.5 provides a hint that this may well be happening in the case of Jamaica. Since 1986, only 21.5 percent of the Jamaicans apprehended entered as temporary visitors in contrast to the average of 54 percent in Table 9.1 for all the English-speaking Caribbean. Furthermore, what is striking about Table 9.5 is the high share (34 percent) of immigrants among those apprehended. Immigrants are permanent residents and are therefore not affected by employer sanctions. Their apprehension must mean that they have obtained their permanent resident status

**Table 9.4**
**Length of Time in United States before Apprehension and Percentage Distribution of Total Apprehended from Jamaica, Haiti, and the Dominican Republic, October 1987 to February 1989**

| Country | At Entry | Within 72 Hours | 4-30 Days | 30-365 Days | Over 1 Year |
|---------|----------|-----------------|-----------|-------------|-------------|
| Jamaica | 4.5 | 6.3 | 7.2 | 24.7 | 57.2 |
| Haiti | 2.8 | 8.5 | 7.5 | 20.9 | 60.3 |
| Dominican Republic | 21.6 | 40.0 | 9.3 | 12.0 | 17.1 |

Source: U.S. Department of Justice, Immigration and Naturalization Service, *Annual Reports, 1987-1989* (Washington, D.C.: Government Printing Office, 1987–89).

**Table 9.5**
**Apprehensions of Jamaican Aliens by Status at Entry**

| Group | 1987* | 1988* | 1989** | Total | Percentage |
|---|---|---|---|---|---|
| Visitors | 248 | 300 | 152 | 700 | 21.5 |
| Students | 19 | 22 | 14 | 55 | 7.7 |
| Temporary Agricultural Workers | 95 | 76 | 52 | 223 | 6.8 |
| Immigrants | 318 | 520 | 285 | 1,123 | 34.4 |
| Other | 358 | 542 | 259 | 1,159 | 35.6 |
| Total | 1,038 | 1,460 | 762 | 3,260 | 100.0 |

*Fiscal Year: October 1 to September 30.
**October to February.

Source: U.S. Department of Justice, Immigration and Naturalization Service, *Annual Reports, 1987–1989* (Washington, D.C.: Government Printing Office, 1987–89).

under false pretenses or that an increasing number of them have been engaging in illegal activities.

We return to the question of the effectiveness of the INS in apprehending visa violators. With the help of data gathered from the amnesty program, which ended in 1988 (see Chapter 8), we developed a methodology for calculating the rate of apprehension.

Between 1963 and 1981, the cut-off year of eligibility for amnesty, over one million non-immigrants from Jamaica entered the United States. The amnesty data indicate that approximately 9,000 Jamaican illegals applied for legalization, a number that represents less than one percent of the total number of non-immigrants for the 1963–81 period. Over the same period, the INS required 16,449 Jamaican illegals to leave the country. If we add this number to the 9,000 who applied for legalization, we get a total of 25,449 illegals. The amnesty data also indicate that 65 percent of those who applied for legalization entered the country legally. Assuming that this percentage applies to all Jamaican illegals, by taking 65 percent of 25,449, we get 16,542 as the number of illegals who entered the country legally. This means that of the one million non-immigrants who entered the country legally between 1963 and 1981, less than 2 percent violated the conditions of their temporary visas. Based on the regional data for Table 9.1 for deportable aliens, it is reasonable to say that the majority of the Jamaican illegals arrived as temporary visitors and students. And based on the last two columns of

Table 9.1, we would also expect students to have a higher propensity to violate their visas than temporary visitors.

To calculate the annual number of visa violators from Jamaica, we proceed on the basis of what we know so far. We know that the total number of non-immigrants who violated their visas over the 1963–81 period is 16,542, and that the INS apprehended and sent home 16,449, 65 percent of whom (10,692) entered the country legally. Thus for every three non-immigrants who violated their visas, the INS apprehended two. The foregoing underscores two important characteristics of illegal migration from Jamaica: a low rate of visa violation and a high rate of apprehension.

Using this apprehension rate of two out of three visa violators, we can calculate the total number of visa violators each year between 1963 and 1981. The procedure is as follows: first we calculate 65 percent of the annual number apprehended in Table 9.3; since the result represents the two out of three apprehended by the INS, we divide it by two and multiply the result by three to get the total number of visa violators. To illustrate, we use the year 1963, when the INS apprehended and sent home 580 apprehendees. Sixty-five percent of that number were visa violators, which is 377. By dividing 377 by two and multiplying the result by three, we get 565.5, rounded off to 566, the number of non-immigrants who violated their visas that year. Table 9.6 shows the annual number of visa violators, temporary visitors for pleasure and business, and students as shares of all non-immigrants.

To find out whether changes in the composition of non-immigrants affect the share of non-immigrants apprehended as visa violators, we tested the hypothesis that changes in the share of non-immigrants who are visa violators (SVV) are determined by changes in the non-immigrant shares of business (SBV) and pleasure (SVP) visitors and students (SS). The results of an ordinary least squares regression analysis of the data for the 1963–81 and 1963–86 periods are shown in Table 9.7.

For both periods, the coefficient of the variable, SS, is not only highly significant, it is the only significant one. This leads to the conclusion that variations in the share of non-immigrants who violate their visas are largely explained by variations in the share of non-immigrants who enter the United States on student visas. The coefficients for business and pleasure visitors are negative, suggesting that the greater the share of these groups among the non-immigrants, the lower the share of visa violators. These coefficients, however, are not statistically significant.

Because education is an important factor in economic growth and development, the greater the number of Jamaican students who acquire higher education in the United States or elsewhere, the greater the long-run benefits to the Jamaican economy are likely to be. Yet the results of

**Table 9.6**
**Visa Violators, Business Visitors, Pleasure Visitors, and Students as Shares of Non-Immigrants from Jamaica, 1963–86**

| Year | Estimate of Visa Violators from Jamaica | Visa Violators as % of Non-immigrants | Business Visitors as % of Non-immigrants | Pleasure Visitors as % of Non-immigrants | Students as % of Non-immigrants |
|---|---|---|---|---|---|
| 1963 | 566 | 1.93 | 3.6 | 43.7 | 2.5 |
| 1964 | 631 | 1.72 | 3.7 | 46.5 | 2.5 |
| 1965 | * | * | * | * | * |
| 1966 | 1,051 | 2.27 | 4.3 | 47.2 | 2.1 |
| 1967 | 2,148 | 4.29 | 3.5 | 44.9 | 2.3 |
| 1968 | 2,053 | 4.18 | 4.5 | 58.9 | 2.7 |
| 1969 | 1,533 | 3.21 | 5.6 | 60.2 | 2.9 |
| 1970 | 1,091 | 1.75 | 5.2 | 60.8 | 2.8 |
| 1971 | 1,320 | 2.26 | 7.1 | 63.1 | 2.9 |
| 1972 | 1,282 | 2.30 | 8.0 | 66.0 | 2.5 |
| 1973 | 1,104 | 1.61 | 7.6 | 68.1 | 2.3 |
| 1974 | 1,014 | 1.39 | 8.9 | 67.5 | 1.9 |
| 1975 | 844 | 1.11 | 7.7 | 71.8 | 2.0 |
| 1976 | 517 | 0.58 | 4.8 | 49.0 | 1.4 |
| 1977 | 418 | 0.50 | 5.1 | 43.5 | 1.7 |
| 1978 | 321 | 0.41 | 5.0 | 44.7 | 1.5 |
| 1979 | 292 | 0.53 | 4.4 | 46.6 | 1.1 |
| 1980 | * | * | * | * | * |
| 1981 | 516 | 0.47 | 7.2 | 83.3 | 1.4 |
| 1982 | 645 | 0.48 | 7.2 | 83.7 | 1.5 |
| 1983 | 675 | 0.43 | 32.4 | 50.2 | 1.8 |
| 1984 | 666 | 0.58 | 24.2 | 57.6 | 1.5 |
| 1985 | 850 | 0.67 | 23.8 | 59.1 | 1.4 |
| 1986 | 775 | 0.53 | 26.0 | 57.5 | 1.2 |

*Not available

Source: Table 9.5 and U.S. Department of Justice, Immigration and Naturalization Service, *Annual Reports, 1963–1986* (Washington, D.C.: Government Printing Office, 1963–86).

**Table 9.7**
**Results of Regression Analysis (t statistics are in parentheses)**

| Dependent Variable | Independent Variables | | | | Adjusted $R^2$ | F Test | Durbin-Watson |
|---|---|---|---|---|---|---|---|
| | Constant | SBV | SPV | SS | | | |
| 1963-1986 SVV | -.522 (-.46) | -1.863E-02 (.84) | -.0112 (-.79) | 1.437 (4.45)* | .55 | 9.69 | 1.75 |
| 1963-1981 SVV | -.8336 (-.67) | -.3002 (-1.35) | -.0025 (.64) | 1.4711 (3.89)* | .50 | 6.52 | 2.29 |

*Significant at the one percent level.
SVV = Illegal aliens as a percentage of non-immigrants
SBV = Temporary visitors for business as a percentage of non-immigrants
SPV = Temporary visitors for pleasure as a percentage of non-immigrants
SS = Foreign students as a percentage of non-immigrants

our analysis indicate that the greater the share of students among the non-immigrants, the greater the share of visa violators. The fundamental problem here, as we indicated earlier, is the inability of students to finance their education while in the United States, an inability aggravated by a persistent shortage of foreign exchange in Jamaica.

## A POLICY PROPOSAL

Since education plays a vital role in the development of Jamaica and the entire Caribbean, a U.S. policy that encourages development should also encourage an increase in the supply of higher education to the Caribbean. If foreign exchange constraints reduce the number of students who come to the United States to study, the human capital stock of the region will grow at a slower rate. If the students who cannot pay for a U.S. education are educated at home, the potential loss to the local economy could be offset. But local institutions of higher learning may have a limited capacity to supply the quantity, quality, and the diversity of education demanded by a growing economy.

To break the vicious cycle that a scarcity of foreign exchange creates, an infusion of external resources is required. Soft loans earmarked for study in the United States could be provided to the governments of the region. Such a U.S. policy would achieve the objective of encouraging long-run development by contributing to the growth of the region's human capital stock while at the same time reducing the propensity of students for illegal migration. Students receiving such loans would, of course, be obligated to return home to work for a minimum number of years after the completion of their studies. The governments of the region would be responsible for ensuring the repayment of the student loans in local currency. The program would operate countercyclically in the sense that more loan funds would be available when there is a shortage of foreign exchange and less when the foreign exchange situation improves.

Access to a dollar fund to finance their education would ensure that the United States continues to be a major supplier of higher education to the region. This, more than the employer sanction under the Immigration Reform and Control Act of 1986, would bring about a sustained decline in the propensity for illegal migration.

## NOTE

1. For a detailed study of the employment of illegal aliens in the United States, see Barry R. Chiswick, *Illegal Aliens: Their Employment and Employers* (Kalamazoo, Michigan: W. E. Upjohn Institute for Employment Research, 1988).

# Index

# About the Editor and Contributors

RANSFORD W. PALMER is graduate professor of economics at Howard University. He received his Ph.D. in economics from Clark University, Worcester, Massachusetts. Dr. Palmer is a former chairman of the Department of Economics at Howard and a former president of the Caribbean Studies Association. His publications include *The Jamaican Economy* (1968), *Caribbean Dependence on the United States Economy* (1979), and *Problems of Development in Beautiful Countries: Perspectives on the Caribbean* (1984).

AUBREY W. BONNETT is dean of the school of Social and Behavioral Sciences, California State University at San Bernardino, and former chairman of sociology at Hunter College, City University of New York. He received his Ph.D. from the City University of New York. A Social Science Research Council's postdoctoral scholar, he is the author of *Institutional Adaptation of West Indian Migrants: An Analysis of Rotating Credit Associations* (1981), *Group Identification Among Negroes: An Examination of the Soul Concept in the U.S.A.* (1980), coauthor of *Emerging Perspectives on the Black Diaspora* (forthcoming), and of several articles on West Indians in the United States.

PETER D. FRASER is a lecturer at Goldsmiths' College, University of London. He received his Ph.D. from the University of Sussex. He has taught at the University of the West Indies in Trinidad and was a fellow at the Institute of Commonwealth Studies and the Institute of Education, University of London. Dr. Fraser is a coauthor of *The Caribbean*

*Economic Handbook* (1985) and *The Central American Economic Handbook* (1987).

MONICA H. GORDON is currently researcher/consultant and adjunct professor in the City University of New York system. She received her Ph.D. in sociology from the City University of New York and has taught at Mount Holyoke College, University of Oregon, and Tufts University. Her teaching and research interests include international migration and immigrant patterns, social/cultural change and development, and race/gender stratification.

GORDON K. LEWIS is professor of political science at the University of Puerto Rico and director of the Institute of Caribbean Studies. Professor Lewis' publications include *The Growth of the Modern West Indies* (1968) and *The Modern Caribbean: A New Voyage of Discovery* (1989).

ALOMA MENDOZA received her B.A. and M.A. at York University, Toronto. She has taught sociology courses at York University on race and ethnic relations and the family. She is currently writing a dissertation on the socioeconomic, cultural, and psychological experiences of Caribbean women in Canada.

PATRICIA R. PESSAR is research director of the Center for Immigration Policy and Refugee Assistance at Georgetown University. She received her Ph.D. in anthropology from the University of Chicago and has done field work in Scotland, Labrador, Brazil, the Dominican Republic, and the United States. Her publications include *When Borders Don't Divide: Labor Migration and Refugee Movements in the Americas* (1988) and a coauthored volume, *Between Two Islands: Dominican International Migration* (forthcoming).

ANTHONY H. RICHMOND, Ph.D., F.R.S.C., is professor emeritus of sociology at York University, Toronto. He received his Ph.D. from the University of London. His numerous books, monographs, and articles on immigration and ethnic relations include *Immigration and Ethnic Conflict* (1988) and *Caribbean Immigrants in Canada: A Demo-economic Analysis* (1989).

LISA S. RONEY is in charge of planning and research as the director of planning of the United States Immigration and Naturalization Service in Washington, D.C. She previously served on the staff of the Interagency Task Force on Immigration Law and Policy and was a senior research associate with the Select Commission on Immigration and Refugee Policy. She has written extensively and made numerous presentations on many aspects of immigration law and policy.

MEL. E. THOMPSON is a research fellow at the Centre for Research in Ethnic Relations at Warwick University, specializing in Afro-Caribbean migration. She is currently working on her doctoral thesis, which examines the migration experience of Jamaicans in the West Midlands, United Kingdom.